ALSO BY JULIE KAVANAGH

Nureyev

Secret Muses: The Life of Frederick Ashton

The Girl Who Loved Camellias

The Girl
Who Loved
Camellias

⌘

THE LIFE AND LEGEND
OF MARIE DUPLESSIS

Julie Kavanagh

Alfred A. Knopf *New York* 2013

THIS IS A BORZOI BOOK
PUBLISHED BY ALFRED A. KNOPF

Published in the United States by Alfred A. Knopf, a division of
Random House, Inc., New York, and in Canada, by Random House
of Canada Limited, Toronto.

www.aaknopf.com

Knopf, Borzoi Books, and the colophon are registered trademarks
of Random House, Inc.

Library of Congress Cataloging-in-Publication Data
Kavanagh, Julie, [date]
The girl who loved camellias : the life and legend of Marie Duplessis / by Julie
Kavanagh.—First edition.
pages   cm
Includes bibliographical references and index.
ISBN 978-0-307-27079-5
1. Duplessis, Marie, 1824–1847.   2. Courtesans—France—Paris—Biography.
3. Paris (France)—Social life and customs—19th century.   4. Dumas, Alexandre,
1824–1895 Dame aux camélias.   5. Courtesans in literature.   I. Title.
DC705.D87K38 2013
944.06'3092—dc23
[B]   2012051103

Front-of-jacket images: *Marie Duplessis,* The Granger Collection, New York;
Camellia © amanaimages / Corbis
Jacket design by Carol Devine Carson

Manufactured in the United States of America
First Edition

To Ross, Joe, and Alfie

Contents

Acknowledgments

My first thanks must go to Jean-Marie Choulet, curator of the Musée de la Dame aux Camélias in the pretty Normandy town of Gacé. A historian and author of the enlightening *Promenades à Paris et en Normandie avec la dame aux camélias,* Jean-Marie entrusted me on our first meeting with his own source material for his book. I came away with a milk crate full of journals, handwritten notes, books, and pamphlets that would save me several months of work. Most valuable of all was an unpublished bibliography of Marie Duplessis compiled as a labor of love by Alain Orgerit. Over the five years that it took to research and write the book, Jean-Marie was always there for me, sending e-mailed replies to my questions, acting as a go-between with other experts, and allowing me privileged access to exhibits in the museum, several of which are included among my illustrations. Jean-Marie's wife, Colette, was also enormously encouraging and hospitable, and my friendship with the Choulets will long outlast the publication of this book.

Also of incalculable importance was my researcher Kristine Baril. We met at the Bibliothèque Nationale's Accueil Général desk, where she still works, and forged an immediate bond. With her impeccable English and passion for all forms of art, Kristine was as much an ideal companion as a heaven-sent collaborator. Her boundless curiosity about Marie Duplessis drove indefatigable online quests that led to several break-throughs in our research. She was doggedly good-natured about helping me to master the Bnf's impenetrable code system, and her elation at any new discovery was just as intense as my own. I consider Kristine to have been a true partner in this project, and owe her more than I can ever repay.

I am indebted to Jean-Luc Combe and his former colleague Isabelle Rambaud, Conservatrice générale du patrimoine, for their guidance about French archival procedures; to Jean Hournon for his expertise on nineteenth-century Bougival, and for the Dumas archive he put at my disposal. Rudiger Beermann was a splendidly informed authority on Baden-Baden, while Dagmar Kicherer greatly facilitated my archival research there. Academician Gonzagues St. Bris was responsible for my gaining access to the venerable Bibliothèque de l'Institut de France; William Bortrick of Burke's Peerage kindly provided me with the genealogical information that an official archivist failed to supply; Eva Guggemos's assistance at Yale's Beinecke Library went beyond the call of duty; Guy Peeters generously consulted Spa's *liste des Etrangers* on my behalf. I owe thanks to Elfgardt and Otmar Wintersteller for their German translations of source material and for their hospitality. Mme Ruault, the owner of the chambres d'hôtes "le Plessis" (a small château that Marie had once coveted herself), provided me with a welcoming, inspirational, and comfortable base in Nonant. At Tricase's Caffé Cappuccini, Vito, Massimo, and Rocco created the simpatico surroundings in which much of this book was written.

I owe profound thanks for the information and kindnesses I received at different stages of my research from: Claude Broux, Jean Darnel, Simone Drouin, Elisabeth Leonetti, Annick Tillier, Pierrette Bodin, Atty Lennox, Arnaud Marion, Joy Moorehead, Jasper Rees, Jonathan Keates, Pascale Lafeber, Isabel Lloyd, Michael Saffle, Michael Shipster, Tariana Shor, Nicola Shulmann,

Guy Thibault, Anne-Marie de Ponton d'Amécourt, and Alan Walker.

I would like to record my thanks to the following institutions:

Alençon's Archives Départementales de l'Orne
Archives Départementales des Bouches-du-Rhône, Marseille
Archives Départementales des Yvelines
Archives Départementales d'Indre-et-Loire
Bancroft Library, University of California, Berkeley
Beinecke Rare Book and Manuscript Library (Frederick R.
	Koch Collection), Yale University
Bibliothèque Nationale de France, Arts du spectacle
Bibliothèque Nationale de France, François-Mitterrand
Bibliothèque-Musée de la Comédie-Française
Manuscript Library Spoelberch de Lovenjoul, Bibiliothèque
	de l'Institut de France
Ministère de la Défense, section des archives historiques
Mulgrave Castle Archives
National Archives of Estonia
Pleyel Pianos Archives
Stadtarchiv, Baden-Baden

The Girl Who Loved Camellias would not exist without the belief and enthusiasm of my agent Lynn Nesbit, and my two Knopf editors Shelley Wanger and Bob Gottlieb. All three encouraged me to pursue what can only have seemed a dismayingly uncommercial venture in today's uncompromising publishing world. I can't thank Shelley enough for her skillful, sensitive shaping of my book, or Bob for his continuing support and generosity in letting me use his rue Jacob apartment as my Paris base.

At Janklow & Nesbit UK, I am immensely grateful to Claire Conrad for her tireless championing of *The Girl Who Loved Camellias*. I also owe thanks to Janklow's Stephanie Koven for her efforts to launch the book into a global market. At Knopf, Shelley's assistant, Juhea Kim, was tremendously helpful in securing images, and unfailingly kind and obliging. I owe sincere thanks to Andrew Dorko for his meticulous care and patience, and to Anne Cherry for her scrupulous copyediting, specialist knowledge, and zeal.

I am indebted to the friends who encouraged me throughout the writing of this book: Lola Bubbosh, Rupert Christiansen, Peter Eyre, and Gaby Tana. The late Patrick O'Connor was its earliest supporter; Julian Barnes cast an aficionado's eye over the manuscript, as did Peter Conrad, who played devil's advocate and urged me to write an introduction placing Marie Duplessis in a wider context. Selina Hastings has been, as ever, my first reader, dearest friend, and lodestar: I can't imagine writing a book without her.

I have dedicated *The Girl Who Loved Camellias* to my family, who will always get my most heartfelt thanks of all.

The Girl Who Loved Camellias

Introduction

MARIE DUPLESSIS WAS the most admired young courtesan of 1840s Paris. A peasant girl from Normandy, she had reinvented herself in a matter of months, changing her name and learning how to dress, speak, and act like a duchess. But this was far more than a *Pygmalion* or *Pretty Woman* transformation. The country waif, scarcely able to read or write when she arrived in the capital at the age of thirteen, was presiding over her own salon seven years later, regularly receiving aristocrats, politicians, artists, and many of the celebrated writers of the day. These were, of course, all men, because no virtuous woman would have anything to do with a courtesan, but Marie's profession had bought her proximity to the most brilliant minds in Paris. Her close circle included Nestor Roqueplan, editor of *Le Figaro,* Dr. Veron, director of the Opéra, and bon viveur Roger de Beauvoir, whom Alexandre Dumas père called the wittiest man he had ever known. Dumas himself was intrigued by the childlike Marie, and his son Alexandre fell in love with her. Franz Liszt came to Paris for a week but was so bewitched by Marie that he stayed for three months and remained romantically attached to her memory for the rest of his life. Such was her fascination that her early death from consumption in 1847 was regarded as an event of national importance. "For several days all questions political, artistic, commercial have been abandoned by the papers," a bemused Charles Dickens wrote to a friend from Paris. "Everything is erased in the face of an incident which is far more important, the romantic death of one of the glories of the demi-monde, the beautiful, the famous Marie Duplessis."

A year later, with the publication of *The Lady of the Camellias*, the novel Dumas fils had based on her life, the beau monde was abuzz again. Dumas père was a national institution in France, and people were curious to see whether the twenty-four-year-old was to follow his father's lead. He certainly had the elder Dumas's lively style and flair for natural dialogue, as well as a freshness and sincerity of his own. But of even greater interest was the subject of the book itself. Alexandre's affair with Marie Duplessis was well known on the Boulevard, and so was the identity of the heroine he renamed Marguerite Gautier. His descriptions of her are pure reportage. Whether sitting in her box at the theater with her signature bouquet of camellias or stepping into her pretty blue carriage, wrapped in a long cashmere shawl, Marguerite was instantly recognizable as Marie: the same tall, thin physique, the same chaste oval face, black eyes, and dark arched brows. As intrigued then as now with the private lives of celebrities, the public read the fiction as fact, thrilled to be taken inside the demimondaine's apartment, allowed to eavesdrop on scurrilous conversations at her dinner table, and be shown her rosewood furniture, Saxe figurines, Sèvres china—even her boudoir with its costly array of gold and silver bottles. Marguerite's friends and suitors also had their counterparts in real life, the passionate young hero Armand Duval being a composite of two of Marie's lovers with elements of Alexandre himself.

In addition to his contemporary setting and characters, the young author drew on French literary tradition. He borrowed the plot device from Abbé Prévost's eighteenth-century novel *Manon Lescaut*, which has a narrator who learns the details of the young courtesan's plight from her grieving lover, and he also made Marguerite a descendant of Victor Hugo's redeemed courtesan Marion Delorme, who gives up her wealthy protectors for an impoverished young man. During an idyllic country interlude, Marguerite devotes herself entirely to Armand, but Dumas fils had a more dramatic transformation in mind for her. In his only significant departure from the circumstances of Marie Duplessis's life, he invented a scene in which Armand's father, the personification of bourgeois morality, begs Marguerite to set his son free. It is a sacrifice she must make in order to save the reputation of the man she adores, but also for the sake of his pure young sister, whose marriage would be jeopardized by the scandal of Armand's relationship. This is the turning point of the story, and it makes a saint and martyr of the wanton heroine, crucially allowing her to be accepted, even pitied, by respectable nineteenth-century society.

Part social document, part romantic melodrama, both ahead of its time and rigidly conventional, *The Lady of the Camellias* was an instant success. Dumas fils had sold only fourteen copies of his first book, *Sins of Youth,* a collection of long poems, including one entitled "M.D.," which intimately details what it was like to make love to Marie Duplessis. Printed at his father's expense in 1847, it had passed unnoticed, whereas his novel received an advance of a thousand francs from the reputable firm of Cadot, whose first edition of 1,200 copies was quickly followed by a sell-out printing of another 1,500. Having grown up in the shadow of his illustrious father, Dumas fils was overjoyed by this first taste of literary fame, confessing, "I should have died of shame and jealousy if I had not contrived to acquire a little glory of my own."

The impact of the novel, though, was nothing compared with the sensation caused by the play. It had been a three-year struggle to persuade a theater to take on *The Lady of the Camellias,* which Dumas fils adapted in 1849. His father's response had been ecstatic—"It's original! It's touching! It's audacious! It's new!," he exclaimed as he tearfully embraced Alexandre, while also warning him that his work was too authentic to be allowed onstage.

Nepotism counted for nothing—"I was the son of the greatest dramatic author of his time, no-one could have a more powerful protector, but I might as well have arrived from the provinces with an unknown name." Dumas père's Théâtre Historique had closed by 1850, and *The Lady of the Camellias* was turned down by the Gaîté, the Ambigu-Comique, and the Gymnase, which had just mounted *Manon Lescaut.* Eventually, the new director of the Vaudeville accepted it, but it was immediately banned by the censors. When Louis-Napoléon Bonaparte became president of the Second Republic in December 1851, the author's friendship with his half brother, the Duke de Morny, helped force a cancellation of the veto, but he was told that it would make no difference; the audience would stop the play. The actress cast as Marguerite, the Vaudeville's diva, thirty-three-year-old Anaïs Fargueil, withdrew after the first reading, and the part was offered to the more suitable Eugénie Doche, a young beauty with something of a louche reputation. Armand, twenty-three-year-old Charles Fechter, was three years her junior, with all the bullish surliness of a conceited young star. When Dumas fils suggested that in Act 4, Armand, overcome by jealousy and anger, should fling Marguerite to the floor, Fechter refused. "It's impossible," he said. "The public will never allow it." Convinced of its effect, the author persisted until finally Fechter shrugged. "As the play will not get to that point, I might as well agree."

Courtesans, romanticized by legend, had regularly been represented onstage, but only in a historical setting. Hugo's *Marion Delorme* took place in the time of Louis XIII, and Scribe's *Adrienne Lecouvreur* was set in the eighteenth century, the actress-courtesan's own time. French theater, with its comedies in couplets and costume dramas portraying kings and cavaliers, was itself embalmed in the past and had never featured characters or situations taken from life. Then suddenly, here was Dumas fils, "a young scamp," transporting the audience directly into the demimonde, using actual dialogue and the spicy expressions of Left Bank cafés and dance halls. Establishment figures, such as the Louvre's director, Horace de Viel-Castel, recoiled in horror. "This play is shameful. . . . During five acts *The Lady of the Camellias* unfolds before civilised people the sordid details of the life of a prostitute. Nothing is left out. . . . The police, the government tolerate these scandals, and seem to ignore the fact that this will result in the demoralisation of the public."

In fact, the public was enchanted. At its premiere on 2 February 1852, the play received a thunderous ovation, and twenty thousand printed copies were sold almost overnight. During the Vaudeville's first run of two hundred performances, Place de la Bourse was blocked by the carriages of grandes dames who found themselves weeping over the fate of a fallen woman, plucking flowers from their corsages and throwing them onstage. Even innocent young girls, chaperoned by their nannies, went again and again, sitting in the upper boxes in floods of tears. "It was the first time I had heard of pocket-handkerchiefs as a provision for a play," wrote Henry James, who remembered as a small boy walking in the Palais-Royal with his cousins, American girls who lived in Paris, and envying them as they recounted how often they had sobbed while watching Mme Doche as Marguerite. Neither he nor they had any idea of the profession of the lady of the expensive flowers, "but her title had a strange beauty and her story a strange meaning."

The fascination endured, and James wrote two essays on Dumas fils, praising his naturalness as a dramatist and the brilliance of his dialogue. French contemporaries were just as admiring. "It's the new theatre—human, true and strange," wrote Arsène Houssaye in his poem "Memories of Youth":

> This is no longer Dumas I; this is no longer ancient
>   drama . . .
> Dumas II, another life, another love, another source . . .
> And even more tragic in its reality.

Making art out of what he saw and being true to his own time, Dumas fils had anticipated by more than a decade the momentousness of Manet's painting *Olympia,* which provoked an uproar when it was shown in the Salon of 1865. While also drawing on traditional precedents, this brazen portrait of an odalisque and her black maid updates the idealized nude in a classical setting to a *grande horizontale's* bedroom in Second Empire Paris. With her immodest, confrontational stare, Olympia is a modern woman (supposedly the courtesan Marguerite Bellanger impersonated by Manet's model Victorine Meurent). And, like Marguerite Gautier, she is not only an uncompromising embodiment of the present but a harbinger of the future. Dumas fils had perfectly judged the appetite and readiness of his audience; as James observed, "He could see the end of one era and the beginning of another and join hands luxuriously with each." *The Lady of the Camellias* became a theatrical phenomenon, bringing its young author the wealth and renown he craved.

In the audience at the Vaudeville one night during the winter of '52 was the composer Giuseppe Verdi with his mistress, Giuseppina Strepponi, a retired soprano. The novel had already inspired him to begin composing an opera, and the play provided even more of an incentive. The vitality of the demimonde offered rich theatrical opportunities, and he had been deeply moved by Marguerite's selfless courage. Verdi saw how music could intensify her spiritual journey, expressing secret doubts and psychological nuances untapped by the play. In Francesco Piave's libretto for *La Traviata* (*The Wayward Girl* in English), the original story would be further distilled into three acts—Love; The Sacrifice; Death—and the heroine and her lover renamed Violetta and Alfredo. The controversial nature of their unmarried love had resonated with Verdi, who had been forced at that time to defend his own relationship with Strepponi. The play's immediacy had impressed him, too, and he was determined to make Violetta a contemporary figure. But with opera implacably bound by convention, the modern setting that he "desired, demanded and begged" was refused. Obliged not only to accept the period of Louis XIII, Verdi failed in his insistence that the soprano must be young and graceful and sing with passion. The first Violetta, thirty-eight-year-old Fanny Salvini-Donatelli, was a prim-lipped, portly matron with a huge bosom, and every time she coughed consumptively, the audience burst out laughing.

If the premiere at Teatro La Fenice, Venice, on 6 March 1853, was not exactly the fiasco its creator described, then neither was it the work he had intended. Just over a year later, the role of Violetta was sung by Maria Spezia, who, though young, was no beauty, and it took the piquant little prima donna, twenty-year-old Marietta Piccolomini, to make a sensation of *La Traviata* and to launch it in London and Paris in 1856. Verdi's insight into the characters had amplified the play's atmosphere of forgiveness, and the emotional core was now the tremendous confrontation between Violetta and Alfredo's father—itself a drama within a drama. At first ruthlessly self-righteous, Germont finds an inner sensitivity that grows into true compassion (made audible in the soaringly beautiful "Piangi, piangi, o misera"). Marie Duplessis's short life had evolved into a masterpiece—a rapturous parable of human redemption through love. And it was this metamorphosis that so impressed Proust on first seeing *La Traviata*. "It's a work which goes straight to my heart," he remarked. "Verdi has given to *La Dame aux Camélias* the style it lacked. I say that not because Alexandre Dumas fils's play is without merit, but because for a dramatic work to touch popular sentiment the addition of music is essential."

Eclipsing its source, *La Traviata* went on to become one of the most popular operas of all time. For many, the definitive portrayal remains that of Maria Callas, who identified with Violetta to the point of obsession. The hefty diva in a ballooning gown of the 1951 Mexican production transformed herself four years later into a slender beauty for Visconti's belle époque version at

La Scala in Milan. Not only resembling the raven-haired Marie with her ballerina shoulders, tiny waist, and lack of décolletage, Callas shared her passion for fine clothes, furs, and jewelry as well as a weakness for wealthy men and marrons glacés. She never again put so much of herself into the creation of a character and went so far in the interest of psychological truth as to allow her voice to suffer. "How could Violetta be in her condition and sing in big, high, round tones? It would be ridiculous," she said, and proved her point in the last act by creating a reedy, gasping sound of a consumptive fighting for breath. Callas was able to combine her phenomenal technique with exceptional glamour, but this vital combination has eluded other interpetators, who sing with seraphic purity but do not look the part. In 1994 an unknown Romanian, the lovely Angela Georghiu, was Violetta in a Covent Garden *Traviata,* her mesmerizing, full-blooded performance making her a star overnight. The great contemporary Violetta is Anna Netrebko, a playful minx who stole the famous Callas detail of kicking off her stilettos after the party scene. Netrebko has completely redefined the character, giving her a stark veracity and sexual audacity that the twenty-first century demands.

Although hardly a night goes by that *La Traviata* is not performed somewhere in the world, the impact of the play has diminished drastically with time. This was something Dumas fils had foreseen when he remarked in the preface to the 1867 edition that *The Lady of the Camellias* was "already ancient history" and owed its survival to its reputation alone. His view was shared by the novelist and critic Jules Barbey d'Aurevilly, who a year later saw "a revival which hasn't revived."

> What is immensely striking . . . is the obsolescence, the sadness, the end of something which seemed for a moment to live so intensely. . . . Compared with the courtesan of today and her monstrous corruption, squalor, language, slang and stupidity, the Marguerite Gautier of M. Dumas

fils, who first interested everyone in courtesans, seems nothing but a faded engraving of some vague design.

It was not until the great Sarah Bernhardt first played the heroine during her United States tour of 1880 that *The Lady of the Camellias,* renamed *Camille* for the American public, came triumphantly back to life. A beautiful, worldly Parisian, Bernhardt went on to play Marguerite around three thousand times, inhabiting the role so entirely that audiences believed she *was* the consumptive courtesan. As her febrile gaiety in the opening scenes deepened into idealistic passion for Armand, the high romance was all the more transporting for its underlying trace of cynicism. Using her knowledge of the pathological details of tuberculosis, she made Marguerite's suffering so harrowing in its authenticity that no other actress succeeded in challenging the supremacy of Bernhardt's interpretation. Until, that is, the Italian actress Eleonora Duse made her Paris debut in 1897.

Watching her rival from a central box was Sarah Bernhardt, bejeweled and exquisitely dressed, like a reincarnation of Marie Duplessis. There in the audience, too, was the first Marguerite, Eugénie Doche, who was now an old lady. Duse's nerves showed, and she made little effect that night. With her plain, melancholy face devoid of makeup and her ascetic personality, she had none of the gregarious sophistication necessary for the first act and so did little with the heroine's transition. But whereas Bernhardt, the star diva, imposed her own personality at every moment, la Duse soon came to discover what she called an inexplicable reciprocity of feeling for women like Marguerite and in this way conveyed far subtler shades of mood. In fact, as Verdi himself recognized, her internal, reflective technique, which could register shifts of conflicting emotion in eloquent pauses and modulations, more closely resembled the vocal coloring of a singer. "If only I had seen her Marguerite before composing *La Traviata.* What a splendid finale I might have put together if I had heard that crescendo invoking Armand that Duse has created simply by allowing her soul to overflow."

For the rest of the century, and well into the next, Marguerite Gautier became a favorite vehicle for the world's actresses—not all of whom were legends. Henry James recalled seeing a fat Marguerite and a coy production in Boston in which the lovers were represented as engaged. Nevertheless, he never lost his regard for the play, which he felt withstood any amount of mediocrity in the performance. "Nothing makes any difference. It carries with it an April air: some tender young man and some coughing young woman have only to speak the lines to give it a great place among the love-stories of the world." For Coco Chanel, even the dismaying sight of Bernhardt as "an old clown" performing Marguerite at the end of her career could not dim her lifelong passion for *The Lady of the Camellias*. In homage to its heroine, Chanel adopted the white camellia as her own emblem, printing it on fabrics, embossing buttons with it, and fashioning it into rings and necklaces.

With the arrival of silent movies, *The Lady of the Camellias* underwent a fourth incarnation. A Danish film of 1907 was followed by a 1911 version in which Bernhardt herself appeared, and a decade later came Alla Nazimova giving a high-camp performance opposite Rudolph Valentino's sloe-eyed Armand. The advent of sound brought Abel Gance's 1934 adaptation, with the sparkling Parisian chanteuse Yvonne Printemps, and then the great classic: George Cukor's 1936 film *Camille* starring Greta Garbo. Of all the legendary interpreters, Garbo may have come closest to embodying the real Marie, bringing an ironical intelligence to the role, ridding it of sentiment, and changing the notion of the heroine as a victim of men. She believed that Marie, whose story she researched, had loved her work and the lifestyle it allowed her, and to Cukor's delight, she took the initiative in her scenes with Armand (Robert Taylor). "She never touches but kisses her lover all over the face. Often she is the aggressor in lovemaking. Very original." Since Garbo's *Camille* there have been movie versions in numerous foreign languages, including Egyptian (the 1942 *Leila, ghadet el camelia*). In Mauro Bolognini's heavy-handed *Lady of the Camelias* (1981), Isabelle Huppert gives a biographical portrait of Marie Duplessis herself. This was followed three years later by an English film in which Greta Scacchi's Camille starred opposite a baby-faced Colin Firth. The list of film spin-offs includes Antonioni's 1953 *La signora senza camelie* and Baz Lurhmann's *Moulin Rouge* of 2001, in which Nicole Kidman stars as a consumptive courtesan in love with an impoverished young writer (Ewan McGregor).

Of the dozen or so ballets based on *The Lady of the Camellias,* the first was the quaintly named *Rita Gauthier* [*sic*], created in 1857 by Filippo Termanini, which ends happily with the lovers' marriage. John Taras made *Camille* for the Ballets Russes in 1946, and Antony Tudor choreographed his own *Lady of the Camellias* for New York City Ballet in 1951. There were Gsovsky's intolerably long *Die Kameliendame,* staged in Berlin in 1957, and Maurice Béjart's 1959 pas de deux *Violetta,* danced by Violette Verdy to music from *La Traviata.* But the only two versions in current repertories are Frederick Ashton's *Marguerite and Armand,* made in 1963 as a showcase for Fonteyn and Nureyev, and John Neumeier's 1978 *Lady of the Camellias,* created for Stuttgart's dramatic ballerina Marcia Haydée. When Ashton choreographed his ballet, the Dumas fils source was considered such an "old hack story" that he avoided a conventional narrative by distilling it into headlines—Prologue, The Meeting, The Country, The Insult, The Death of the Lady of the Camellias—which must be bafflingly elliptical to people unfamiliar with the plot. In today's audiences they are the majority. The play still resurfaces from time to time (in 2002 it was staged as a West End musical, *Marguerite,* set in German-occupied Paris with a TV soap star in the title role), but the name Marguerite Gautier has barely survived the twentieth century. As for Marie Duplessis, it was her love of camellias and romantically early death that provided the spring-board for all these reinterpretations, yet she is unknown now to anyone apart from the (mainly French) cognoscenti.

I first discovered her while researching the life of Ashton and learned more when working on my biography of Nureyev. Wanting to say something new about *Marguerite and Armand,* I began casting around for background material on Marie Duples-sis. There wasn't much. She appeared in English anthologies of courtesans or in syrupy fictionalized versions of her life, and as her hold on me grew, I had no choice but to improve my O-Level French. A year or two later, with Marie becoming more and more seductive as a subject in her own right, I had begun working my way through just about every book, article, obituary, and tribute ever written about her. Most of these were stored in the Biblio-thèque Nationale's intimidatingly vast repository in the concrete wasteland of Quai François Mauriac, a ten-minute TGV ride from Paris's Saint-Michel station. I'd been warned of the chal-lenge of locating BnF material, but I hadn't anticipated that this search would require cryptanalysis skills to crack its codes, as well as the patience and nimble fingers of a lace maker to prevent the microfilm machines from wildly unraveling their spools of archival treasures.

In the notes to a French paperback edition of *La dame aux camélias,* I had been intrigued by the mention of "a mysterious friend" from her native village who was one of the few mourn-ers at her funeral. I remember wishing at the time that Marie had lived a century and a half later so that I could track down this man as the key source for her Normandy background. And then I found him. It was her first biographer, Romain Vienne, the son of Nonant innkeepers, who knew everything about her upbringing—and a great deal more. Before this discovery I couldn't see how it was possible even to attempt a rounded por-trait of Marie: no diaries existed and almost all her letters had been destroyed. But in Vienne's *The Truth about the Real Lady of the Camellias,* her voice could be heard as vividly as if it had been tape-recorded, and her character—witty, skeptical, modest, sophisticated, merry, subdued—emerged on page after page. Like countless others before me, I fell in love.

I think a large part of Marie's appeal was the fact that, as Nureyev would have said, she made her own luck. The mythical versions begin with the courtesan at the height of her success, giving no idea of her trajectory—of what she overcame. Abandoned by her mother and abused, degraded, and sexually exploited by her father, she used her burgeoning beauty to make a new start for herself. From the moment of her arrival in Paris Marie took charge of her destiny: she was a survivor—she knew what she wanted and how to get it. The money she earned from selling her body did not make her a victim; it bought her independence, a privilege generally available only to women who were aristocrats. But Marie was freer than they were. As she was not required to conform to the ethics of the age, conversations in her presence could be as lewd as they were enlightening, which was the reason why a particular coterie of Parisian wits and intellectuals preferred demimondaines to grandes dames at their dinners. Often two or three of the Opéra's most beautiful ballerinas would be there, magnificently dressed and bedecked with diamonds, but rarely did they speak a word. As the poet and essayist Théodore de Banville explained, "No one had told them to remain silent. But they instinctively guessed that the sparkle of their eyes and their scarlet lips had more value than anything they could say." Marie, by contrast, was too clever and observant to remain appealingly mute in such company. An autodidact, avid reader, and regular theatergoer, she was determined to profit from Parisian culture and sample the same hedonistic pleasures available to men.

As Marie's story mutated into different genres, her own personality became overshadowed by the dominant themes of sickness, sacrifice, and death. Dumas fils and Verdi softened her, capitulating to the romantic ideal that sought to exonerate and desexualize the fallen woman. Psychologically, Marie had less in common with Violetta than with two other operatic heroines: Carmen, the sultry rebel, whose grave danger is that she acts like a man; and the remorselessly materialistic Manon Lescaut. Like Manon, whom she recognized as an alter ego, Marie was practical, willful, grasping, and manipulative. But these are human flaws, whereas Violetta, who renounces her own happiness, can seem infuriatingly and unconvincingly saintly to modern feminists. "What rankles in me is that male composers and writers create women who are such gleaming ideals," remarks Rebecca Meitles in *Violetta and Her Sisters.* "So few women have been able to be true to themselves." Sophie Fuller agrees. "Why on earth didn't Violetta simply ignore the self-righteous Germont?" she asks—a point that also troubled the singer Helen Field: "She wouldn't actually have done that—at least *I* wouldn't have done that! You find yourself asking who would." And yet, Dumas fils was perfectly aware that he was stretching credibility. "One looks around in vain for a young woman who could justify the novel's progression from love, through repentance to sacrifice. It would be a paradox," he wrote in his 1867 preface. "Young people in their twenties who read it will say to themselves: 'Were there ever girls like that?' And young women will exclaim: 'What a fool she was!'; It is not a play, it's a legend."

La Traviata has survived for the reason recognized by Proust. It is Verdi's music, with its transfiguration of the human voice, that reconciles an audience to the heroine's conversion, signaling her capitulation by a key change and expressing pure, altruistic virtue in a surge of beatific sound. But for those moved by Violetta's noble nature, the prosaic reality of the model may come as a shock. "You're actually demolishing the myth," the writer Peter Conrad, a friend of mine, remarked in an e-mail after reading my manuscript. "I regard Violetta as one of the great characters in drama. She acquires a true tragic grandeur, and Marie can't help but be morally dwarfed by her. She's the sow's ear."

Marie is a different woman to different people. To Garbo she was strong and controlling, to Fonteyn she had "something of that vulnerability of the feminine woman, like Marilyn Monroe." Duality was part of her nature; like Violetta, she was addicted to pleasure but beset by misgivings. And if their circumstances had been the same, who knows whether Marie would have made Violetta's selfless choice? She believed herself capable of an infinite capacity to give—"Oh how I could have loved!" she once exclaimed—and she, too, underwent a spiritual journey, begging forgiveness and wanting to atone for her moral irresponsibility. Performance history has made this a love story between an older woman and a possessive youth, but it should be remembered that Marie was only twenty-three when she died. To the men whose sexual needs she served she brought beauty, grace, and distinction, and at the same time she elevated every aspect of her own life with the sensibility of an artist. This is what Dumas fils meant when he described Marie to his father as "far superior to the profession she practises." It was something also recognised by Liszt, whose attachment to Marie may have had consequences far more profound than their brief liaison. "Without her knowing it," he wrote, "she put me into the vein of poetry and music." Marie Duplessis was one of the great romantic muses, and that, to me, is reason enough to tell her own, unsung story.

Part One

Alphonsine

❧

Waif

ON AN EARLY summer afternoon in 1841, the stagecoach from Paris drew up in front of the Hôtel de La Poste in Nonant, a village in Lower Normandy. Among the alighting passengers were two girls in their late teens: the tall one, pale and elegantly dressed, was Alphonsine Plessis, a fledgling courtesan; the other, plump and pink-cheeked, was her maid, Rose.

Alphonsine had spent her early childhood in Nonant, where she was born on 15 January 1824. This was the first time she had returned home since leaving for Paris three years before. In spring she had given birth to a child fathered by the viscount who was her protector and on her doctor's orders was coming to convalesce in the country. She had arranged to stay with her older sister, Delphine, who lived nearby, but the long journey had exhausted her, and she decided to rest at the hotel for a couple of days before moving on to Delphine's cottage. At around five o'clock, refreshed by a siesta, Alphonsine came downstairs and said, smiling, to the proprietress,

—Bonjour, Madame Vienne. You don't recognize me but you know me well. I'm the little Plessis girl.

—Ah, certainly, my poor child. No, I wouldn't have known you.

"La pauvre Plessis" was still a subject of conversation in Nonant and its neighboring hamlets. Tales were told of her angelic mother, who had been forced to abandon her two children to escape the murderous abuse of her husband. It was said that Marin Plessis, a man whose infamy had earned him the reputation of an evil sorcerer, had sold the thirteen-year-old Alphonsine to Gypsies, and even more disturbing were the rumors of incest. Mme Vienne had last seen Alphonsine as a wild urchin exploiting her precocious sexuality as a way of begging for food, but the young woman who had arrived that day, wearing a lace-edged bonnet that prettily framed her ingenue face, had indeed changed beyond recognition. Her burnished peasant complexion had gone, replaced by the smooth sheen of white china, and she had acquired a self-assurance and social ease that completely belied the misery and degradation of her adolescence.

Eager for news of relatives and mutual friends, Alphonsine asked Mme Vienne if she and Rose could join the family table for dinner. The son of the house, twenty-five-year-old Romain, was also there that night, and although he did not remember Alphonsine, he still had a vivid picture of her mother, Marie. It had been market day and Mme Vienne had stopped to greet Mme Plessis, whose pallor and air of sadness had conveyed even to the twelve-year-old boy that something must be very wrong. Soon after came word of Mme Plessis's flight. Romain, who wrote poetry and had spent several years in Paris studying medicine and law, was a sympathetic, sharp-witted young man, and Alphonsine warmed to him immediately. As soon as dinner was over she asked him to show her round the garden, and while he picked her a bunch of flowers, she chattered away, intriguing him with hints of piquant episodes in her Paris life.

The following day was a Sunday, and Alphonsine went out early for a walk. This is the gently undulating countryside that Degas described in his notebooks twenty years later: "Continuously going up and down green humps. . . . Exactly like England, large and small fields, surrounded entirely by hedges. Damp foot-paths, ponds/greenery and shady ground." The Merlerault region of L'Orne is pastureland whose lushness feeds into the creamy richness of the cuisine: Camembert is a regional speciality, not surprisingly, as the grass is the best in France. Le Merlerault–bred horses, such as Napoléon's stallion Acacia, were renowned for their speed and agility—the reason that the English formed their cavalry here during the Hundred Years' War. And it was while staying with a friend at a château in nearby Exmes that Degas began his series of equine paintings, inspired by the sleek beauties stabled at Le Pin National Stud outside Nonant, which is still active today. Since the time of the first Normans, the rais-ing of horses has been an aristocratic pursuit, and for Alphonsine, ownership of a fine mare or stallion, the symbol of her Normandy childhood, was something she coveted more than anything else.

Watching her leave the hotel, Romain had presumed she was going to mass, but if this was Alphonsine's intention, she changed her mind, having come across a handsome peasant boy with nostalgic associations. As a seventeen-year-old, Marcel had been her first conquest, his seductress of no more than twelve or thirteen at the time. Intent now on impressing him with her new prosperity, Alphonsine invited Marcel to lunch at the hotel, where she proceeded to order some of the finest wines in the house. He, however, was impressed only by Rose, so giggly, frisky, and radiantly healthy that she all but eclipsed her deli-cate mistress. Nevertheless, he and Alphonsine parted like old friends, embracing affectionately, before she set off to spend the afternoon visiting acquaintances from her childhood.

When she returned that evening, there were half a dozen new arrivals in the dining room, a rowdy group of men, laughing, smoking, and lasciviously eyeing the two girls. Anticipating a barrage of "banal remarks and insipid compliments," Alphon-

THE GIRL WHO LOVED CAMELLIAS

sine again asked Mme Vienne if she and Rose could sit at their table, and afterward Alphonsine withdrew alone to the garden with Romain. Enlivened by the wine, she was more forthcoming now about her debut in the demimonde; her attentive companion put her completely at ease, and she surprised him by her frankness—even replying to his blunt query about her state of health. "I've told everything to your mother. I gave birth to a beautiful little boy two months ago and I've come to the country to recuperate." The only subject on which she refused to be drawn was the loathsome reputation of her father. Marin Plessis had died earlier that year in miserable circumstances, and Alphonsine begged Romain not to compound her sorrow by questioning her about him.

As they were talking, two of the travelers sitting on a nearby bench came over and tried to strike up a conversation with her. As part of the management, Romain felt he could not appear to be monopolizing a guest and so tactfully got up to go—only to be followed by Alphonsine. Taking his arm, she suggested they walk together on the Paris road, saying that she needed an excuse to get away from the tiresome men. They hadn't gone far when they came across a wedding party returning from the town of Le Merlerault—a young couple followed by a jubilant procession of parents and friends. "Now that's the kind of gaiety I like," said Alphonsine. "*Look* how they love each other." "They'll love each other more in a very short while," added Romain.

His suggestive tone was deliberate, intended to coax the young courtesan into revealing further confidences, but it was also an act. Romain may have been eight years older than Alphonsine, but he was an innocent when it came to women; his poems, published before he was twenty in a collection called *Le berceau,* are melancholy Petrarchan odes to chaste young girls, to a cruelly unattainable married woman, and to the soprano Mme Damoreau-Cinti—the juvenilia of a sentimental idealist. Alphonsine, with her paradoxical appeal—the childlike demeanor counteracted by knowing black eyes and coarse banter—was unlike anyone he had met before. Darting into a wheat field to pick her a bunch of cornflowers, Romain found himself one moment courting her like a lovesick boy, the next listening pruriently to her risqué stories of her Paris nightlife. Alphonsine was only too aware of the effect she was having on her companion. She amused herself by observing him as he struggled to overcome his attraction and teased him about his "most veiled of allusions to a project everyone is discussing"—presumably his engagement. Sulkily dropping his arm, she told him that she expected confidences in return, something she gradually coaxed out of him over the coming weeks. The bond they established in Nonant that summer was the beginning of a lifelong friendship.

Alphonsine's father, Marin Plessis, was born as the result of a quick, illicit union between a priest and a prostitute. Marin's father, Louis Descours, had grown up in a lower-bourgeois family who saw the church as the best career opportunity for their son. A simple, weak young man with no real vocation, Louis was easy prey when, in the early spring of 1789, the daughter of a neighboring farmer set her mind on seducing him. The louche ways of Louise-Renée Plessis—"as infamous for her foul tongue as for her misconduct"—had earned her the sobriquet La Guenuchetonne, meaning a debauched woman—half beggar, half prostitute. But if the illiterate, maligned Louise had derived some self-satisfaction from corrupting a member of the clergy, it was shattered by the discovery that she was pregnant. On 15 January 1790, she gave birth to a son, who was baptized on the same day in the village church of Lougé, held by the midwife who delivered him. The baby had been named Marin after his paternal grandfather, Marin Descours, but the birth certificate records his father's identity as "unknown," and only Louise and her parents attended the ceremony. As a rule in the Normandy countryside the illegitimate offspring of a bourgeois father was provided for by the paternal family, who regarded this as an obligation. It was not the case with the Descours, however, even when Louis became vicar of the same village, Lougé, where his bastard son lived in a hovel of a cottage with his mother.

As soon as Marin was ten or eleven, he was sent to work as a farmhand, joining the large number of child laborers in Normandy. By the time he reached puberty, he had developed into a tall, slim, virile youth. Emboldened by his superb looks, Marin made a play for the daughter of his employer—unwisely, as the farmer found out and ordered him off the premises. By his early twenties Marin had become a peddler roaming the countryside and selling his trinkets and utensils from door to door. Dressed in the costume of his profession, short culottes and a waistcoat, he had all the swagger and sophistry of the traditional mountebank and could woo his female customers with fantastical stories of far-flung places and the novelty of his wares. "He was of an ideal beauty," remarks one local chronicler, "but it was a beauty that contained something fatal: he had, as the Italians say, the Evil Eye." Marin's sexual magnetism had an almost hypnotic power over women, some of whom were swept away against their will, while others succumbed out of fear. Then, after more than a decade of countless fleeting encounters, he decided that the time had come to take a wife.

Marie Deshayes was plaintively beautiful and more than usually intelligent for a country girl. She and her sister, Julie, were outgoing and hardworking and, having reached their mid-twenties unmarried, were resigned to a future of spinsterhood and caring for their widowed father. Marie was then employed as a maid by the Count and Countess du Hays, who owned the nearby turreted Château de Mesnil in Saint-Germain-de-Clairefeuille. It was in this manor kitchen that she first set eyes on Marin Plessis. "As soon as she saw him she fell in love," E. du Mesnil, a local historian, wrote in a letter of 1882. Descendant Charles du

Hays confirms this. "Marie Deshayes fell in love at first sight. She wanted Marin Plessis and she got him, despite the alarm and pleas of her family."

If Alphonsine inherited her promiscuous nature from her father, then her grace and natural distinction may have been the result of her mother's aristocratic blood. For more than a century her French biographers have mistakenly claimed that her maternal great-grandmother was Anne d'Argentelles, a descendant of the noble seigneurs of Mesnil, who married a servant, Etienne Deshayes. Among their six children was Louis Deshayes, wrongly identified as the grandfather of Alphonsine. In fact, there was another Louis Deshayes in the neighborhood. This Louis Deshayes was married to Françoise Leriche and farmed a small holding in Courménil, about ten kilometers north of Nonant. The younger of their two daughters was Marie Louise Michelle Deshayes, and it is she who was Alphonsine's mother.

However, according to E. du Mesnil, it was local knowledge that sometime after the marriage of his tenant farmers, the count had exercised his "droit du seigneur," leaving Françoise Deshayes pregnant. It was this, du Mesnil suggests, that explained her granddaughter's taste and manners, her passion for beautiful things and for thoroughbred horses. "Because the Count du H was a gentleman to the ends of his fingernails. His family went back to the celebrated Alou, who was one of the companions of Guillaume at the Battle of Hastings."

If the rumor is true and the countess was aware of her husband's transgression, she was exceptionally forgiving, as she loved Françoise Deshayes's younger daughter as much as her own children. Marie was brought up at the château and encouraged to remain with the du Hayses instead of helping her parents on the farm. Her role was to take care of the family linen, and the countess had plans to marry her to a good local man. But then Marin Plessis appeared. As Vienne put it, "She was seized by a furious, blind passion for someone totally the opposite of herself."

The couple were married on 1 March 1821 at the mairie in Courménil, the groom's side of the family represented by Marin's mother and two Plessis relatives, a laborer and a weaver, and the bride's by her father, aunt, and uncle. "From that moment an impossible life began for the poor woman," continues du Mesnil. "One would see her following her husband from fair to market, sleeping sometimes here, sometimes there, selling cotton scarves and little items of haberdashery." It may have been either a relative or the du Hayses who came to the rescue, helping the couple to raise enough money to open a shop selling haberdashery and basic groceries in Nonant. This was a large village of around eight hundred inhabitants, which, since the recent completion of the Rouen-Alençon *grande route* intersecting with that of Paris-Granville, had become an important junction. The Plessis house and shop, a simple little square building with a double façade, was situated at the crossroads. Marin now had a respectable profession, he had made a good marriage, and he was adored by his wife—the years of humiliation were over. But it was on the very day of the wedding, according to Charles du Hays, that his true character revealed itself, and Marie was forced to realize how unsound her judgment had been.

Alcoholism was rife in nineteenth-century rural Normandy. An official inquiry of the time discovered that children from the day of their baptism were given a spoon of eau de vie—80 proof Calvados or *poire*—in the belief that it was as natural as the apples and pears from which it was made. Strong cider accompanied most meals, but just as it was considered effeminate to drink this without fortifying it first with eau de vie, no inn would serve a man coffee without the accompaniment of "calva." Like most of his male compatriots, Marin was rarely sober, but in his case, drink could unleash a fury so irrational that it terrified his new wife. Feeling trapped by domesticity, he became more volatile by the day and decided to return to his itinerant trade. Marie was left to run their Nonant shop alone, an arrangement that sparked a new problem even more incendiary than alcohol: Marin had become consumed by jealousy and began neglecting his business in order to return home unannounced.

A Maupassant tale called *Le colporteur* plays out a scene of striking similarity. A Normandy peddler with a persuasive tongue travels the French countryside with his merchandise on his back while his wife looks after their haberdashery shop. At the beginning of the story he speaks of her with tenderness, but once back home, he turns surly and consumes a dangerous amount of wine. Observing his change of mood, the narrator is sure that he will beat his wife once the couple are alone. "He had a hard look about him . . . the air of a brute in whom violence was dormant." Maupassant's peddler had good reason. In the two minutes when he goes to the cellar, a beautiful youth with bare feet and shoes in hand charges out the front door. "It was a scene of eternal drama which is played out every day in all different forms, in all different worlds," Maupassant concludes. The husband had seen nothing and was furious without knowing why. "Perhaps by an obscure feeling of foreboding, the instinct of a cuckolded man." It's unlikely that Marie, admired for her perfect conduct, ever gave Marin cause for his suspicions, but the son of La Guenuchetonne, irrevocably damaged by the deplorable conditions of his upbringing, needed little to persuade himself that all women were whores.

A few months into the marriage, Marie found that she was pregnant. "She hoped that the cradle would be her protection and the child her guardian angel," recounts Vienne. This was not to be. Delphine-Adèle Plessis was born on 19 February 1822, and that evening Marin arrived with two friends at the mairie of Saint-Germain-de-Clairefeuille to register the birth. He had wanted a son and must have numbed his displeasure with drink, as his signature on the certificate, unusually elegant in other examples, is barely legible. E. du Mesnil describes how Marin, so possessed by fury, beat Marie mercilessly and then disappeared.

After her recovery the unfortunate victim arrived with her child to beg for help from her one-time benefactors [the du Hays]. They welcomed her like a prodigal daughter. A long time went by before we heard again about "le beau Plessis," but one day he reappeared in the area, and, with a touching solicitude, the count du H gave an order to all his workers not to tell the young woman of her husband's return. But despite this precaution, somehow the couple found out about each other, and mother and child disappeared from the château. The unhappy woman began again her errant life of before, made more miserable still by the torture that "le beau Plessis" often inflicted on her by preferring some inn keeper's daughter, Gypsy girl or willing seamstress. The poor woman endured everything because her husband and master would honour her sometimes with a warm look and tender caress. She became pregnant a second time.

Rose-Alphonsine came into the world at 8 p.m. on 15 January 1824. Her birth was declared the next day at Nonant's mairie, witnessed by August-Jean Cornet, a shopkeeeper, and baker Louis Pignel. Marin, who was around at the time and enraged by the arrival of another girl, told his wife he was leaving for good. During the next months, however, he would continue to return, venting his aggression not only on his family but on their neighbors, who began to instigate costly lawsuits. Having resigned herself to her husband's brutality, Marie did her best to run the business while looking after their baby and toddler, but with resources practically exhausted, the shelves were bare and the shop deserted. Forced to find cheaper lodgings, the family moved a few kilometers away to a small cottage on the hillside hamlet of Les Orgeries.

It was there one evening that a passing roofer heard a child's terrified screams and stopped to investigate. While Marie was in the cellar, Marin, furious with one of the girls, had flung her to the back of the room. She had fallen unharmed on the bed, but nevertheless the twenty-year-old Gouet was shocked enough to report Plessis to his landlord. Weary of yet another brutal scene, the landlord evicted the family, who moved into a dilapidated cottage near the church. By the following year they had moved again, to an even shabbier place in the nearby village of La Porte, but then a charitable landlord offered them a three-year lease on a more suitable dwelling less than a kilometer away in the village of Le Castel. The abuse continued. On the night of 6 January 1825, coming home drunker than ever after celebrating the Feast of Three Kings, Marin flew into a psychotic rage and tried to set fire to the house, dragging his wife toward the flaming hearth. Vienne continues:

> As strong as she was courageous, and understanding the terrible danger threatening her life, Marie managed not to lose her head and for ten minutes was able to resist by hanging on to a table and the legs of the bed. Her cries went unheard, her strength was giving out, and she was about to succumb when the door was flung open and a saviour entered who grabbed Plessis with a grip that almost pulverised his bones.

It was the Nonant-Rouen messenger, Henry Aubert, a young colossus "as sweet as a lamb," who insisted that Marie should take the girls and leave the house immediately. Stopping a neighbor returning from the Gacé fair, Aubert offered to lend him his horse and trap to drive the victim and her children to a friend who would protect them.

Marie knew she had no choice. The next morning, learning that Marin would be absent all day, she went back to La Castel to fetch some belongings, and then, walking with the children to her aunt in the next village of La Trouillère, she covered them with kisses and bade them goodbye. At first she hid herself away in a neighboring barn belonging to a couple named Dupont, but she was spotted by a local gossip and forced to find another refuge. Mme du Hays took charge, offering to send Marie to one of their tenant farmers, and at midnight Monsieur Dupont drove her to her hiding place. Charles du Hays remembered going as a child with their maid several times to visit Marie. "She seemed to me as beautiful as a saint and all the stories I'd heard made me shudder with fear. 'It's the wife of Pluto,' this servant told me. 'Her husband intends to kill her and if ever he finds her he will kill all those who helped to hide her. If ever you talk of this he will burn down your house and poison your cattle.' And so I scrupulously kept my secret."

About a week later, through the intervention of a retired English jockey who had worked at the family's stables, Mme du Hays found Marie employment as a lady's maid to a well-born Englishwoman, who lived in Paris in the winter and on the shore of Lake Geneva in summer. "As we had remained on terms of affection with her," wrote Charles du Hays, "my mother wrote telling her of the misery which we had before our eyes and asked her to help." One morning, escorted by two loyal farmhands, Marie was driven to the *grande route* to take the stagecoach to Paris, where her new employer was waiting.

It was Marie's aunt and uncle, Marie-Françoise and Louis Mesnil, who for the next two years looked after the Plessis girls in La Trouillère, a hamlet a few kilometers north of Nonant. Marin reappeared from time to time, promising to send a monthly allowance for his daughters' upbringing, but no money ever arrived. As Mesnil earned very little as a laborer, the couple made the decision to keep Delphine and send Alphonsine to their cousin in La Corbette. Marin promised to provide eight francs a month as upkeep, but he never sent a sou. And yet, although money was tight, this was a relatively happy period for Alphonsine. The cousins, Agathe Boisard and her husband, Jean-François, who was a roadsman as well as clogmaker, were welcoming, kindhearted people, and their son, Roch, who was exactly Alphonsine's age, became the brother she never had. And if separating from Delphine had been a wrench at first, the sisters found they were only a short walk away from each other, La Corbette no more than a kilometer away from La Trouillère.

These Merlerault hamlets, linked by dirt tracks shaded by ivy-clad oaks and made up of no more than three or four cottages, remain virtually unchanged to this day. In the nineteenth century, the heart of almost every house was a large earthen-floored space serving as both kitchen and family bedroom, with hocks of salted pork suspended from the beams and a curtained partition for the husband and wife. With food cooked on the fire and the windows rarely opened, the interior was as snug and murky as a Normandy proverb suggests—"Warm smoke is better than cold wind." A meal consisted of several galettes per person made with sarrasin flour and milk, or vegetable soup flavored with beef or pork fat. Poultry was reserved for Sundays and holidays, and once or twice a year there was a special occasion when a family killed a pig and summoned parents and friends to eat *fricot de cochon.* The day that the sarrasin was harvested was another excuse for a celebration. The workers who had taken part were invited with their families to a dinner lasting through the night, sitting at a long table strewn with bread, jugs of cider, and baronial platters of meat.

For six-year-old Alphonsine, the high point of the year was the Saint-Mathieu fair, which brought a horde of strangers to Nonant—strolling players, puppeteers, fire-eaters, and merchants selling everything from bonnets, ribbons, and frippery to tinware, fruit, and charcuterie. "Locals waited for Saint-Mathieu to buy their umbrellas, soap, crockery and fabrics. . . . Young girls waited for the fair to have their ears pierced and adorned with pendants of silver or gold; fiancés bought rings to fulfill their promises, and farmers found all the tools and objects necessary to cultivate their land." The sense of anticipation was always justified by the festive atmosphere of the day itself, September 22, when inhabitants of neighboring villages joined the Nonantais picnicking on the grass and strolling between the stalls and café tents.

Nothing, however, would equal the excitement of the historic summer day that not only affected every inhabitant of the region but forged a link to Alphonsine's future. This was 7 August 1830, when the dethroned Charles X and his cortège arrived in Le Merlerault en route to the Normandy coast. A week earlier, on July 31, following the republican insurrection in Paris, Louis-Philippe d'Orléans had been named "lieutenant general of the kingdom" and on August 2 ordered that Charles and his family be chaperoned with the greatest respect to Cherbourg. "The immense convoy was watched by a double row of people who had hastened there from ten leagues away to contemplate this unique spectacle: the exodus of a king and his court." Following the king's coach, drawn by eight splendid horses, its gold facing and glass windows sparkling in the blazing August sun, were carriages containing the dauphin, the dauphine, and their children; other members of the king's entourage with their respective households and servants; escorting bodyguards, commissaires, and policemen; plus wagons and carts loaded with furniture, silver, luggage, and bales of hay serving as fodder. For the crowd, gaping at the procession through clouds of dust raised by the horses' hooves, the effect was as poignant as it was thrilling.

In Le Merlerault, the fifth stop on the long, slow route into exile, a modest town house on the main street had been offered to Charles X by an ex-member of his guard. The bodyguards had set up a bivouac on the lawn by the side of the house, and curious locals could spot the old monarch strolling around after dinner, while the domestics cleared away the meal. Earlier in the day the elegant Duchess de Berry had spent several hours sitting sewing on the grass with her daughter and the two princesses. There was more excitement that night when a rider from Paris came thundering into Le Merlerault bringing a note to Charles from Louis-Philippe suggesting that the royal family leave the young Duke of Bordeaux behind in France. The crowning of King Charles's grandson as Henry V was the old monarch's greatest wish, but there was no question that his daughter-in-law, the Duchess de Berry, would ever leave the country without her ten-year-old son. On the morning of Sunday the 8th, the royal party moved on to Argentan, and on August 16 arrived at their destination of Cherbourg, where two *paquebots* were waiting to transport them to England. Had Alphonsine but known it, in one carriage, bearing the royal arms of the dauphin, was the father of the young duke who was to become her first love.

———

In September news came that Marie Plessis had died. She was thirty-three years old. Marie had written the du Hays family sometime earlier from Paris, where she lived on the rue du Faubourg-Saint-Honoré, saying that she was being treated with great affection and care by her English employer. She gave as an example the privilege of attending a special mass in the presence of the royal family, claiming that during the service the king had eyes for her alone. Nothing, though, could assuage Marie's memory of her suffering or the loss of her children. While spending the summer of 1830 in Châtelard, Montreux, she fell ill and made no effort to recover.

Alphonsine was then twelve years old and attending a small girls' school in Saint-Germain-de-Clairefeuille run by a nun from La Providence order in Sées. Sister Françoise Huzet taught her charges to read and write, but her main role was to prepare them for their First Communion. For Alphonsine, this took place in Saint-Germain's pretty church dating from the twelfth century, where one of the stained-glass windows has an image of a soulful-eyed Virgin, believed locally to have been modeled on Marie Plessis. After this, Alphonsine's school days were over.

In her role as surrogate mother, Agathe Boisard continued to be kind and supportive, though having given birth to two more boys, she had little time to devote to Alphonsine. With the arrival of a girl in 1836, the situation became impossible, and Agathe pleaded with Marin to take his daughter back. He refused, as did other relatives and friends to whom she appealed. Alphonsine became one of 965 Ornaise children to be abandoned that year; she still spent nights with the Boisards but was left to her own devices to feed herself, scavenging meals from relatives or from neighboring farmers. When she begged the harvesters for bread or soup, some took advantage, indulging their fantasies by making lewd advances in return. "She had understood, she had seen," writes Vienne. "Her education in vice had begun."

Hearing what was going on, Agathe took Alphonsine to visit her father and insisted that he take responsibility for his daughter by finding her a job. Delphine, set up by her great-uncle Louis Mesnil, was already working locally as a laundress, and, at Agathe's suggestion, Marin went the next day to a laundry in Nonant asking the owner to employ Alphonsine as an apprentice. But his reputation had preceded him, and the woman was too intimidated by the Sorcerer to consider employing his daughter. "He made everyone tremble," wrote one local historian. "People were more afraid of him than of the King's attorney or the police." However, another laundry mistress agreed to take Alphonsine on for ten francs a month. All went well to begin with. Mme Toutain was pleased with her adroit, eager assistant, while Alphonsine appeared to enjoy making herself useful. Having reached the age at which girls become aware of fashionable clothes, she found herself coveting the prettier items she handled and loved to spend time with her dressmaker aunt and godmother, Julie Deshayes. In September, as a reward for her hard work, Aunt Julie asked her what she would like as a present from Saint-Mathieu fair. "My wonderful aunt," she exclaimed, "please buy me a ring!" The two went round the stalls together and chose a simple silver band encrusted with a few blue stones. It was worth only forty sous, but it meant far more to Alphonsine than all the diamonds and emeralds she would later acquire.

In the evenings after work she reveled in her freedom from family contraints, choosing the company of young farmhands who sang smutty songs and swilled pitchers of *beire,* the most lethal Normandy cider. Still only twelve or thirteen but discovering an appetite for sex, Alphonsine was impatient to lose her virginity, and it was at this time that she propositioned Marcel, whose initial reluctance challenged the child's seductive powers for the first time. Coquettishly suggesting, "You play Alfred and I'll be Josephine," she led him into the shade of a hedge bordering one of du Hays's fields and committed what Vienne calls her first *polissonnerie*—or sexy escapade.

Every Sunday Alphonsine would walk to Saint-Germain-de-Clairefeuille to spend time with her father. One day he took her to the hill town of Exmes, to a gloomy house at the end of an alley belonging to a man Vienne names as Plantier—a septuagenarian with "a detestable reputation" as a debaucher. That night, after the three had dined together, Marin returned home, leaving his daughter behind. It was not until Monday evening that Alphonsine went back to work, and, to compensate for her absence, she handed over twenty francs to her employer—the equivalent of two months' salary—saying, as the old bachelor had suggested, that it was from her father. As the weeks went by she regularly spent long weekends with Plantier, who sent her away each time with a five-franc coin. The pittance she earned working in the laundry was making her careless about the hours she kept, and one week she failed to appear until the Tuesday evening, defiantly brandishing the ten francs she had been given. Perplexed, Mme Toutain interrogated her:

—Where have you been these past few days?
—With Monsieur Plantier.

—Who gave you the ten francs?

—Monsieur Plantier.

—What do you do there?

—He plays with me and I play with him.

—I'm going to tell your father.

—You won't be telling him anything he doesn't know. He's the one who sent me there.

Mme Toutain instructed her husband to go to Exmes to find out more.

"The information was deplorable," Vienne reports. "It was, in effect, Plessis who had taken his fourteen-year-old daughter to Plantier. It was evident that the two scoundrels were in perfect accord, and that they had made an infamous pact." Worried about the possibility of scandal, Mme Toutin decided to get rid of Alphonsine, who had anyway become capricious and slapdash. Not only that, but there had been complaints from the parents of other apprentices whom the girl was corrupting by teaching them about what she had learned, in shockingly indelicate language. Alphonsine was given no alternative but to return to Exmes.

"What went on during the next months in this isolated house, sheltered from curiosity, between the child and the hideous satyr?" writes Vienne. "One can guess without any trouble." The ménage of *la petite* Plessis and Plantier had become a topic of such concern that the police were informed and began to make inquiries. Had the old man employed Alphonsine as a maid, or had she been "sold"? No one knew, but the fact was that she was living alone with an old man, and most people imagined the worst. When they were together a few years later, Vienne pressed Alphonsine about what had taken place, but was met with bitter silence. "This only confirmed my suspicion that there were passages in the story that would make even a *grande horizontale* blush."

The 1981 film *Lady of the Camelias* shows Alphonsine complicit in the arrangement. A dirty urchin begging in the rain, she first encounters the Plantier figure when he gives her a coin, which she delightedly hands over to her father, who is watching from a café window. She willingly moves in with the old man and becomes sullen and resentful only with the onset of puberty. Her father is there in the bedroom with Plantier when Alphonsine first sees menstrual blood on the sheets, a moment Bolognini uses to dramatize the origin of one of the best-known aspects of the *Dame aux Camélias* myth. Wiping away her tears, Marin mawkishly whispers, "Don't let that upset you. It's quite natural at your age. . . . When it happened to your mother she wore a flower on her dress. A red flower. It was her way of letting me know not to bother her. There was a time when she didn't wear any flower and you came into the world nine months later." The truth, however, which Vienne claims that Alphonsine confided to him, was chillingly different. Completely ignorant about female matters, she was panic-stricken by the flow of blood and, seized by a primal terror of mutilation and defilement, fled from the house.

A couple named Denis, who ran a reputable inn on the Grand-Rue, took pity on the child and engaged her as a servant. Marin dared not object, as the mayor of Exmes had summoned him and questioned him at length. Earning a salary of sixty francs a year, Alphonsine remained for about eight months in this honest, tranquil house where Mme Denis kept a motherly watch over her charge—even having her sleep in a box room next to the couple's bedroom. But one evening in October 1838, Marin arrived and announced that he had found employment for his daughter in an umbrella shop in Gacé. It was an opportunity too exciting to resist. Compared with the sedate Ornaise villages Alphonsine had known, Gacé was a city of light, a vibrant center with forty cafés, a dozen dress shops, and regular fairs and markets. Maison Fremin, the umbrella shop where she began work as a maid and apprentice, was one of eleven in the town. Women in modish bonnets and shawls wandered among the lime trees of Place du Château (its thirteenth-century tower now houses the Musée de la Dame aux Camélias), and, admiring them, Alphonsine felt as if she had been given a new life. There was also a louche element to Gacé; the livestock market drew farmers from all around—men spending nights away from their families, who were only too glad to pay for the company of local girls. But after only two months, Marin arrived to take Alphonsine away.

This was another period that triggered a barrage of rumors. There was the possibility of incest, something Bolognini's *Lady of the Camelias* makes much of. In the film, Alphonsine's father is a swarthy male whom she nuzzles with adoration and kisses like a mistress. Theirs is the forbidden bond depicted by Edith Wharton in her semipornographic fragment "Beatrice Palmato"—the sexual collusion between a father and his consenting, highly aroused daughter. Beatrice's father is an adept lover, his silver-sprinkled head between her parted knees, conjuring in her "the old swooning sweetness," "the lightnings of heat" that her new husband, with his rough advances, can never achieve. And in Wharton's fantasy, the sexual expertise is reciprocal, with the father expectantly pressing into his daughter's palm "that strong fiery muscle that they used in their old joke to call his third hand." Was this also the case with Marin—was he deliberately grooming his daughter in preparation for her future career? Twice Vienne broached the subject with Alphonsine but obtained first denials and tears and then an order to cease his questions.

There are various stories about Alphonsine's life at this point, but what is clear is that she was on her way to Paris. Charles du Hays said that she had been only eleven years old when Marin tried to sell her to Gypsies.

She wasn't old enough to be handed over, and he had to wait another two years. Then when she was thirteen he took her into the forest of Saint-Evroult, and left her in the hands of these new masters. They brought her to Paris, but as she was still found to be too young for the purpose they had in mind, she was employed there as an apprentice.

Delphine told a curious local lawyer who questioned her in later years about Alphonsine's upbringing that their father had sold her to mountebanks, a claim also made by E. du Mesnil. "Seeing in the sweetness of the child, a source of income in the future," he writes, "they dressed Marie and taught her how to appear in public." Vienne, however, insists that it was Marin himself who delivered her to Paris. Weighed down by an enormous pack made from rabbit skins, they left Le Merlerault on foot, traveling in stages, sometimes sleeping in stables. During the journey, Alphonsine was given a stuffed green lizard in a box for good luck—a talisman that had a special meaning for her and which she kept for the rest of her life.

Marin went back to Nonant alone, and to those who demanded to know why he had not brought Alphonsine with him, he replied dismissively, "What do you expect? Paris is so big that I lost her. In this devil of a town, there's no drum you can beat to find stray objects." The Sorcerer's violent character, combined with the sulfurous rumors, had made him an object of such universal contempt that his return sparked what amounted to a witch hunt. He found that all his possessions and furniture had been thrown out, and no one was prepared to offer him lodgings. Eventually, out of pity, the proprietor of a house in Ginai let him stay in an outbuilding used for sheltering animals. Vienne describes him at this time as a filthy, railing alcoholic clad in rags—a picture he would have been given by his brother-in-law, who was the local doctor and treated Marin at the end of his life. He had been afflicted by leprous sores (probably caused by syphilis), which made him even more of a pariah, and only the doctor and Nonant's curé would visit him. On 7 February 1841, at the age of fifty-one, Marin Plessis died in Ginai. His body was discovered by neighbors.

And Alphonsine? What was to become of this "child full of fear, who spoke of the devil, ghosts and werewolves"? The infamous Saint-Lazare hospital, where prostitutes were treated for venereal diseases, was full of girls from the provinces forced to survive in Paris as *filles publiques à vingt sous,* soliciting in the streets and sleeping in warehouses or abandoned buildings. One report claims that Alphonsine did in fact "pay for her promiscuity with a visit to Saint-Lazare," a place whose very name expressed the ultimate in misery and humiliation. There she would have joined the 1,300 other detainees imprisoned in the penitentiary for a minimum of six weeks or until they had been cured. The writer Gustave Claudin heard that she had been seen in "the most suspect places," and the first recorded sighting of Alphonsine in Paris has it that one of these was the Pont-Neuf.

The bridge crossing the Seine from the Latin Quarter to the Louvre was a place where all classes of the population converged. It was a street theater of teeth extractors, pimps, purse snatchers, quack doctors peddling purgatives and ointments, jugglers, singers, bootblacks calling from their boxes, stalls selling sweets, chickens, delicacies, secondhand clothes, and books. To Alphonsine it was like an urban version of the Saint-Mathieu fair, and she was drawn to one booth in particular, held by the aroma and sight of potatoes turning golden brown in a bubbling cauldron of fat.

Watching her was the distinguished dandy Nestor Roqueplan. A bachelor and *flâneur,* he had recently given up the editorship of *Le Figaro* to become director of the popular Théâtre des Variétés. Cane in hand, top hat inclined over one ear, he was considered to be the most Parisian of all Parisians, whose urbane loathing of the countryside was well known. (Pointing to a row of elms on the boulevard des Italiens, he once declared, "Look—they were so bored they had to come here to get away.") The Boulevard, with its exclusive cafés and restaurants, was Roqueplan's domain, and it was only his eye for fetching working-class girls that had brought him to the hubbub of the Pont-Neuf.

He spotted Alphonsine straightaway. "She was nibbling a green apple which she seemed to despise," Roqueplan recalled. "Fried potatoes were her dream." These were a delicacy with a special significance for the poor, as Théodore de Banville noted in his book on Parisian mores: "Not only delicious, but sacred like everything that costs only one sou." Alphonsine, however, did not have one sou, and between her and the *pommes frites,* which she was eyeing "like a peasant craving gold coins," was an abyss. Reading her mind, Roqueplan went up to the stout *friteuse* and bought a large cornet, which he handed to the waif. "This made her blush, but she dropped her apple core and devoured the chips in three minutes." For Alphonsine, it was the defining moment of her arrival in the metropolis—the first time that she had tangible proof of the luxuries her beauty could buy.

Grisette

ALPHONSINE'S FIRST FRIENDS in Paris were students. She may have come across them among the Pont-Neuf crowd or in the Luxembourg Gardens, where young men headed between lectures to have assignations with the girls who strolled along its paths or sat sewing demurely under the willow trees. But the most likely meeting place was at one of the lively public balls. The undergraduates' favorite was Le Prado, near the Louvre, where women were exempt from paying, and it was not unusual for them to arrive alone. "Most of those without cavaliers left better accompanied," remarked one contemporary, while another described a typical first encounter. Sitting at a table drinking punch, a student urges his friend to act as go-between by charming a pretty girl in a corner on her own. Ten minutes later, after many peals of laughter, the conquest has been achieved, and she is introduced to her admirer. "Louise was one of those birds of passage who, through fantasy, and often through need, make their nest for a day—or rather a night—in the attics of the Latin Quarter and remain there voluntarily for several days. Provided, that is, one knows how to keep them."

To be the mistress of a student living in a garret near the Sorbonne was a situation envied by the street girls of the city. Equally at home by the fireplace of a grand salon as at the rough table of a Left Bank café-cabaret, these would-be lawyers, doctors, philosophers, musicians, artists, and writers provided strays like Alphonsine with their first experiences of a worldly, learned society. The Latin Quarter of the mid–nineteenth century had a certain clannish charm, being totally free of the tourists who swarm its sidewalks today. If top-hatted interlopers ventured there from across the Seine, they rarely stayed after nightfall and were never seen inside the smoky student cafés. Here, long-haired youths wearing workingmens' caps, a pipe between their lips, played cards and billiards or conversed intently over a beer or shot of absinthe. Most were on an allowance of no more than two hundred francs a month, which bought them breakfast of a buttered baguette and bowl of milk at a *crémerie* and dinner for three francs somewhere like Magny's, a cheap restaurant on the rue Mazet. Toward the end of the month, when funds ran low, they would move en masse to brasseries such as Viot's or Bléry's, where you could eat for twenty-two sous, or survive on a meat pie from one of the *charcuteries*.

The Bobino theater on the rue de Madame was another student hangout. It was where vaudevilles rather than serious plays were performed, and audiences would join in the choruses of well-known songs or drown out the dialogue with raucous interpolations. On Monday and Thursday nights the grand salon of La Grande Chaumière, a public ball on boulevard du Montparnasse, was packed with young people watching the dance celebrities of the day. Clara Fontaine, a curvy brunette with a pale, round face, had been awarded the title *la reine des étudiants* (the students' queen). Her rival was Elise Sergent, a beautiful Gypsy with black hair and olive skin, known as *la reine* Pomoré, (the queen of Tahiti), because of her exotic appearance and copious bangles and beads. Although untrained as a dancer, she was brilliant at improvising and always attracted a cheering crowd with her version of the polka, a craze she is said to have launched. Clara Fontaine is credited with inventing the cancan, which first appeared at the La Grande Chaumière and quickly caught on.

On Sunday nights in the summer, the students and their girls—*les biches étudiantes*—went dancing themselves in the rotunda of La Chaumière. Determined to challenge the conventions of the time, they adopted wild alternatives to the more formal dancing then in vogue. The quadrille's square patterns could be embellished with countless variations—"Jumps, fluttering, twisting, foot-stamping, contortions and undulations of the whole body would vary according to the inspiration of each one, becoming more and more animated, expressive and eccentric." The polka was instantly controversial, with more bodily contact between partners than ever seen before. The cancan—or cachucha, as it was also known—could escalate into a bacchanalian frenzy. The public ball version was nothing like the high-kicking chorus line of the belle époque with its swishing skirts, flashing knickers, and jump splits. It began sedately, a dance for a couple in a quadrille, with the student in an academic position—left foot forward, hand on one side, back curved, right arm around his partner; she rested one hand on his shoulder and held her skirt in the other. Once the music started, according to a contemporary, all propriety was cast aside.

A helter-skelter of bewildering dash, of electrifying enthusiasm, one dancer leans languidly over, straightening himself again with vivacity; another races the length of the ballroom, stamping with pleasure. The girl darts by as if inviting a fall, winding up with a saucy, coquettish skip; that other passes and repasses languidly, as if melancholy and exhausted; but a cunning bound now and then, and a febrile quiver, testify to the keenness of her sensations and the voluptuousness of her movements. They mingle, cross, part, meet again, with a swiftness and fire that must have been felt to be described. . . . What then shall we call the cancan? It is a total dislocation of the human body, by which the soul expresses an extreme energy of sensation.

The French Cachucha is a superhuman language, not of this world, learnt assuredly from angels or from demons.

Every public ball was policed by municipal guards who were there to uphold decency, but La Chaumière's director, *le père* Lahire, a gigantically tall, rotund man, had obtained government permission to keep order himself. If one of the students danced in an excessive, disorderly manner, he would take him in his arms like Hercules and carry him to a quiet corner of the boulevard to compose himself. On hot nights he patrolled the garden outside the rotunda, where alleys wound through bowers of hornbeams with benches hidden in the groves. It was the scene of numerous trysts, though morals were strictly maintained by Lahire, who, while brusque with the youngsters, was a good man with a dry wit, and greatly liked.

Between university terms, La Chartreuse, on the rue d'Enfer, became the place to go. It had the advantage of being lively during the dead season, although it was simple to the point of being grubby. The orchestra was third-rate and the atmosphere so riotous that the rickety floorboards trembled under the dancers' stamping feet, throwing up choking clouds of dust. To Albert Vandam, an Englishman in Paris, the pleasures of high society paled beside the noisy bohemia of student balls, theaters, and restaurants. "I preferred the Théâtre Bobino to the Opera and the Comédie-française; the Grande-Chaumière . . . to the most brilliantly lighted and decorated ballroom." There was a special camaraderie among students, who spoke a patois colored with jargon from painters' studios, theater wings, lecture halls, and newspaper offices. Their high ideals and good humor had such romantic appeal that graduates who went on to lead bourgeois lives, making respectable marriages and establishing themselves as notaries, "would recount their misery as artists with the kind of relish a homecoming traveller might brag about his escapades with tigers."

This was the world of *La Bohème,* where every day presented a new challenge to find enough money for food or lodgings. "Since when have we eaten two days in a row?" quips one student to another in Henri Murger's *Scènes de la vie de bohème,* the source for Puccini's opera. In *La Bohème,* the quartet of jovial young friends is used to dodging debt collectors and living a routine of bed without supper or supper without bed. Murger's Rodolphe, an aspiring playwright with a daytime job as editor-in-chief of a fashion magazine, first meets his mistress, Mimi, when she timidly knocks on his door. An impoverished seamstress living on the floor below, she has come in search of a light for her candle. For Alphonsine, too, it was hunger that drove her one day to the lodgings of a young man she knew called Henry. When she turned up on his doorstep, she was in great distress, saying that she had not eaten for the last forty-eight hours.

—Well, let's see . . . what can I get you? asked Henry.
—If it's not too extravagant, replied a blushing Alphonsine, I would ask you for some cherries. It's mid-June now and I haven't yet tasted any.

They went out together to buy a pound of cherries, and her young benefactor was rewarded by watching Alphonsine's "explosion of joy" as she received them; the sensuality with which she devoured each cherry—"her lips even more brightly scarlet than the pulp of the fruit"—was an image he still vividly recalled more than a decade later.

Observing the ravenous Alphonsine on the Pont-Neuf, Nestor Roqueplan had immediately identified her as "one of those girls of the Latin Quarter improperly known as grisettes." *Grisette*—a term that first appeared in the mid–seventeenth century to describe the gray fabric, *grise de serge,* worn by young working women—had come to describe almost any pretty young girl of easy virtue. The grisette may, like Alphonsine, have been brought up in the country, but she was a specific Parisian type, often the heroine of popular novels and stories, like Henri Murger's Mimi or Rigolette from Eugène Sue's 1842 *Mysteries of Paris.*

Nubile, coquettish, sincere in love and light without being immoral, she was the poet's muse, the painter's model, and the ideal mistress of a frugal student. She may have taken responsibility for the sentimental education of these sons of the bourgeoisie, but she would not accept the gauche offer of a young man's money. Instead, she adored being given cakes, trinkets, and treats—"A dinner tempts her, the theatre seduces her, a ball wins her heart." Honest and gay, the *étudiante,* as she was also known, was gifted with the kind of spontaneity lacking in girls of the students' own class; she danced, she sang, she drank and smoked, and she was quite content with a meager dinner of soup or a plate of vegetables costing three sous. Accustomed to hearing intellectual conversations day and night "on anatomy, physiology, philosophy—and every other subject ending in 'my,' 'by,' and 'phy,' " some grisettes found themselves absorbing serious abstract ideas, whereas others were completely out of their depth. It was Murger's Rodolphe who had picked up the enticing Louise at Le Prado, but it soon became clear that he expected more of her than she could give; Rodolphe wanted to speak *le beau langage* and write her reams of moonlit verse, while she spoke only the patois of love and would have far preferred the gift of a hat or a pair of boots.

By now, Alphonsine's fustian skirt and heavy Normandy clogs, which she had worn on her arrival in Paris, had been replaced by a modest silk dress and black leather ankle boots, while a coquettish little bonnet encircled her lovely face—an effect that "sparked a revolution" in the students. "It was even reported that aspiring doctors of law, in spite of the gravity of their future position, proved themselves assiduously attentive and gallant towards her." But while enjoying the students' company, unfazed by scholarly conversations about legendary jurists

Cujas and Barthole, Alphonsine is said to have spurned the young bohemians as lovers, choosing instead to bestow her favors on the lead violinist at Le Prado.

There are several versions of Alphonsine's first weeks in Paris. Delphine declared that her sister had been "welcomed by two students, one of whom was very rich, educated her and made her his mistress." Alternatively, she may have been working at the age of fourteen in a dress shop on rue Saint-Jacques, where she was maltreated, even beaten. "Tired of this miserable life the Sorcerer's daughter escaped one day and was taken in by the students of the Latin Quarter, who made her their companion and their servant." Or it was the dress shop in the arcades of the Palais-Royal, where Alphonsine's employer will die of cholera? Thrown out without money or shelter, she wanders off crying into the street, where "a blackguard offers her his friendship and bread."

Vienne, presumably passing on Alphonsine's own version of her Paris debut, tells a lighter story. It was always Marin Plessis's aim, he says, to take his daughter directly to his Parisian cousins, a couple named Vital, who lived on the rue des Deux-Ecus, an alleyway in the old quarter of Les Halles. This was Zola's belly of Paris, a decade before the ironwork and vast glass expanses of the covered market were built. Bordered by gabled, ramshackle houses, the medieval streets were crowded before dawn with horse-drawn carts arriving from the countryside full of fresh produce. Market gardeners brought bundles of vegetables and handfuls of fruit; wholesalers piled their huge baskets with artichokes, lettuces, celery, and cauliflowers, stacked symmetrically like cannonballs; cart axles bulged under the weight of damp, seaweedy sacks of mussels, coops of squawking poultry, whole carcasses of sheep and beef. Throughout the early hours there were the cries of wagoners unloading their wares and the constant rumble of wheels on cobbles "lulling the dark city with the sounds of food on the move."

The Vitals had a vegetable stall of their own, but their business was too modest to employ Alphonsine, so they asked an acquaintance, Mme Barget, who owned a laundry business, to take her on as an apprentice. This establishment was on the rue de l'Echiquier, way out in the Tenth Arrondissement near the dreaded Saint-Lazare prison-hospital, but the opportunity of a job there would have been greatly appreciated by Alphonsine. Though factory workers were women of disrepute in the professional hierarchy of the mid–nineteenth century, the feminine trades associated with couture—laundry maids, seamstresses, shop assistants, milliners, florists, and corsetmakers—were considered, in the main, to be respectable. "They're virtuous because they spend the day making clothes that are the most indispensable to modesty," wrote the poet Alfred de Musset, singling out laundresses for particular praise. "They are very caring and clean, given that they're constantly handling washing and fabrics which they can't spoil without forfeiting their pay."

To Nestor Roqueplan, *blanchisseuses* were, for the most part, irresistibly pert and appealing—"the prettiest working girls in Paris"—although Zola paints a far harsher picture in his novel *L'Assommoir.* In a large hangar containing enormous reservoirs of water and zinc cylinders are lines of about a hundred kneeling women working for one sou an hour, their arms bare to the shoulders, their skirts gathered up as they lean over their tubs, beating furiously. The heat from coke-fired stoves is intolerable, the air thick with steam and the acrid stench of bleach, and as they laugh and shout at each other above the racket of machines, their flesh turns ruddy and gleams with sweat. Zola's laundresses are bawdy and rumbunctious—a dispute ends with two of them locked in a catfight—but in Mme Barget's atelier, there was never any unruly behavior or risqué talk. "She was an upstanding woman," writes Vienne, "proud of the honour of her household, and more importantly, of the honour of her two daughters, whom she had brought up with strict surveillance." Alphonsine would have worked beside these two girls, using an iron filled with hot charcoal and starching lace petticoats that were frothier and more delicate than anything she had ever seen.

Having slaved for six days in succession, most grisettes, as described by Musset, "frisked about like fish in the water as soon as their work was over," and Alphonsine was no exception, living for the fun and freedom of Sundays with her Latin Quarter friends. She told Romain Vienne that one night she accepted an invitation to a ball followed by supper. Her escort had chosen a tavern renowned for its rabbit stew and wine priced at six sous a bottle, and after they had eaten, he took her to the Bois de Boulogne. In spring, when the acacias and linden trees were in flower, or on summer evenings, the Bois became a grand boulevard attracting the most elegant Parisians, who strolled down its long, central avenue, or paraded past in their carriages. After dark, however, it took on a mysterious, clandestine aspect, and couples secluded themselves amongst the trees or in coupés with shaded windows. "It's the intimate hour of the Bois, the hour of abandon and sweet talk . . . when the wood becomes the confidant of a thousand charming adventurers whose secrets it guards." Alphonsine laughed as she recounted how the young man had caressed her on a footpath overhung with flowers while swearing eternal love, although the consequences turned out to be far from amusing at the time. She claimed to have been spotted by her employer, who was out walking with her daughters, but this seems too far-fetched. Whatever the circumstances, Mme Barget discovered that her apprentice had lied to her about being at home with her relatives that night, and Alphonsine was abruptly sacked.

Mme Vital, on the other hand, was understanding and forgiving. Although her reprimand was severe, she softened her words with advice and kindly warnings, pardoning Alphonsine on the condition that she behave from now on. She needed to find her young ward a situation more likely to engage her interest, and since Alphonsine was developing a real interest in fashion, Mme Vital went to see a friend who owned a dress shop near the Palais-Royal. Mélanie Urbain had had her own share of misfortune and been forced to bring up an illegitimate child alone. Consequently, she was sympathetic toward the wayward Alphonsine and willing to employ her.

There were "pretext shops" in Paris that were actually brothels run by procuress-dressmakers, who offered to lend fine clothes to attractive young women they had spotted, with the intention of launching them as prostitutes. Vienne says, however, that there was nothing disreputable about Mlle Urbain, who kept a close, motherly watch over her apprentices, to the point of employing porters to make deliveries in order not to expose the girls to the dangers of the street. With food and lodging provided as part of her job, Alphonsine left the Vitals' household, although she now chose to spend her Sundays with them instead of keeping company with her Latin Quarter friends. "She found that work was the best way to escape temptation," writes Vienne, "and she remained in this honest establishment for about six months, tranquil, wise and relatively happy. The good Mme Vital was enchanted by the progress and conduct of her little cousin, while Mlle Urbain began to be proud of her young assistant. Only one thing troubled these two women: "Alphonsine was becoming disturbingly pretty."

By this time, Alphonsine had made two close girlfriends, both a couple of years older: a fellow shop assistant called Ernestine, and Hortense, who worked in another boutique nearby. Neither was particularly attractive, but they were spirited and a lot of fun. Vienne, who met them later, describes Ernestine as the most mischievous of the trio, with a devilish side and a particular suggestive look in her eye that raced the heart of anyone who met her gaze. The three had decided to go on a trip one Sunday to the annual fair in the park of Saint-Cloud, just outside Paris, and Alphonsine, eager to have enough spending money, had persuaded a sympathetic colleague to lend her five francs. But on this particular September Sunday the weather was dreadful, and so they decided to go window-shopping in the Palais-Royal instead. After making five or six tours of the galleries, the girls went into a restaurant to have lunch, their entrance making the kind of effect captured by social historian Edmund Texier in his description of a typical *demoiselle de boutique:* "Her hat is not much more than a piece of woven straw with very little trimming, her dress a piece of cotton fabric, her shawl a square of printed material; and yet altogether it makes a captivatingly graceful and elegant ensemble. Her eyes glance and sparkle beneath the modest hat brim; she moves with a gently swaying motion of her figure, her skirt rippling in an undulating, provocative way." The girls had immediately caught the attention of the *patron,* who, with complete tact, offered them a glass of old Burgundy. M. Nollet, as Vienne calls him, was an amiable widower in his late forties, who upon hearing of the canceled excursion to Saint-Cloud, volunteered to be the girls' escort the following Sunday.

This time the weather was beautifully sunny, and, dressed in their finest outfits, the three arrived at their agreed meeting place in the place de la Concorde. M. Nollet ushered them into a carriage and took them straight to a popular restaurant, where a friend of his was waiting. This M. Fleury, a rich bon vivant, paid court to Hortense, while M. Nollet, who also came from a small village in Normandy, made it clear that he was seriously taken by Alphonsine. Conversation during lunch was animated, but at the same time courteous and respectful, and after they had eaten, they made a tour of the fair, where there was plenty to amuse them. Young men on raised platforms tried their strength at hitting punch balls, others blew into yardlong mirlitons that amplified the voice; there were puppet shows and stalls selling all kinds of trinkets. The girls' companions bought them more gifts than they could carry and then treated them to a lavish supper, after which M. Nollet drove them back to Paris. Before taking leave of each other, he and Alphonsine made a plan to meet again.

One meeting led to another. Hortense, who was the most practical and cynical of the trio, took it upon herself to advise Alphonsine how she should proceed. She had been well trained to avoid the traps of seduction because her employer, Mlle Urbain, who had worked her way up from streetwalker to her position of proprietress, spoke crudely in front of her girls about the exploitative nature of men. "They're all monsters," she would spit venomously. "Even the best are of no value." Hortense had resolved to accept only a protector who agreed to her conditions, but Alphonsine had things under control. It was about a month later that M. Nollet asked if she would come and see a little furnished apartment he had found for her in the rue de l'Arcade, near the Tuileries gardens. Alphonsine, whose lodgings can have been no more than a grisette's narrow little room with an iron bed, was charmed and excited by the place. "Then will you allow me to offer it to you?" asked M. Nollet. "I will rent it in your name, and when you move in, you will find in this drawer three thousand francs* for your initial needs."

This was a critical turning point. To accept would propel Alphonsine from a respectable working girl to the status of kept woman—what Nestor Roqueplan deemed the "ugly, improper" term of *une fille entretenue*. The alternative, however, was even less appealing. In a boutique like Mlle Urbain's, the average wage was twenty-two francs a month, with a six-day week beginning at seven in the morning and ending at eight at night—a punishing routine in which it was all too easy to become trapped for decades. "Today working girls can't freely give their love, they have to find a complement to their salary," writes the anonymous author of *Paris dansant; ou, Les filles d'Hérodiade*. "Each of them

---

* In the 1840s, the exchange rate of French gold and silver francs stood at approximately 5 francs to the U.S. dollar.

has her lover as she has her bonnet, her shopping bag . . . the celibate working girl is disdained."

In Alphonsine's mind, there *was* no alternative, although the shame she felt in succumbing to M. Nollet's offer would not allow her immediately to confess to Mlle Urbain that she would not be coming back. She stayed away from work for several days before summoning the courage to return to the shop. Splendidly dressed in her new acquisitions, she effusively embraced her employer, thanking her over and over again for her kindness, and wept as she bid goodbye to her colleagues. The elderly Elisa Vimont, who had lent her five francs for the Saint-Cloud outing, had become a real friend. (As a young girl she had been the image of Alphonsine, so deliciously pretty that the well-known portraitist Achille Devéria asked her to model for him.) As well as returning the money she owed, Alphonsine begged Elisa to accept as a token of remembrance her precious Saint-Mathieu fair ring that her aunt had given her. The prospect of breaking the news to her cousins was far too daunting, and so, instead, Alphonsine wrote them a letter. The reply was pitiless. "If ever you set foot in my house again," Mme Vital replied, "I will chase you away like the vermin you are."

Lorette

IN THE EYES of the respectable world, Alphonsine had fallen irrevocably into disrepute. As far as she was concerned, however, she had achieved the ambition of every grisette: to attain the status of lorette. "The lorette is a grisette who has swopped her bonnet for a hat, her Indian dress for one of silk, her small shawl for a cashmere," writes one historian, while a contemporary notes: "The lorette sleeps in an acacia gondola, the grisette makes do with a folding bed. . . . Lorettes have an aesthetic eye and regard with contempt the commode of fifteen francs, the mirror of five francs with which the working girl is satisfied. Their furniture has to be of mahogany, of lemon-wood and rose-wood, their mirrors and shelves coverered with objects of bronze, crystal and porcelain."

The term came from the Ninth District's church of Notre-Dame-de-Lorette, a quarter where many lorettes lived, the church itself described by Alexandre Dumas père as more boudoir than temple. Lorettes were a new genre of women first identified by Nestor Roqueplan in his gossipy, palm-size society bulletin *Nouvelles à la main*. They were a product of contemporary Parisian life—girls who had set out to take a lover, not through attraction or affection but for financial gain. They would never ask for money or accept it from suitors whose offer was too direct, but they were acutely aware of their market value. "The grisette gives, the lorette receives." This element of calculation had to be practiced with skill and exercised with elegance, even modesty. It was essential to be beautifully dressed—"to this aim one sacrifices everything . . . it is more important to be well-adorned than to eat"—and a lorette would think nothing of spending forty francs, nearly two months' salary for a shopgirl, on just a shawl of crêpe de chine. Casting aside her grisette wardrobe of two shirts, one skirt, one bonnet, and a pair of woollen stockings, she would replace it with marvels of the season bought from boutiques of the Palais-Royal and rue de la Chaussée-d'Antin. Outfits for a ball detailed in the fashion pages of the January 1839 edition of *Paris Elégant* describe dresses of pale pink crêpe garnished with lace and velvet roses and accessorized with white gloves, silk stockings, and white cashmere or taffeta shawls. In the spring of that year, misty tulle bonnets came into fashion worn with capes of Alençon lace—"little masterpieces of lightness and freshness."

Confronted with such unimaginable luxuries, Alphonsine had been gripped by a wild, sensual excitement and within a month, according to Vienne, had spent M. Nollet's three thousand francs. "He gave her another two thousand but this sudden affluence made her ambitious," he writes. "She'd already dreamt of moving on to millionaires capable of satisfying her foibles and fantasies. She disdained M. Nollet's third handout and, knowing he could not continue, he stopped seeing her."

The goal of the lorette was to be noticed in public places, to attract the attention of admirers who could offer dinners and theater outings. Alphonsine no longer frequented the student balls of the Latin Quarter but the more exclusive Jardin Mabille, near the Champs-Elysées, whose proprietor had been an eminent professor of dance. "At Chaumière the woman dances for pleasure, at Mabille it's for business; at Chaumière she's open to caprices, at Mabille, she speculates." At Mabille, women whose appearance was as strikingly stylish as that of any society beauty could dance only with men to whom they had been presented—a select group from the world of literature, finance, arts, journalism, and politics. "From these acquaintances the lorette must learn to distinguish unproductive suitors whose pockets are empty and who only know how to offer their love. . . . Before long she will have mastered the art of finding unexpected compensations in gray hair and physical flaws."

Alphonsine's friend Ernestine had already led the way. A wealthy banker had installed her in a sumptuous apartment on the rue Tronchet, where she kept a carriage, coachman, and groom, and gave extravagant, Rabelaisian dinners behind thick curtains. It was on one of these evenings that Alphonsine met a colleague of Ernestine's protector, to whom Vienne gives the pseudonym of Valory. This agreeable young man, elegant and at ease with himself, made Alphonsine his mistress within two days, joining the ranks of what were known as "Arthurs." These were the bourgeois young men who had given up simple, modest grisettes for more sophisticated, fashionably dressed women with whom they were proud to be seen. Good families considered that a son who kept company with lorettes was lost, and this was certainly the case with the likable Valory, who in three months spent tens of thousands of francs on Alphonsine. Intelligent enough to realize that his entire inheritence would disappear if he continued to see her, he resolved to bring the arrangement to an end, claiming that he was forced to go away on business. But while Valory's passion had decreased as fast as the money in his wallet, Alphonsine had allowed herself to become extremely fond of her lover, whose youth and insouciance, combined with his generosity, were aphrodisiacs after the unwelcome attentions of middle-aged M. Nollet. When she realized that Valory had abandoned her, she was mortified. "Oh how she ranted," says Vienne, "vowing to revenge herself on her next lover, and to be more clear-sighted in the future in imitation of her two friends." Even Hortense, who claimed to be waiting for a husband and still worked in her dress shop, had played things to perfection with M. Fleury, who, despite having been allowed no more than prim rendezvous, had assiduously wooed her since the girls' Saint-Cloud outing. It was only six months later, after the desperate promise of "a small fortune, a dazzling wardrobe, an equipage, and all the rest," that M. Fleury had succeeded in his conquest.

With no protector for two months, Alphonsine squandered her savings to the last sou. She was on the verge of becoming one of those lorettes who regarded every admirer as the source "either of a hat, or a scarf or the rent which is overdue, or at least lunch for the next day." These were the women you saw waltzing at Mabille in their hats, muffs, coats, and scarves, either because they wanted to parade their hard-earned treasures or because they did not have fifty centimes to give the cloakroom attendant. In society's view, they were not victims but dangerous "blood-sucking parasites," whose only ambition was to siphon off the fortune of every man they met. But to the women themselves, this marketing of their sexuality was the only way of transcending their fate, the opposite extreme of the opulence they sought being an abyss of poverty, misery, and disease.

By the early summer of 1840, Alphonsine's circumstances had radically changed. In Hortense's salon she had met a viscount whom Vienne calls de Méril, a handsome, kind man attached to the minister of the interior. Delighted to be the mistress of such a distinctive figure, she wrote excitedly to her great-uncle Mesnil, who had become her guardian on the death of Marin Plessis. Exclaiming how grateful she was, she described her lover as "a true friend" who took a constant interest in her. "I lack nothing, and I'm filled with hope that I will now have the means to live as I please."

When Alphonsine found out that she was pregnant, she realized she had only herself to blame, telling Louis Mesnil, "It's not his fault that I didn't follow his good advice." But the viscount had no intention of abandoning his sixteen-year-old mistress. On the contrary, he was sweetly solicitous toward Alphonsine, giving his word that he would take care of her and their child. Keeping her condition a secret even from Ernestine and Hortense, she rarely went out and, when the delivery date grew near, moved into the modest apartment the viscount had rented for her outside Paris. There, a midwife was employed to take care of her, and after the birth a wet nurse took over. Alphonsine, who seems to have taken next to no interest in her son other than a concern for his future, was impatient to return to her city life, but her doctor would hear none of it, insisting that she spend three months recuperating in the country.

It was that summer of 1841 that Alphonsine spent in Nonant—her first visit since 1838. Having sent her maid, Rose, back to Paris, she stayed with the Mesnils in La Trouillière, sleeping in a cupboard-sized room off the kitchen and paying her great-aunt sixty francs a week toward her upkeep. Her nineteen-year-old sister still lived nearby with the elderly aunt, Mme Lanos, who had brought her up. Delphine was a typical country girl, described by an Ornais lawyer who had met her as "moderately pretty among her peasant sort, a brunette like her sister, although between them there was no comparison." Vienne is more critical, commenting on Delphine's rude manners and brusque, imperious ways, which had made her unpopular with her young colleagues. "Alphonsine, by contrast, was sweet, cheerful and warm; she made friends everywhere because she never prejudged or uttered a disobliging word against anyone." However unlikely it was that Delphine could thrive in the demimonde— since there was nothing at all sensual about her—Alphonsine was determined to improve her sister's prospects by persuading her to come to Paris and had asked a couple of lorette friends to write an enticing portrayal of its attractions.

On the day she expected these letters to arrive, Alphonsine took Delphine with her to the post office, stopping en route at the Hôtel de La Poste and inviting Romain Vienne to accompany them. Hortense's account, which he was asked to read, was full of intimate details and protestations of friendship, while the other letter, signed Georgina, gave a deliberately seductive picture of their twilight world. But while Delphine had previously seemed tempted to follow in her sister's footsteps, her response to the letters was bitterly reproachful. This may have been brought on by embarrassment in Romain's presence or genuine distress over the choices her sister had made; whatever the reason, Delphine turned the situation into an opportunity to castigate Alphonsine for her conduct, reminding her of the shame she had brought on the family by giving birth to a bastard. Deeply hurt, Alphonsine turned her back on Delphine and was silent throughout the journey when Romain drove them home. After dropping her in La Trouillère, he took Delphine on to her aunt Lanos's house, seizing the opportunity of their being alone to try to prevent an irreconcilable breach between the sisters. "I scolded Delphine for her harsh language, and encouraged her in her resolution to marry and to continue her work as a laundress. She promised not to bring up the subject again."

Two or three times a week, when she passed by the inn on her way to collect her letters from the post office, Alphonsine had long talks with Romain, who always accompanied her home. They discovered a Parisian friend in common in Elisa Vimont. "You were her mother's lodger when you were a student," Alphonsine reminded Romain, who then guessed that the shop where she had worked must have been Mlle Urbain's, "because to know one was to know the other." Romain promised to visit Mlle Urbain and Elisa the next time he was in Paris, and Alphonsine said she would do her best to widen his circle of women friends by introducing him to Ernestine and Hortense.

On one occasion, suspecting he did not believe that she was the mistress of a man with such an illustrious name, she invited him to read a letter she had received from de Méril. Now living in Burgundy, where he had been transferred, the viscount was, as Hortense put it, "lost to Alphonsine." He assured her, however, of his intention to oversee the upbringing of their son, whom he had installed with a family nearby. His letter, Vienne reports, was affectionate and full of details about their vigorous child. What was lacking, though, was any sign of love. "But I kept this observation to myself. To avoid the subject of how long their relationship was likely to last, I told Alphonsine that I was enchanted by her good humour and complimented her on her joyful expression—the sign of a healthy nature."

Alphonsine's health had indeed improved significantly. On fine days she went for walks in the afternoon, and this regime, combined with long, tranquil nights of sleep, had added a sparkle to her eyes and a glow to her complexion. But her sense of well-being was not to last. She had had more than enough of the countryside and longed to return to the boutiques, cafés, and balls of her beloved Paris. The Saint-Mathieu fair, which she had no intention of missing, was on September 22, and Alphonsine announced that she would be leaving Nonant the very next day. Romain was with her as she wandered from stall to stall, buying numerous trinkets to hand out to the peasant urchins scampering around. "Aren't you going to give me a present?" she teased Romain, who told her to choose something she fancied. Picking out a knickknack of no value, she said, "This is what I'd like, and nothing else. I may never return to Saint-Mathieu, and this little thing will remind me of it."

The following evening she arrived at the Hôtel de La Poste with Mme Mesnil, who had come to see her off. When they embraced, she whispered to her great-aunt to look for three little packages that she had left under her pillow. These all contained money, she told Vienne, including a hundred francs for Delphine—"My wedding present to her if she marries."

The Hôtel de La Poste was full that night, and as Alphonsine had left it too late to reserve a room, she had the option either of traveling to an inn in Laigle or settling for a corner of the attic. She chose the latter, steeling herself to climb up the ladder under the gaze of lascivious eyes. Romain came to her aid, protecting her from the stares of the carousing onlookers by holding her skirts pressed against her thighs—an image he describes with a suppressed erotic charge.

Two months after her departure from Nonant, Louis Mesnil received a letter from his great-niece. Enclosing another hundred francs, ten of which she asked him to give to Delphine, she told him that she had arrived safely in Paris, but her health was still poor and she had been obliged to see a doctor. This was not, as might be assumed, the onset of tuberculosis (whose symptoms would not appear for another three years) but rather the ill effects of an overhectic city routine. Vienne maintains that a month after her return, Alphonsine had begun a new affair, her lover this time an aging baron who was even richer than de Méril. It lasted eight months, he says, although this can not have been the case. In a second letter to Louis Mesnil, written a fortnight later (November 25), Alphonsine tells him that the reason she has not been in touch is because she has returned to work in the shop. She also thanks her great-uncle for sending her money. Clearly, there was no beneficent protector in her life at this period. Alphonsine had assured Vienne in Nonant that she could count on continued support from de Méril; "He has no intention of abandoning me." But the viscount's letters and payments had then stopped, she told him later, after news came that their child had contracted pneumonia and died.

———

For Alphonsine to return to the lowly rank of shopgirl was a humiliating setback. Proof that this can have been only a momentary reversal of fortune, however, is an 1842 bill found among her papers for a "plush white hat" priced at 25 francs. Nothing denoted status in the demimonde of Paris more than a woman's choice of hat. No grisette would dare wear the bonnet of a lady, but a lorette was proud to be seen in one. Alphonsine had bought the hat at Mlle Urbain's new boutique on rue Louvois. The shop's former assistant was now one of its most affluent customers.

Her benefactor, Vienne eventually learned from Hortense, was the "duke de R," the head of a noble family who had an income of eighty thousand francs a year. He was, she enthused, "the real thing" and was so passionate about Alphonsine that he refused her nothing. "She has a brilliant equipage, a profusion of jewels and a splendid wardrobe of lace and cashmere. Professors of French, drawing, music and dance come every day to give her lessons; this duke seems to want to transform his mistress into a duchess." Having been promised that she would be launched that season in the fashionable spa resort of Baden-Baden, Alphonsine sent a euphoric letter to Delphine, urging her to come and see her before she undertook the long journey. "Our cousin Marie Lanos could accompany you, and I will be responsible for all your expenses," she wrote on 28 February 1842. "When you have once seen this delightful city of Paris you'll never want to leave it again."

> Rare lorettes made their fortune by their beauty or their spirit; they bid adieu to the quartier, and to the Arthurs they despise, and establish grand existences in respectable houses with a salon, and the company of men whom society women envy; they write letters and make remarks that are quoted. . . . Each day, from two to four, the boulevards and the Champs-Elysées are filled with these Amazons riding towards the Bois on rented stallions.

The account is Nestor Roqueplan's, and it could very well be a description of Alphonsine—or rather, of her new incarnation. He had seen her for a second time at the Ranelagh, the only aristocratic public ball, where she was accompanied not by her magnanimous, elderly protector but by one of the most eligible young aristocrats in Paris.

I felt myself tapped on the shoulder by a tall youth, as fresh as a rose, with hair as blond and curly as Cupid's—the duke de . . . , who had on his arm a charming person, elegantly dressed. It was none other than my gourmande of Pont Neuf, whom he was exhibiting with all the pride of an inventor. She had passed through all the preliminary stages of *la galanterie*, appearing in dubious places and with dubious people, and had at last fallen into the hands of a man who had instilled her with dignity.

Her name, Roqueplan discovered, was now Marie Duplessis.

Part Two

Marie

⁒

THE YOUNG DUKE'S name was Agénor de Guiche. He was the eldest son of the Duke and Duchess de Gramont, and he could hardly have been much grander. His descendants were linked to the royal blood of Aragon and Navarre, and his parents were as influential at court as their own parents had been before them. His elegant mother was feted and admired, while his father, a remarkably handsome nobleman, served the dauphin in the household's most prestigious position of First Gentleman. As a child, Agénor's playmate was Charles X's grandson Henri, Duke of Bordeaux, who, for one week, at the age of nine, would be king of France.

Agénor was one year older than Henri, and when Paris fell under siege in the July revolution of 1830, both he and his younger brother, Augustus, were trapped by the barricades in their college of Sainte-Barbe. Their father, refusing to forsake the royal family in adversity, had accompanied the Bourbons at the start of their journey of exile, traveling through Normandy to Cherbourg, while his wife and children remained in Paris. When an angry mob planted two cannons in front of their gate, the duchess fled to the Gramonts' country estate, a perilous journey owing to the fact that their carriage bore the royal arms and livery. Agénor and Augustus were rescued from the college by a family friend charged with conducting them to the country, and once the duke had dealt with the disposal of the dauphin's property, the Gramonts joined the royal family in the refuge offered to them in Scotland.

For the next two years Agénor was brought up in Holyrood Palace, in the Old Quarter of Edinburgh. A vast edifice built around a quadrangle, it looked magnificent but made a dismal home, and to the ex-king and his little band of devotees, Holyrood was a prison: the Duke de Gramont referred to the exiled court as "inmates." Agénor took Holy Communion in the Catholic chapel, standing beside Henri, and he was almost certainly schooled by the two tutors chosen to mold the mind and morals of France's legitimist heir to the throne. But this was by no means a lavish upbringing. The duke mentions in a letter the family's need for money and their ongoing miseries, offering to sell one of his wife's diamond-and-emerald jewels. Conditions were no better in the exiles' next place of refuge, Hradschin Palace in Prague, which the duchess left in disgust, soon followed by her husband. From 1833 the family remained in France, at Versailles. "The Gs have retired from Court and keep themselves aloof," Benjamin Disraeli, Britain's future prime minister, wrote to his sister in 1837. "The Duke devotes himself entirely to the education of his three sons." Gramont's efforts were rewarded when, at the age of eighteen, Agénor entered the Ecole Polytechnique, a unique educational establishment reputed to be one of the best in the world.

It was the Polytechnique that had intellectually formed the male elite of France—leaders of the armed forces, politicians, magistrates, wealthy industrialists—and when Agénor was promoted to underlieutenant in the artillery service in 1839, he seemed destined for a brilliant career. A portrait of him as a student painted by his uncle, Count d'Orsay, the famous dandy, shows a young man with a black moustache and magnificent side whiskers who exudes privilege and self-confidence. The Gramonts' days of glory may have been over, but Agénor's beauty and rank allowed him to maintain a charmed position in society. Even knowing him to be "absolutely without fortune," the Duchess de Dino included the nineteen-year-old Duke de Guiche on her list of four aristocratic suitors for her daughter. Agénor, however, living in his bachelor apartment in a backwater of the Eighth Arrondissement, had no intention of relinquishing his freedom. He preferred an evening at a demimonde café or public ball to any grand soirée, and he was always on the lookout for a pretty girl. One, according to the journalist known as "Méjannes," was Alphonsine. "The Duke de G. . . . was still an elegant Polytechnicien when, twice a week, he would gaze through the window of the shop where she worked in the rue Coq Heron [*sic*], admiring the little one's arresting profile."

Over the next couple of years, to the despair of his parents, the youth whom Disraeli had admired as "quiet with great talents" was acquiring a reputation as dissolute as that of his ancestor Armand de Gramont, Count de Guiche, one of the most infamous playboys of the seventeenth century. Agénor had become a typical Parisian "lion," frequenting the fashionable cafés and restaurants of the boulevard des Italiens dressed, even at noon, as if he were going to a ball. Very tall, with startlingly blue, caressing eyes, he was irresistible to women, whom he courted and admired but only as an aesthete and epicurian. "He never wasted his time by loving them," writes Vienne. "It was said that a young and sweet dressmaker had been able to captivate him for several months, but then he abandoned her like all the rest."

Instead of progressing, as expected, to the artillery and engineering school of Metz, Agénor took an illegal absence from the army for more than a year and then in September 1841 received an order forbidding him to return to military service. Enforced civilian life meant only one thing to this "beautiful lion"—the pursuit of pleasure. And one of his hunting grounds was Le Prado.

On a day of mourning, of desolation for the Latin Quarter . . . a pure-blooded lion of the boulevard des Italiens, shod in the shiniest leather boots, wearing the whitest kid gloves, the Duke de G., slipped amongst the ungloved bear cubs at le Prado, drunk with latin and legal articles, and swept off Marie Marin [*sic*] who became Marie Duplessis. A week later, the only talk on the Italiens, at the Opera, in the galante society of Paris was of the beautiful mistress of the Duke de G.

Charles Matharel de Fiennes, a literary critic at *Le Siècle,* dates Agénor's coup as 1840, but Vienne, as usual, takes a different line. Barely disguised in his memoir as the Viscount de Tiche, Count de Grandon, Guiche, he says, had met Marie on earlier occasions and even been received in her salon, but they had become lovers only when she was established as a young courtesan. Their affair, Vienne claims, began at La Maison d'Or (also known as Maison Dorée).

Situated on the corner of the boulevard des Italiens and rue Laffitte, this elegant restaurant, with its Aubusson-hung doors, its sculpted paneling, paintings, mirrors, and silk curtains, was a favorite meeting place of the city's gilded youth. Its owner, a Monsieur Hardy, had introduced to France the English "grillroom" and would stand in front of the enormous white marble chimney supervising the barbecuing of succulent slabs of meat. After an evening at an Opéra ball, a boisterous young crowd descended on La Maison d'Or, calling for bottles of champagne, gambling, and crashing out tunes on the piano until dawn. One half of the restaurant was for customers from the street, but the other, overlooking rue Laffitte, was reserved for important regulars, who sheltered themselves from curious eyes in private booths piled high with soft cushions. (An engraving from the time of a *salon particulier* shows a ribald scene of two lorettes and their conquests, one a bearded rake with unfastened shirt, who rests his hand on the pretty girl's rump as she ladles out punch from a steaming cauldron.)

Accompanying Marie that evening was a delicate eighteen-year-old blonde whom she had adopted as a protégée. Well brought up and from a good family, Lili had fallen for a cad who seduced and then abandoned her, leaving her without resources. Aware that a sense of shame prevented Lili from returning to her parents, Marie befriended her, and, for a brief period when she was between lovers, the two young women became insepa-rable. If their intimacy was a sapphic interlude, it was something that Marie would have kept strictly to herself: lesbianism in nineteenth-century Paris was regarded as an abomination. Not surprisingly, Vienne provides no clues, but he does cynically sug-gest that this was a mentorship motivated by aesthetic consid-erations. The striking color contrast of their blond and jet-black hair was guaranteed to attract attention as they rode beside each other in an open carriage through the Bois de Boulogne.

At La Maison d'Or the pair was again the focus of all eyes, and it was not long before a group of young men came to sit at an adjoining table. One was Agénor. Reminding Marie that he had met her before, he introduced his friends and graciously invited the girls to join them. What would have been a modest dinner became a princely feast, and after midnight and much champagne, Marie participated in a heady round of vingt-et-un. Vienne continues:

> Lili, who had never touched a card in her life, allowed her-self to be wooed by the eager Marquis de Carizy, who had a face like a furnace; Marie, as usual, played for the high-est stakes and lost huge sums, but [the Count de Guiche] settled her debts with marvellous tact. At two in the morn-ing the young women returned to their carriage on the arms of Carizy and [de Guiche], who asked to have the honour of seeing them again that evening before dinner.

They met around six pm at the Café Anglais, with the same flirtatious routine as the night before but with greater intimacy. The next day they were reunited in a box at the Opera and after midnight had supper at la Maison d'Or. The fourth day, resistance had ceased. A treaty of alliance was concluded: the marquis, a gallant man and extremely rich, offered Lili a brilliant situation, and the count became the successor of the Duke de R.

A portrait painted around this time captures the young girl Agénor found so desirable. It is a watercolor of a plump-cheeked, unsophisticated Marie at the theater painted by Nestor Roqueplan's brother Camille. As yet unable to afford a box of her own, she is sitting in the stalls wearing a lace-edged shawl and beribboned bonnet—still more grisette than courtesan. Her hair is parted and demurely swept back, not styled into modish *anglaises* (ringlets), like that of the pretty Parisians around her, but it is on her that a grandee has his opera glasses trained. Alluring and defiantly unescorted, Marie would have been considered a threat by the society women in the audience—as much of a threat as the young actress a contemporary describes sitting in a reserved enclosure at the races.

Her presence produced a vivid emotion, all the more because she was extremely attractive. A bailiff was told to escort her off the premises, but Mlle responded victoriously by showing her ticket. The law was on her side, and she, no doubt, would have capitalized on this, had it not been for an amiable, persuasive young dandy who offered her his arm, and with all kinds of compliments and galanteries, conducted her elsewhere. This delicate mission, accomplished with talent and success, would no doubt have its recompense.

With Agénor as her beau, Marie gained entrance to an opulent new world peopled with suave, manicured young men who bowed to her as though she were their equal. She was a forerunner of Stefan Zweig's lowly post office girl whose change of name had felt completely natural, convincing her that she was "another person, that other person." And in becoming what she feigned to be, Marie, too, must have experienced what the novelist called "the delirium of transformation," her metamorphosis wiping out all but the faintest memories of her miserable past. If she was fearful of revealing her unworldliness, she soon learned how to disguise it by studying the arrogant poise of the women who disdained her, learning to walk and to move as they did. She had left Normandy barely able to read and write but now began to discover classic and contemporary novels and was soon to build a library as comprehensive as that of any man of letters.

In Vienne's account, it is the mysterious Duke de R. who acts as Alphonsine's Pygmalion, overseeing her education and developing her into "an incomparably distinguished woman." Agénor, however, as Nestor Roqueplan noted, also considered Alphonsine to be his creation. He may even have been the powerful friend said to have attempted, through royal connections, to secure the title of duchess for Marie so that she could attend grand balls and court marriages. "The matter did not take place without administrative obstacles," writes Georges Soreau, an early biographer. "I was told that mayors from various townships received orders to produce false papers so that she could get the official document required to authorise the very genuine title."

This was probably no more than a rumor, but had it been true, and had Agénor been involved, the scandal would have brought unimaginable disgrace to his family. And yet, if Marie had been a respectable potential fiancée for her son, the Duchess de Gramont would have taken her in hand, as she did her close friend, Lady Blessington, who was given what today would be described as a makeover by the duchess, "an oracle of fashion." Accounts of Ida de Gramont, sitting in a swan-shaped sledge, wrapped in a coat of the finest Russian sable, her handsome duke holding the reins on each side of her, show her to have created a near-mythical impact in public—the kind of impact that Marie herself went on to cultivate, framed in her box at the theater, her black hair threaded with diamonds. Through Agénor, brought up in the family house on the rue du Faubourg-Saint-Honoré—"a picture of English comfort and French elegance"—Marie absorbed elements of the duchess's exquisite taste. Lady Blessington describes the Gramont salons filled with pretty furniture, pictures, and vases of old Sèvres; Marie, too, would have only antique Sèvres on her shelves.

But in fact Marie needed little mentoring. "She possessed to the highest degree the art of dressing herself. . . . She had *du particulier* . . . inimitable originality" (Gustave Claudin). "Who can explain to us by what prescience or divination certain women with no notion of art or taste suddenly become the most fervent priestesses of beauty? . . . Succeeding the Normandy peasant, the servant of the Latin quarter students, was a woman of the greatest elegance, aristocratic taste and delicacy" (Charles Matharel de Fiennes.) This sense of delicacy was the quality most praised in Marie, who presented herself in an artfully understated way. Being slender and not voluptuous, she never wore décolleté necklines but covered her shoulders with a cashmere shawl and chose dresses of white or pearl gray, which gave her an angelic, innocent appearance. Matharel de Fiennes never forgot the one time he caught sight of her at a public ball.

> I can still see her now: large black eyes, alive, sweet, astonished, almost anxious, in turn full of candor and vague desires, the brows like black velvet and placed there on her forehead to offset the whiteness of her skin and the brilliant crystal of her eyes. Lips which were half-parted, hair that

was Spanish by nuance, French by grace, an effect so charming, so poetic that whoever saw Marie Duplessis—cenobite,
octogenarian or student—fell instantly in love.

The early days of Agénor's love affair with Marie passed in
an intoxicating blur—the nights given over to pleasure, performances, balls, and fine dinners, the days reserved for sleep. But
unlike Marguerite's Armand, who was partly modeled on Agénor, he does not seem to have been at all tormented by Marie's
profession. In her only existing letter to him—a touchingly frank
confession of her situation and dependence—she writes, "Someone you don't know has made me a proposition which I'll tell you
about in my next letter, if my affairs don't bore you too much."

Marie's other lovers at the time were ferociously possessive
by comparison. Count Fernand de Montguyon, a middle-aged
dandy, famous for his taste in corps de ballet girls, had been
outraged when he spotted Agénor not only riding in the carriage that he, Montguyon, had given Marie, but also with the
black spaniel that had been his gift to her. "What should I do?"
he exploded to a friend, who, after reflecting for a moment and
judging his man, replied, "It's quite simple. I see the choice either
of a duel . . . or a very witty word." A remark made by Marie
suggests that Agénor's sudden departure for London in July 1842
may have been triggered by the reappearance of another propri-
etorial protector, whom they referred to as The General. "We
would have been so happy if he hadn't come to surprise us," she
wrote. "Our life was so well organised!"

Agénor's London sojourn was almost certainly a banishment
imposed by his parents to end his degrading liaison (Vienne himself uses the word *exile*). There are no surviving letters from Agénor to Marie, and all his personal papers were later destroyed in
a fire at his château. The Gramont family left no compromising
letters, and the confessional journal of Agénor's uncle the Count
d'Orsay—admiringly described by Lord Byron as a "History of

His Own Times"—was burned by d'Orsay himself. Decadent, witty, outrageously extravagant, and exquisitely elegant, d'Orsay was a glamorous mentor to young Agénor, whom he worshipped in return. Hearing how his nephew had plunged a knife through the heart of a wild boar that had attacked him, d'Orsay compared him to a romantic hero—"a modern Raoul de Courcy." There was scandal attached to Count d'Orsay's own amorous situation. He had married Lady Blessington's fifteen-year-old stepdaughter but kept the stepmother in his life, and may also have been the sexual partner of Lord Blessington. All of which makes it likely that Agénor could have counted on d'Orsay's support over his youthful transgression.

A banishment, then, it may have been, but certainly not a punishment. The Duke de Gramont, who had been brought up in England and served in an English regiment, ensured that his son was received in the best circles of London society, which included the Blessington-d'Orsay salon at Gore House, where Dickens and Thackeray were frequent guests. Marie, meanwhile, sorely missing her young lover, had only her forthcoming trip to Baden-Baden to distract her. The letter she wrote to Agénor in a neat, confident hand was sent to him at 11 Little [*sic*] Maddox Street, Hanover Square, and postmarked 24 July 1842.

> *My dear Agénor,*
> *Although you have not been gone for long, I have some things to tell you. First, my angel, I am very sad, and very bored because I can't see you. I do not know yet when I will leave, but I would like it to be soon, because I am being bothered by The General who insists that I receive him and continue to be with him as before. He has no intention of changing his conduct towards me. . . . But let's talk of the present, my poor angel—and not regret the past. . . .*
> *I would like to ask your advice: whether or not I should travel with Mme Weller, I am very bothered because I hardly under-stand this woman who at times is excessively nice to me and at*

*others changes her manner completely. So I am waiting to get your
response as a friend.*

*Write me a long letter soon—tell me everything you're thinking,
and what you're doing—tell me also that you love me—I need to
know this and it will be a consolation for your absence, my good
angel. I am very sad, but I love you more tenderly than ever. I
embrace you a thousand times on your mouth and everywhere else.
Adieu my darling angel, don't forget me too much, and think
sometimes of she who loves you so much.*

  Marie Duplessis.

———

In the 1840s, the journey from Paris to Baden-Baden was still
undertaken by stage or mail coach and lasted several days. The
passport Marie ordered specially for the trip records her age as
twenty-one, as French subjects had to be *majeur* to travel abroad,
but she was still an impressionable eighteen-year-old, completely
unprepared for what was in store. Having known only gentle,
Normandy pasturelands, Marie must have been intoxicated by
the panoramic sweep of her new surroundings; it was the first
time she had left France, and every new impression roused her
love of life and adventure. Baden-Baden itself, enfolded by the
summits of three mountains and surrounded by fields with graz-
ing cattle, was unlike anywhere else she had ever been—a country town with all the sophistication of a European city.

We know she arrived there on Friday, 22 July 1842, because
an entry in the *Badeblatt,* the newssheet distributed at midday with a list of foreigners who had reached there the evening
before, records that "Dem. Duplessis" was staying at the Hôtel
de l'Europe. Like the two single Englishwomen, Miss Morris and
Miss Aytmer, who came the same day, she had brought two servants with her (presumably her maid, Rose, and the fickle Mme
Weller). But was she also accompanied by The General? Vienne
quotes from a subsequent letter he claims that she wrote to

Guiche saying that she had gone to Germany "to guard her fidelity" and had been obliged to borrow forty thousand francs "for this platonic excursion." And yet he also says that her companion in Baden-Baden was the "Duke de R." The *Badeblatt* offers no possible contender at the Hôtel de l'Europe. Arriving on the same day from Paris and staying at the Hôtel d'Angleterre was one Marquis de Rodes, but a week earlier, on July 15, a Duke von Skarzynsky had arrived with his servants from Paris and moved into the Hôtel du Rhin. Skarzynsky was a general.

The Hôtel de l'Europe, with its magnificent sweeping iron staircase and river frontage was considered to be one of the choicest places to stay—favored especially by the Russian aristocracy. It was perfectly situated, facing Conversation House, where a ball took place three times a week, and minutes away from the modish promenade of Lichtentaler Allee. As the Prussian military band played its weekly concert in the pavilion, the blare of wind instruments carried up the avenue accompanying the parade of victoria and tilbury carriages, cavaliers in military uniforms, strolling dandies, and crinolined women holding parasols in matching pastel shades. For Marie, Baden-Baden was a little Paris. Lichtentaler Allee was its Bois de Boulogne, the villas that overlooked the park adorned with caryatids were like those of the rue de la Madeleine. The names of hotels, restaurants, and menus were all in French, and even the Russians spoke French among themselves. In May, just before the start of the season, milliners, couturiers, hairdressers, pedicurists, and corset makers traveled from Paris to set up shop in the town. The *Badeblatt* also records the arrival that summer of one Jean-François Utz, a painter who would be "practicing the art of making portraits à la Daguerreotype"—in other words, one of the earliest pioneer photographers.

A time would come when Marie, enfeebled by symptoms of the tuberculosis that was to kill her, would seek the healing properties of the waters and other treatments for which Baden-

Baden was famous. Dumas fils's Marguerite is "so frail, so changed that the doctors ordered her to take the waters in the spring of 1842," but the earliest of Marie's many medical bills is a pharmacy receipt for a gargle solution, dated 1843. In all probability, like the majority of visitors to Baden-Baden that summer, Marie was there for its social pleasures. For Parisians these were centered primarily around the casino. In the French capital, although gambling still went on in the cafés and restaurants of the boulevard des Italiens, since midnight on 31 December 1837, all the casinos in the Palais-Royal—the most famous in Europe—had been forced by law to close. Quick to seize an opportunity, one clever entrepreneur, Jacques Bénazet, had secured the license to run Baden-Baden's casino, and within a year not only transformed it into a beautiful palace of rich baroque elegance but also made himself the patron of the town. The spectacle of the casino's dignified, savvy croupiers and their quickly moving scoops, the piles of gold and silver on the green baize, the ivory ball spinning into the bottom of the roulette wheel were thrilling to Marie, who, though she had gambled with cards, now discovered the adrenaline rush of casino gambling. But while she was in her element, admired and flattered by men of all ages, Vienne claims that the Duke de R.—"a grand seigneur, who was a serious man, correct and a little cold"—had tired of Baden-Baden's frivolous routine and announced that he would be leaving the following day.

If this was the case, Marie was not alone for long. The account of what happened next is her own, recorded in the memoirs of the actress Mme Judith. On her daily walk under the firs of the promenade, Marie told Mme Judith, she had noticed a distinguished old man who was always there, and who would stare at her with adoration, sometimes even walking beside her so that he could observe her longer. One day he felt bold enough to approach her. "Do not fear, Mademoiselle, that I am trying to woo you," he said. "It would suit neither my age nor my taste. You are very beautiful. But you will understand the kind of feelings your beauty inspires in me when I tell you that I have recently lost a daughter whom you resemble like a sister. . . . More than a sister." He stopped a moment, and his look, fixed on Marie, was lit with great tenderness. He went on, "Mademoiselle, I have a favour to ask you: I would like to see you often to remind me of my daughter. It is not unusual to commission artists to paint portraits of those one has lost, and you would be the living portrait of my child."

He told her that he was the Count von Stackelberg and admitted that he'd made inquiries about her, while finding it hard to believe what he had learned. "The purity of your features reveals a soul at odds with your conduct," he said, adding that as an extremely wealthy man he was in a position to help her. "Will you renounce the existence you lead?" he pleaded. "You yourself can name the figure of income which I will undertake to provide. Accept the offer I am making you. . . . Help me to accomplish a doubly pious act—that of honoring the memory of the deceased, and of bringing honor to the living."

"I can't explain how much this proposition moved me," Marie confided to Mme Judith. "It was the first time that anyone had spoken to me in this way. I looked at this old man who was giving a lost girl the charity of comparing her to a child untouched by vice, and stayed silent, but as a response, I dabbed at my eyes." The count took this to be an assent, and gravely thanked her.

The seventy-six-year-old Gustav Ernst von Stackelberg had arrived on July 17 with his family and servants—ten people in all—settling into one of the town's grandest private houses. He was Estonian by birth, his family having made their fortune in the Baltic states, and like his father before him he had been a diplomat and a favorite of Catherine the Great. A colleague, Charles (Karl) Nesselrode, who spent three years working alongside Stackelberg in Berlin forty years earlier, was astounded, even at this early period, by his profligacy: "He has just rented a house for 4,000 florins, which in this country is an exorbitant amount," Nesselrode told his father in 1802, adding that his own rent was thirty-three florins. It was unclear why Stackelberg, who let it be known that he found women of the diplomatic corps very disagreeable, then chose to marry the Austrian ambassador's daughter. But Countess Caroline von Ludolf made an excellent wife, and went on to bear Stackelberg twelve children. Nesselrode described him as a bizarre character with a hot temper, but he was universally recognized as a superb diplomat, having received the Order of Saint Andrew, Russia's most prestigious award, for service to his country. As special envoy for the czar, Stackelberg represented Russia at the 1814 Congress of Vienna (the result of which was a balance of power in Europe and forty years of peace), and he is part of Jean-Baptiste Isabey's group portrait of the illustrious participants, who included Wellington, Metternich, and Talleyrand. On his retirement in 1835, Stackelberg settled with his wife in Paris, but any possibility of a tranquil final phase was shattered when, in 1840, a double tragedy struck, and the couple lost not one but two daughters—Maria and Elizavetta, aged twenty-nine and thirty-three—who both died in Turin.

Was Marie a reincarnation of either one? Different scenarios featuring the bereaved old man have been produced time and again, although in each case there is only ever a single adored daughter whom Marie was said to have resembled. She had "the same waxy virginal pallor, the same black eyes enlarged and elongated by misfortune, the same smile, the same size, same hands, same feet," writes Alfred Delvau in *Les lions du jour,* claiming, too, that Stackelberg had promised to make Marie his sole legatee. Dumas fils in his novel sets Marguerite's encounter with the old duke in the French spa town of Bagnères, where she actually meets his daughter. "She had not only the same illness, but also the same face as Marguerite—to the point that they could be mistaken for sisters." Dumas goes on to say that the young duchess was in the third degree of consumption, and that she died a few days after Marguerite's arrival.

In Vienne's memoir the initial meeting place has become the Belgian town of Spa, and Stackelberg is "The Duke de Kelberg . . . an eighty-year-old beau, former German diplomat and a fabulously rich landowner." Marie, he said, had attached no importance to the insistent attentions of this affable, gallant octogenarian and had readily accepted his arm for a daily walk in the park.

Stackelberg, who had a gift for making women of any rank feel special, was immensely enjoyable company. "He's a unique character, and I am sure that his extraordinary style is having an effect on me—for better or worse," wrote one grand duchess in the 1820s. And it is more than likely that it was he, described in the *Badeblatt* as "Rittmeister," a cavalry officer, who sparked Marie's passion for riding (Agénor was known to hate horses). If so, the pair would have been among those galloping at exhilarating speed down Lichtentaler Allee, beating up the dust and causing the promenaders to scatter. High-spirited, fresh, and hungry for new experiences, Marie must have been more of a tonic to a father in mourning than any recuperative treatment the spa had to offer. But she, according to Vienne, had no delusions about his fixation on her. "She was certainly far from doubting that she inspired in him an emotion which had nothing paternal in it, and that it would not be long before he began courting her with the conceit of a young hero."

"The poor old man, he would have been embarrassed to be her lover," counters Marguerite's friend Prudence in *The Lady of the Camellias*—a belief apparently shared by its author, who writes, "The feelings of this father for Marguerite had a motive so chaste . . . anything else would have seemed to him like incest. . . . He never said a word to her that his daughter could not have heard." Dumas fils himself, however, was unequivocally damning. In the notes he gave to actors while rehearsing his subsequent play, he insists that the lachrymose story of the consumptive daughter whose double Stackelberg had discovered in Marie was a complete fiction. "The count, in spite of his great age, was not an Oedipus looking for an Antigone, but a King David looking for a Bathsheba," he writes, though, as one biographer has pointed out, he has confused the story of Bathsheba with that of Abishag the Sunammite. What Dumas had in mind was a comparison between Marie and the young virgin brought to cherish David in his old age, lying in his bosom so that the king might "get heat." "The essential fact," says Francis Gribble, "is that Marie Duplessis, for the sake of money, submitted to the intimate caresses of a man old enough to be her great-grandfather."

Vienne, who—unlike any other chronicler of the time—knew all about Alphonsine's sexual history with an old man, was himself in no doubt of the reality of the situation. "After short preliminaries," he says, "the triumphant octogenarian was honored by admission to the bedroom and to the privileges reserved for a protector-lover." According to him, this consummation took place soon afterward in Paris, although accounts in the *Badeblatt* may suggest otherwise. By July 29, Stackelberg had moved—alone—to the Hôtel de Hollande, and by August 2, Marie had moved out of the Hôtel de l'Europe.

Back in Paris, the count made frequent visits to Marie "every morning at an hour when Parisians are not yet awake," Vienne says. A receipt dated October 1842, detailing the redecoration of a new apartment at number 22, rue d'Antin, suggests that he had found premises for her, a five-minute walk from favorite haunts like La Maison d'Or. It was also equidistant from Stackelberg's own house on the rue de la Chaussée-d'Antin. Just as he and his wife worked at polishing the manners of their grandchildren—"they were taught not only to dance but also to walk elegantly"—Stackelberg set about enhancing the style and surroundings of his teenage mistress. Improvements to rue d'Antin amounted to a total of 11,952 francs, and two bills settled by Stackelberg for Chinese vases, candlesticks, and a clock are evidence of his lavish patronage and attention to aesthetic detail. "From this moment, he took care of all my expenses," Marie told Mme Judith. "He would not allow me to decrease these; on the contrary, he insisted that I increase my standards of luxury."

Her developing taste was simple in that she was satisfied only with the best. And now that she could have anything she wanted, Marie made sure that not only her apartment but everything to do with her appearance was of the highest standard. There is an account of one Stephen Drake searching England for thoroughbreds that had been inscribed in the Stud Book because Marie wanted only equine nobility to draw her carriage. And she found them. Sporting chain-mail breastplates, buckskin culottes, and coronets of embossed, polished leather, her horses were as beautifully dressed as she was. For her *promenades à cheval,* Marie had ordered from the renowned French tailor Humann a riding jacket of chestnut velvet and downy cashmere, a Basque-style, richly ornamented petticoat and bodice to be worn over a shirt with tight sleeves buttoned at the wrist. Marie's coiffeur, M. Degoutter, came every day; her pedicurist was Joseph Pau, whose clients included the Opéra's star ballerinas; her suppliers were the finest in Paris: gloves—buttoned and laced à la Medicis—from Mayor, "supplier to the Queen and the Court, Empress of Russia and Mesdames the Grandes-Duchesses"; shoes from Jacob, who also had a boutique in London's Bond Street; Portuguese soaps from Postansque, perfumer to the Duchess de Nemours. When Marie entertained at home, elaborate meals were brought in from Chevet or La Maison d'Or, whose specialties of the house were *l'omble chevalier,* a rare freshwater fish, and sautéed livers of monkfish.

Her household expenses alone, Vienne reckons, amounted to forty thousand francs a month, paid by the count, who, in addition, gave her everything she could possibly want. And in return?

"The reader may wonder what she did with an eighty-year-old lover. I do not intend to dwell on unpleasant details. . . . I know no more. I deliberately abstained from questioning Marie, who was grateful for my reserve."

Romain Vienne was now living in Paris and working as a journalist. Soon after leaving Normandy he had established a flirtatious bond with Alphonsine's two grisette friends Ernestine and Hortense, and he had also renewed his acquaintance with her ex-colleague Elisa, whose mother had been his landlady when he was a student. Still renting cheap lodgings, he was a nineteenth-century Herr Issyvoo, whose memoir of Marie, like a nonfiction version of Christopher Isherwood's *Goodbye to Berlin,* would eventually capture the personality of a wanton, born-to-be-legendary young woman.

Not having seen Marie since her move to rue d'Antin, Romain had left his card with the concierge in the rue de l'Arcade, only to be told that Mlle Plessis was no longer living there. It was Hortense who took him to the new address, where Rose answered the door and led them into a sumptuously furnished drawing room. Waiting to receive her two friends, with what Vienne describes as charming coquetry and incomparable grace, was Marie. The transformation was astounding. "Her manners were not affected, her dress was skillfully correct, her attitude irreproachable, her walk aristocratic and her conversation of an admirable purity. Her voice had acquired melodious tones. . . . It was an apparition."

Still addressing her as Alphonsine, Romain was surprised to learn that she had changed her name to one that was much more common. This was because it was the name of the Virgin, Marie told him—a reply he found amusing. "There's an original idea! Do you intend to add that of Magdelene?" he teased, asking her also to explain the prefix *du* added to Plessis. "Call it a project, a fantasy—whatever you wish," she answered, "but if it comes up for sale I intend to buy the beautiful château of Plessis in Nonant—which *you* know better than anyone." For all her newly acquired sophistication and wealth, Marie would always remain for Romain "la petite Plessis." Only with him could she call up memories of her childhood and of people they knew in common—a fact she acknowledged when she said, "You are alone in my entourage in knowing everything about my life that I have kept hidden from the world." Mindful of how she was always surrounded by idolators, he prided himself on never flattering Marie and, as he grew to know her better, would tell her truths about herself that only a trusted friend could broach. But, while she valued Romain's frankness and loyalty, she became increasingly aware of his deepening feelings for her. She noticed how he stayed away when she took on a new protector, yet she spotted him almost every day in the street outside her house. His ardor—palpable between the lines of his memoir—was all the more intense for being suppressed, but he knew he could never confess his feelings to Marie. To do so would be to lose her; she had told him as much herself. "Our lovers often bore us, our protectors always do, our friends never. . . . I was very happy when I was certain that you were not going to try to be my lover. If it had been otherwise, our splendid, uncomplicated relationship could never have existed."

———

Within a few months after returning from Baden-Baden, Marie had broken the tacit vow she had made to Stackelberg. In her conversation with Mme Judith, she explains, "For some time, I lived without lovers. I had hoped to reform, believing it possible to accept the life which he offered me. But what can you do? I found I was dying of boredom." Dumas fils's picture of Marguerite confirms this. "She kept her promise to the duke . . . but once she had returned to Paris it had seemed to this girl, accustomed to the dissipated life, to balls—and even orgies—that her solitude, broken only by periodic visits from the duke, would make her die of boredom."

In the novel, it is the old man's friends—"always on the watch for a scandal on the part of the young woman with whom he had compromised himself"—who break the news that she is betraying him, reporting that she sometimes received visitors who stayed until the morning. Having seen one of the duke's servants hanging around her street, Marguerite knew that she was being watched and referred to her protector as "My Old Jealous One." When questioned she confessed everything, telling him that he must stop caring for her because she did not want to carry on receiving benefits from a man whom she was deceiving. "The duke stayed away for a week, but on the eighth day he came to beg Marguerite to allow him to see her, giving her his word that he would accept her as she was."

Shortly after this, Stackelberg lost his third daughter. Living in Naples and only twenty-three years old, Elena died in February 1843. The effect on her father, who had suffered from depression most of his life, can only have been catastrophic (his recurrent nervous attacks were described by a friend as "like fits of madness"). We will never know if Marie was supportive of him during this period. No letters between them exist, although there is a stamp on the reverse of her passport confirming that she was not in Paris in February but had gone to London. Was this to be reunited with Agénor? There is no mention of any trip at this time in Vienne's account, although a paragraph in *The Lady of the Camellias* suggests that it was indeed Guiche whom she went to see. "I traveled over to join the Count de G," remarks Marguerite. "He gave me a marvellous welcome, but he was the lover of a society lady there, and was afraid of compromising himself by being seen with me. He introduced me to his friends, who organized a supper party for me, after which one of them took me home with him."

A beautiful young woman who was not only wealthy but free, Marie had reached a turning point. "I thought I might perhaps find a young man who would understand my remorse and make me his companion" she told Mme Judith, "but the only ones to appear were adventurers drawn by my money. The young men who might have attracted me mocked my ideas of marriage, questioned my self-restraint, and constantly threw my past at me. I felt that my faults of old irrevocably condemned me and that in the society of today the once-fallen woman can never reform—however sincere her contrition might be."

She said much the same to Vienne. "We lost girls will be eternally reproached. Every honest door to me is closed; it is in vain for me to invoke pity; social conventions are without pity. Rehabilitation? Never! Pardon by men? Never! I know them too well in that regard to retain the smallest illusion." Was she right? Indistinguishable in dress and manners from women of the noblest birth—"a duchess could not have smiled differently"— Marie now had the ability and the independence of means to invent a new life for herself, a "retired existence" as pictured by Albert Vandam:

> She might, like so many demimondaines have done since, bought herself a country house, re-entered "the paths of respectability," have had a pew in the parish church, been in constant communication with the vicar, prolonged her life by several years, and died in the odour of sanctity.

But not Marie. Her very nature, as he rightly says, "revolted against such self-exile," and she admitted her "horror of hypocrisy" to Vienne.

> I don't feel I'm blessed with a virtue sufficient enough to become a hermit. I have been, for too long, accustomed to the pleasures of my era to consider attempting to deprive

myself of them . . . to break off, without transition, without hope of return, the past habits of the flesh, of the blood, of the character to which I am enslaved. . . . Alas, it is too hard.

So it was not out of despair, as Marie disingenuously told Mme Judith, that she went back to a life of vice: it was her own choice. In refusing to submit to the punitive moral code of her day and accept "a monastic existence, with no parties, no amusements, no lovers," she entered a world denied to any respectable woman. Marriage and motherhood were what society expected of her sex, but the role of *femme à partie*—a courtesan of the highest rank—was a far more seductive option. "Mixing only with men of wealth and education, they themselves were refined and quick-witted," writes nineteenth-century social historian Alexandre Parent-Duchâtelet. A woman's qualities of beauty, grace, and charm were not sufficient for these men; they expected her also to be cultivated and intelligent. To this end, Marie became part of a distinguished group of intelligentsia, sharing a table at the Café de Paris with a secret society of twelve members of the city's elite—men whose appetite for stimulating conversation, gastronomy, fine wines, and infernal pleasures exactly matched her own.

Part Three

The Lady of the Camellias

〰

PARIS OF THE early 1840s was a ferment of creativity, learning, and social change. The July revolution of 1830 had replaced the old nobility of the House of Bourbon with a wealthy bourgeoisie who thrived under the reign of Louis-Philippe, "the citizen king." It was an era of entrepreneurs and parvenus, and with this new democracy came a felling of traditional barriers. Writers, like the poet Alphonse de Lamartine, a liberal thinker and critic of despotism, had risen in stature by involving themselves in affairs of state. Women were more emancipated, some entering the aristocracy through marriage, others discovering the power of money and using it to their own gain. Fortune seekers by nature, courtesans could flourish in a city Balzac saw as dominated by two passions: gold and pleasure. But even respectable women began showing examples of conduct previously only enjoyed by men. "In novels," wrote Arsène Houssaye, "we find heroines who go hunting, carry arms, play the stock market, ride horses intrepidly and swim without fear. They light your cigar; they let you smoke only because they smoke themselves. . . . The days are over for women as they used to be—obedient, servile, in the shadows. Yesterday they ruled the home, today they rule the government."

Not only the scientific and medical center of Europe, Paris had replaced Vienna as the musical capital, and it was where theater, ballet, and the visual arts were at their vibrant best. Parisians could see exhibitions of current work by Delacroix, Ingres, Corot, and Courbet; attend recitals by Liszt and Paganini; hear the latest compositions by Berlioz and Rossini, who, as director of the Théâtre-Italien, had revolutionized the public's response to opera. Rachel, the great French classical tragedienne, was conquering Paris; Marie Taglioni, the legendary star of romantic ballet, though past her prime, was still captivating audiences by seeming to float above the stage; her successor Carlotta Grisi had inspired poet Théophile Gautier to create *Giselle.*

Paris was also a city of readers. Foreign visitors would be surprised to see a flower seller or street porter with a book in hand—very likely the latest novel by Eugène Sue or Alexandre Dumas père, both at the peak of their fame and revered by rich and poor. This was the age of serialization. A popular triumph like Sue's *Mysteries of Paris,* a naturalistic novel set in the city's underworld, was published in enticing intallments in the *Journal des Débats* between June and October 1843. Even illiterate people, eager to know what happened next, would form a crowd as the next installment was read aloud to them. At the other end of the social scale, readings were held in grand salons as a way of testing reactions and publicizing new works. The Boulevard cafés and restaurants, frequented by the prominent writers and journalists of the day, provided another lively stimulus for literary conversations—as did the Boulevard itself.

An elite strolling ground with the boulevard des Italiens as its epicenter, this area was like an exclusive club with a perpetual flux of famous and familiar faces. During one promenade in October 1840, Liszt ran into, among other friends, Heine, Balzac, Chopin, and Berlioz. For Balzac the Boulevard was "the poem of Paris"—what the Grand Canal is to Venice; for Alfred de Musset it was "one of the points of the earth where the pleasure of the world is concentrated." Paved in asphalt and lit with gas lamps, the Boulevard had very distinct parameters, extending from the rue de la Chaussée-d'Antin to the passage de l'Opéra (the avenue and place de l'Opéra did not yet exist) and ending at the corner of the rue de la Grange-Batelière (today's rue Drouot). It was considered bad form to show oneself beyond these boundaries, and *flâneurs* rarely strayed from beyond the Théâtre de Variétés, a deserted area Musset called the Far Indies.

There was usually a triple circle of tilburies and coaches parked in front of Tortoni on the corner of boulevard des Italiens and rue Taitbout. Founded at the end of the eighteenth century by a Neapolitan gelaterio, it was taken over by a man called Tortoni, who turned the café into a Parisian landmark due to the excellence of its ice creams and sorbets. Frock-coated dandies sat at outdoor tables or congregated around the staircase posing, chattering, and eyeing passing beauties. A carriage and four might pull up with two postilions, one of whom would run in to buy a sorbet for madame, who sat studying the comings and goings through her lorgnette. Nestor Roqueplan was a regular at Tortoni, telling witty anecdotes while leaning against the banister or preventing the impatient waiters from clearing tables and going home. There almost every night between 11:30 p.m. and 1:00 a.m., he would then move next door to the Café Riche because of its late closing hours, joining other insomniacs, who included the writers Gustave Claudin and Henri Murger. Earlier in the evening, Roqueplan would have dined either at La Maison d'Or, sitting at his usual table by the door, or at the Café de Paris, which was considered to be the headquarters of the noble company of the Boulevard.

Facing Tortoni, in part of an *hôtel particulier,* the Café de Paris had the understated elegance of an aristocratic family house, furnished with superb antiques, paintings, and mirrors and lit by candles, oil lamps, and the glow of wood fires. It was not only the best restaurant in Paris but reputedly the best in Europe. The chef had once worked for the Duchess de Berry and could make an art of the simplest dish, such as veal casserole—a "culinary glory" and specialty of the house. Dumas père, who loved cooking almost more than writing, would frequently be taken down to the kitchens for a consultation on a recipe. Almost every evening there was a tasting exchange between clients. "For instance," writes the English journalist Albert Vandam, "Dr Veron, who was very fond of Musigny vintage, rarely missed offering some to the Marquis du Hallays, who, in his turn, sent him the finest dishes from his table." The headwaiter, the urbane, deferential Martin Guépet, would not turn chance customers or sightseers away, but there was rarely a strange face or discordant voice among the diners. To Gustave Claudin, novelist and chronicler of Parisian mores, there was an unspoken, uncontested rule of selection at the Café de Paris: "Nobody was tolerated who could not lay claim to some sort of distinction or originality. A kind of invisible moral barrier existed, shutting out the mediocre, the insipid, and the insignificant, who passed by, but did not linger, knowing that their place was not there."

Marie, herself, was a regular, always welcome at Dr. Louis Véron's table—the most prestigious in the restaurant. A stout, jovial bachelor who dined there almost every night, Véron had trained in medicine and made his fortune from a chest ointment, using some of the proceeds to found *Revue de Paris* and revive *Le Constitutionnel,* the most widely read newspaper of the day. Thanks to his business flair (and the lure of his star ballerina, Marie Taglioni), his five-year stint as director of the Opéra had been a financial triumph and is regarded to this day as a golden age. Véron was immensely popular because he was generous to the point of profligacy—always picking up the bill and offering his authors double the going rate—his conspicuous materialism typical of the money-fixated middle classes who had risen to prominence over the last decade. Although disagreeable to look at, with sagging cheeks and blinking, piggy eyes, Véron was as vain and mannered as a Regency roué, wearing a massive cravat to hide his scarred, scrofulous neck. He loved the company of young women, over whom he seemed to wield a mystifying power. "I gave in because he had a hold over me," said the actress Rachel, explaining why she had chosen Véron as her first lover when she was just seventeen.

Nineteen-year-old Marie was also impressed by Véron's wealth and influence. As the daughter of a peddler and child of the streets, like Rachel, she could understand his arriviste brashness and may even have shared the actress's bizarre attraction to him. Professionally, he was the key to a legion of important contacts, and his table at the back of the restaurant was a magnet for them all. "*Le Tout Paris du Boulevard* files past from six o'clock until midnight," wrote one observer, adding that Véron had hardly sat down before twenty hands shook his and ten people stopped to linger by his side. Marie's lowly origins intrigued Véron. One evening, after she had left the table, he remarked, "I confess, Alphonsine Plessis interests me very much. She is, first of all, the best-dressed woman in Paris. Secondly, she neither flaunts nor hides her vices. Thirdly, she is not always talking or hinting about money. In short, she is a wonderful courtesan."

It was the chance to be part of a rarefied, fascinating milieu like this that encouraged Marie to make the most of her profession. "I wanted to know the refinements and pleasure of artistic taste," she once said, "the joy of living in elegant and cultivated society." It had allowed her not only to indulge her sybaritic nature but to choose her world. The writers who frequented the Café de Paris—Musset, Sue, Balzac, Dumas—were the writers whose books Marie bought. She owned a ten-volume edition of *The Three Musketeers,* and her library of carved oak contained more than two hundred books: classics by Rabelais, Walter Scott, Marivaux, Byron, Molière, and Cervantes as well as works by contemporaries such as Lamartine and Victor Hugo. As Charles Matharel de Fiennes wrote, "These were the men with whom she wanted to keep company."

The Café de Paris literati were also regular guests in the most brilliant salon of the decade, hosted by Mme de Girardin, herself a writer, whose drawing room was a center for men and women to meet on equal terms. Prowess in intellectual conversation was crucial to French culture, and like the great *salonnières* before her, Mme de Staël and Mme Récamier, Delphine de Girardin challenged the accepted notion of passive virtue for women— remaining silent on topics outside their domestic sphere. And yet even she was circumscribed by convention. When Arsène Houssaye's first novel, *The Lovely Sinner,* was published, Mme de Girardin remarked in her *Courrier de Paris* column that she had enjoyed the charming first volume but had refrained from reading the second, having heard that it was too indelicate. This had rankled Houssaye at the time, but twenty years later he felt that Mme de Girardin was right, and in his preface quotes Rousseau's own warning about his novel *The New Héloïse,* a passionate exchange of lovers' letters, saying that no chaste girl must ever read it: "Whoever dares look at a single page of mine is a lost woman." When Gautier examined Marie's books after her death, he found that *The New Héloïse* was one of the two most-thumbed volumes in her collection. The other was *Manon Lescaut,* Abbé Prévost's story of a beautiful young courtesan.

Through the Café de Paris, Marie had the best of both worlds: no inhibitions of propriety and access to the civilizing advantages of a salonlike atmosphere—an informal university for women. But how could a country girl, who a few years earlier could barely read or write, hold her own in this setting? Beauty was appreciated, but it was not a prerequisite of acceptance: Esther Guimont, another "friend of the Café de Paris band," was as plain as she was ill educated, yet known as the *courtisane des lettres* because of her influence on the distinguished writers and politicians of the day. She was said to have lured away Delphine de Girardin's husband, Emile, the most powerful journalist in Paris, because she made him laugh, and her wit and audacity had also won the heart of Nestor Roqueplan.

It was Roqueplan who had discovered Alphonsine as a starving waif on the Pont-Neuf, and he can only have been astonished by her transformation. A raconteur of great originality, he kept his Café de Paris companions amused by mocking everything and everyone (his nickname for Dr. Véron was The Prince of Weals). But although anyone invited to Roqueplan's table was expected to be as cultured and satirical as he was, he nevertheless remained indulgent toward his little *gourmande*. She was, he said, "without intellect, but with a rich instinct."

Others were more skeptical. A romantic revolutionary in his twenties, Arsène Houssaye had belonged to a bohemian group that included Gautier and the artist Gavarni. Now approaching middle-aged respectability, with a patriarchal beard, Houssaye felt that Marie was clever, "but she talked nothing but nonsense. And yet with all this, or without all this, she achieved her renown by way of charm. When you were with her you had no wish to leave." Marie's candor about her lack of education only increased their interest, Albert Vandam said. "She had a natural tact and an instinctive refinement which no education could have enhanced. She never made grammatical mistakes, no coarse expression ever passed her lips." A bright young journalist of Dutch descent, Vandam was not one of the café's literary lions, but he had been introduced to them at the age of twenty-one and was there many a night. His main talent was as an observer, but his reputation for repeating what he overheard had made him something of an outsider. Perhaps because of this, or because he was so much closer to her own age, Marie welcomed his company. "She would often sit and chat to me. She liked me, because I never paid her many compliments."

The infamous Lola Montez was another young courtesan who had made it into the inner circle. She arrived in Paris in early March 1844 armed with letters of introduction from Liszt, her most recent conquest, and had soon begun several other important liaisons. Dumas, one possible lover, remained wary— "she has the evil eye," he told Vandam—and, indeed, Lola Montez was not what she seemed. Born Eliza Gilbert in Ireland's County Sligo, she had adopted the persona of a Spanish dancer, despite having no talent other than a natural grace. She covered her shortcomings with a wild audacity, and, convincing herself that a course of lessons by the renowned ballet master Hippolyte Barrez was enough to prepare her, made her debut in late March on the hallowed Opéra stage. Facing a house full to bursting, she struck a provocative pose before removing her garter and tossing it into the stalls. The roar of approval turned to impatience as soon as Montez started to dance, and this first performance, like the one that followed two nights later, was a fiasco. But while everyone agreed that Lola Montez was no Taglioni, her singular, entertaining personality, enticing beauty, and mad ardor had made her something of a star. Twenty-one-year-old Gustave Claudin, just beginning work as a journalist, felt bewitched by her: "There was about her something provoking and voluptuous which drew you."

Her brazenness was witnessed by Romain Vienne at a party given by Marie. He had hardly sat down before a sparkling young woman with a heavily made-up face came prancing up to them, singing a popular opera tune. Placing a dainty foot on the arm of Vienne's chair, she appeared about to repeat her garter trick but this time challenged him to slide the ribbon from her thigh. Determined not to appear fazed, he did just that, only to be roundly slapped by Lola, who ran off laughing. "Excuse her," Marie said. "She behaves like this with all men—it's her way of amusing herself."

To onlookers it was hard to believe that the pair were friends. "The Irish woman confronted this world with head erect and flashing eyes," Claudin remarked, "the Lady of the Camellias with a blush and trembling lips." And yet, there were some similarities: the same pale oval face, huge dark eyes, and little *Mona Lisa* mouth. Lola's phony Spanish look must have been admired by Marie, as she copied it exactly when she was painted by Olivier, wearing a full-skirted black dress with long tight sleeves, her head shrouded, *à l'espagnole,* in a black lace mantilla pinned with a red rose. Certainly both young women had reinvented themselves, feigning aristocratic refinement while acting as if they were entitled to the sexual freedom of men. As far as the public was concerned, they belonged in the same category, although Albert Vandam insists that they could not have differed more. "Lola Montez could not make friends. Alphonsine Plessis could not make enemies."

Marie's demure appearance touched just about every man she met. "Only the large black eyes, lacking innocence, protested against the purity of this virginal physique," wrote one admirer. Intensifying the effect was her simplicity of dress. Her favorite garment was a shawl—cashmere in winter; crêpe de chine or Chantilly lace in summer—which artfully complemented her tall, thin frame. Balzac, however, would have regarded such subtlety as cynical provocation. Marie epitomized his delicate, decorous-seeming girls who enliven the orgy scene in his novel *The Wild Ass's Skin*—the "make-believe virgins, whose pretty hair breathed out pious innocence . . . wrapping themselves in a mantle of virtue in order to give greater charm and piquancy to the prodigalities of vice."

Marie also embodied the paradox of the sylph. Since Gautier's 1832 ballet *La Sylphide,* a romantic masterpiece, this airy creature had become a contemporary icon—the subject of poems and essays, even the title of a fashion magazine. Expressing the spiritual sensibilities of the eighteenth century, the sylph was an intellectual symbol capable of conjuring up a lost world, the world painted by Watteau, and prized by writers like Gautier and Houssaye. The creator of the role had been Marie Taglioni, whose grace and fragile charm were the qualities most admired in Marie, a resemblance she enhanced with frothy white dresses, her face framed by neat, parted black hair and a diadem of flowers. Taglioni's landmark performance, which first established the preeminence of the ballerina, corresponded to the sylph's own emancipation. Cherishing her freedom and unconstrained by bourgeois conventions, the ballet's heroine is, in the words of one recent historian, "a woman of unnerving contrasts . . . strong but frail, sexually alluring but chaste." It could be a description of Marie.

And yet to have won "the devotion of the erotic Boulevard," Marie was required to be there on their terms. These were all men who sought the society of women of the demimonde, and their familiarity with grisettes, courtesans, and actresses fed their work, creating Balzac's Esther, Sue's Rigolette, Musset's Mimi Pinson. In one of the Café de Paris's private salons, all decorum had to be left at the door. This was the condition for a woman to participate in *Le Souper des Douze*—a dinner held by the dozen "Disciples of Eros," who included Dr. Véron, Alfred de Musset, and Nestor Roqueplan. Seated with the men, at a large table decorated not with flowers but with a cluster of figurines in acrobatic lovemaking positions, was a selection of "pretty girls, lorettes and mistresses" who were unlikely to be discomfited by the male after-dinner conversation. "Because when dessert was served with champagne, frothing in its glasses, we were accustomed to recount, without any reticence, our amorous adventures."

Examples of these erotic vignettes, which take the form of a letter to a fellow "apostle" who has been obliged to leave Paris, were privately published in a volume entitled *Voluptueux souvenirs; ou, Le Souper des Douze*—available only to subscribers. The collection, now in the Bibliothèque Nationale, must be read in the rare books salon with the protection of white gloves and located by its code ENFER—French for "hell." Seeming today to be quaintly risqué, one describes how a frigid courtesan, whose only passion was money, was transported to near nymphomania by the sight of her lover's state of arousal. In another, the narrator plans to cure his mistress of her jealousy with the help of a complicit blonde. When Valérie receives an anonymous note telling her that her lover is being unfaithful, she rushes to his apartment, opening the door with the key he has given her, and catches him with his breeches down. "Madame . . . this is mine and I forbid you to touch it!" she shrieks, launching into a catfight, and rolling on the floor with her rival. The man watches voyeuristically as the two women enlace, and the story concludes with a consensual threesome.

The author of *Voluptueux souvenirs* was Roger de Beauvoir, "the most audacious of this band" and an escort of Marie. He, too, came from Normandy and had aggrandized himself by changing his name and adding "de" to his patronymic (Beauvoir was the name of the land he owned there). His friends nicknamed him Roger Bontemps because of his love of pleasure and extravagant lifestyle. With a cigar in his left hand, a cane of rhinoceros horn in his right, he was a persuasive charmer, a tall bachelor in his early forties, and one of Paris's most elegant dandies. He was born rich—"thrice rich," wrote Dumas, "through his mother, his father and the second husband of his mother." His black beard and long, curling tresses gave him the air of an Italian nobleman. (The writer and photographer Maxime du Camp thought he resembled one of the young Venetians whom Veronese painted in his *Wedding at Cana.*) Almost always good-humored, he was an original, brilliant conversationalist and compulsive scribbler, who composed more than three hundred poems, songs, and madrigals and kept notebooks full of quatrains and epigrams on his friends and enemies. "I have known almost all the witty men of our time," remarked Dumas, "and I am not afraid of saying that not one had the verve of Roger de Beauvoir."

That Beauvoir liked Marie enough to see her outside the confines of the Café de Paris is confirmed in a letter written to poet Félix Arvers, another member of the Twelve.

> *My dear Arvers,*
> *d'Anthoine has just told me that M. Roger de Beauvoir is bringing Mlle Marie Duplessis this evening. Without being prud-*

ish, the women there may not wish to meet Mlle Duplessis, so it
falls to me to ask you to explain to Roger why she cannot come. . . .

In fact, Marie got much closer than others in her position
to gaining access to le monde. Vienne claims she was received
at balls where young women of her kind were never admitted,
and even the most meticulous observers of form would greet her
while pretending not to know her name. The social rigidity of
the ancien régime had relaxed under Louis-Philippe, and dowagers and titled women of fashion had begun to mix with the
demimonde at charity balls and the races. "At first glance they
were the same women, dressed by the same dressmakers, the only
difference being that the demimonde seemed a little more chic,"
writes Houssaye. This, of course, was especially true of Marie,
whose elegance and dignity had made her indistinguishable from
the grandees. Lola Montez also had the comportment of a duchess, but, Vandam claims, the moment she spoke the illusion vanished.

Montez was also incapable of humility—a concept Marie had
discovered to be an effective way of breaking down social barriers. It was certainly how she had endeared herself to Mme Judith,
who would one day find herself impersonating the courtesan in
the role of Marguerite Gautier.

Marie was at the Variétés the night the actress collapsed
onstage from a cerebral fever. Finding out her address (Nestor
Roqueplan was the theater's director), Marie went every day to
her home while she was convalescing, leaving a bouquet of flowers but not revealing her name. Told by her maid that the young
woman was beautiful and aristocratic-looking, Mme Judith left
a note, urging the mysterious visitor to disclose her identity.
Signing her reply "Your devoted and unworthy admirer, Marie
Duplessis," Marie admitted the reason for her anonymity: "I
feared that if you had known my identity you would refuse my

flowers. And I am afraid that in learning it today you will regret having received them."

This may seem overly self-abasing, but Marie knew what she was doing. It was precisely Mme Judith's reaction when she discovered that another "*fervente admiratrice*" was a celebrated figure in the demimonde. Every day at the theater a bouquet had arrived with a note from a woman signing herself Céleste and expressing concern about the actress's ill health. Mme Judith was in her dressing room one evening, entertaining a group of writers and artists, when the latest missive was delivered. She passed it around to her friends, one of whom recognized the signature and exclaimed, "Don't you know who this woman is? It's Céleste Mogador!"

An exact contemporary of Marie, Mogador, whose real name was Elisabeth Vénard, had spent part of her youth in a Parisian brothel until Alfred de Musset took her under his wing. She was now a star dancer at Le Bal Mabille, her brilliance at performing the polka and cancan having challenged the fame of *la reine* Pomaré. Shocked by this, Mme Judith was then informed about Mogador's reputation as a lesbian, which shocked her even more. Taking out one of her cards for her maid to deliver to the young woman waiting expectantly at the stage door, she wrote, "Good for a strong shower at La Salpêtrière" (the prison for prostitutes). The flowers were thrown in the rubbish.

Mme Judith's response on learning that Marie was "the famous *marchande d'amour*" surprised even herself. "I don't know why her letter pleased me so much. The modesty it revealed was so unexpected in a courtesan, and I resolved to bury my prejudice. I invited Marie Duplessis to come and see me." Marie returned the invitation, and they met several times, once in the Bois de Boulogne, where Mme Judith was on foot and Marie promenading in her carriage. They spotted each other, but Marie made only an imperceptible sign of recognition so as not to compromise her new friend. When Mme Judith went up to the carriage and suggested they walk together, Marie hesitated for an instant before springing down and strolling beside her. "The Bois was crowded that day and we were noticed," writes Mme Judith, who years later still remembered Marie's outfit of a magnificent blue velvet coat lined with pink satin over a pale green dress braided with black velvet. On her head she wore a plumed black velvet cap, its feather secured with diamonds. Some people, said Mme Judith, were critical of this public display of friendship, but others, who could not help admiring the beautiful young courtesan, showed approval. Marie, she claimed, felt touched and indebted to her.

Daughter of a lace vendor and earning her living in a flamboyant profession still regarded as morally suspect, Mme Judith's attitude defines the meaning of *folie de grandeur.* It was not rash for an actress—many of whom had similar lowly backgrounds—to form an attachment to Marie Duplessis. There was, however, no possibility of friendship with a woman of society—even though, as Vienne puts it, "their curiosity was constantly put on alert by men's conversations about this marvelous sinner who was the talk of Paris."

But if Marie could not belong to the world of these women, she already belonged to the world of their men. She was an invisible presence in the Jockey Club, an exclusive male bastion, to which the grandest *salonnière* would have been forbidden entry. Also known as Le Club des Lions, the Jockey had introduced to Paris the concept of gentlemen riders, and was such a closed environment that even Alfred de Musset had been blackballed. "Some of the most fashionable habitués of the Café de Paris, though not knowing a fetlock from a pastern, were all too pleased to join an institution which, with the mania for everything English . . . then conferred upon its members a kind of patent of 'good form,' " wrote Vandam. The members' hedonistic routine, in which it was considered proper never to get up before noon, was Marie's own. She frequented the same restaurants, cafés, parks, boulevards, and theaters, and, had she been permitted, she would have lingered on at the Jockey Club until four or five in the morning. On a page of the Register of Requests, someone had added her name in a feminine hand to the signatures—"evidence of the consecration of Marie Duplessis in this grand milieu."

One of her ex-lovers was Fernand de Montguyon, whose reputation was largely responsible for the Jockey Club's being seen as a place of depraved behavior. It was in Montguyon's name that the infamous Loge Infernale was rented for first nights at the Opéra. Virtually onstage, between the curtain and the orchestra pit, this was a special box whose access bestowed great cachet. With the Jockey Club then situated on rue de la Grange-Batelière, a few minutes' walk from the Opéra on rue Le Peletier, the route to the stage door entrance could not have been simpler—an alleyway led directly there. A dandy's destination was either a ballerina's dressing room or the *foyer de la danse,* which Dr. Véron had opened to privileged outsiders so that the performers could arrange assignations with their wealthy admirers. There is a painting by Eugène Lami of this grand salon, ornately decorated with pillars, mirrors, and sculptures, a marble bust in one alcove of the eighteenth-century *ballerina assoluta* Mlle Guimard. *Le foyer de la danse* is a busy portrayal of half a dozen costumed dancers, a couple of whom are in off-duty, Degas poses, with the great Fanny Elssler (Taglioni's rival), taking center place. Seated or standing among them is a scattering of formally dressed men—the key figures from Marie's own circle: Dr. Véron, Alfred de Musset, Fernand de Montguyon, and Nestor Roqueplan.

By the early 1840s, the Opéra had lost its two stars (Taglioni to Russia and Elssler to America), but French ballet had by no means lost its luster, due largely to the appointment of the remarkable Italian ballerina Carlotta Grisi. The first Giselle in Gautier's 1841 ballet, Grisi had became the poet's muse, creating the title role in *La Péri* in 1843—another personal triumph. For romantic writers such as Musset the idealized, supernatural world of *ballet blanc* fired the imagination, its dancers representing in visible form their evanescent ideas. As in Tannhäuser's Venusberg, however, spirituality was inseparable from sexual excess—an antithesis captured in the illustrations to *Voluptueux souvenirs; ou, Le Souper des Douze*. These were drawn by the celebrated Achille Devéria, whom Roger de Beauvoir claimed was a member of their group. In one, a dreamy, top-hatted, baby-faced youth sits alone in his box, a manicured hand resting on its velvet ledge, the other clasping an impressive erection. In a second, a Taglioni-pure sylph, with roses in her hair, kneels while performing fellatio on a good-looking dandy. No wonder the Goncourts viewed the ballet as a debauched stock exchange of women:

> From the stage to the auditorium, from the wings to the stage . . . invisible threads criss-cross between dancers' legs, actresses' smiles and spectators' opera glasses, presenting an overall picture of Pleasure, Orgy and Intrigue. It would be impossible to gather together in a smaller space a greater number of sexual stimulants, of invitations to copulation.

Alexandre Dumas *fils* suggests that Marie, too, did not go to the theater for intellectual stimulation. Sitting in her box, sniffing at a bouquet and nibbling sweets from a bag, she paid very little attention to what was happening onstage: "hardly listening, making eyes in every direction, exchanging looks and smiles with her neighbors." Vienne, however, insists that she was a cultivated judge of the arts, and that the actors and actresses, whom she received in her box, profited from the notes she gave them on their interpretations. She loved the company of performers and took an equal, if different, kind of pleasure in the atmosphere backstage: "The directors knew her and would provide her with a behind-the-scenes pass without her even having to ask," says

Vienne. She even considered going on the stage herself, an ambition that, as Houssaye remarks, was not unusual among her kind. "All these girls wanted to be actresses. The theater provided the baptism which saved them from original sin."

Acting was one of the few lucrative options open to women, and it was also virtually the only profession in which independence was possible. A grand actress could, and often did, flout sexual norms, and society was prepared to accept behavior that they would denounce in a demimondaine. (Rachel's reputation for loose living had not prevented her from being sought out by Parisian *salonnières,* including the venerable Mme Récamier.) Marie was already a practiced role-player in life, whether mimicking aristocratic ways or acting out passions she did not feel, and she was clearly confident about her talent. In the middle of recounting her life story to Mme Judith, she suddenly broke off and exclaimed, "Everything I've told you about my unhappiness is to make myself more interesting—and you've been taken in! I act well, don't I! Almost as well as you!"

Marie studied for a short time with the well-known drama teacher Achille Ricourt, who vowed he had spotted Rachel's genius when she was a street urchin and who was constantly on the lookout for exceptional pupils. His public classes at the Ecole des Jeunes Artistes on the rue de la Tour-d'Auvergne were made up mostly of respectable young girls watched by their mothers, but Marie would not have felt out of place as Ricourt did not exclude the occasional demimondaine among his pupils. Charles Monselet provides a lively picture of Ricourt at work. He rarely remembered anyone's name, and he would catch a girl's attention by calling out things like "Mademoiselle, you, the little blonde . . . over there . . . yes, you!" After some initial warm-up euphonic exercises, his favorite pupil, Agrippine, demonstrates his method, an eccentric distillation of the three facets of theater—comedy, drama, and tragedy—into three words. The first, "elegant," enunciated by Agrippine as *"Eé-liéé-gan-tiéé,"* delights the teacher. *"There* you have the tone of comedy, there is the spirit, the brio, the piquancy!" Agrippine then inflates her cheeks as if about to play trombone and prepares to tackle the second, "montagne," a challenge which Ricourt warns requires "biceps in the throat." But only the maestro himself can demonstrate the essence of tragedy, the invented word "superbatandor": "You must emphasise the 'r,' everything rests on the 'r'—it's the great secret: *Superrrbatandorrr!"*

It could have been a dislike of the passionately febrile Ricourt, dropping names of prominent literary friends, reciting alexandrines, and intoning "in the manner of Diderot," or it could have been the strain of arriving at the school by 10:15 in the morning, but Marie's enthusiasm for the stage did not last long. Dumas père, who had learned of her ambition, was not surprised.

> The theatre, you understand, demands study, rehearsal, performance, it is a great challenge to undertake, a great determination which disallows common pleasures. It is much easier to rise at two in the afternoon, to dress, to promenade in the Bois, to return for dinner at the Café de Paris or Frères Provençaux, to go from there to spend an evening in a stage-box at the Palais-Royal, or Vaudeville or Gymnase; to have supper after the theatre, to return at three in the morning to one's home or to someone else's—than to pursue the metier of a Mlle Mars. . . . The débutante forgot her vocation.

Instead, Marie used the proscenium of her theater box as her stage. "It's there above all that she gave to the mute, disdainful audience, the impact of her beauty," remarked Paul de Saint-Victor, whose portrayal of Marie confirms that she already possessed the inner radiance of a star—the ability to be a cynosure while remaining stationary and silent. "Her presence never failed to cause a sensation; every eye avidly took in this fresh, Raphael-ite face." Aware that the positioning of her box was of key importance, Marie went out of her way to compete for a choice one—as this flirtatious note indicates. It was sent to the *distributeur des faveurs* of the Théâtre de Vaudeville.

> *Once again I'm asking for your help with a box. I dare not ask you for one of the best. You would only send me to the devils. On the other hand, if you want to be one of these devils yourself, then fair enough, you will do me great pleasure. Otherwise a good box on the second tier. . . . I will be very grateful to you {although} you really do owe me a favour. I visited you and you weren't there. With my best wishes and thanks. M. Duplessy. {sic}*

In a painting believed to be by Eugène Lami, Marie, wearing a sylphlike white dress, reclines languorously in her box with two admirers by her side. One man scans the upper tier opposite; the other is very attentive, but Marie is ignoring him, reading from a large, single-page program. On the ledge are the props with which she came to be identified: a pretty pair of opera glasses, a small *bouquet à la main,* and a flower pinned to her corsage, which appears to be her namesake camellia.

This was a flower much in vogue. With an out-of-season stem of hothouse blooms costing up to twenty francs, camellias were also a symbol of status. And not only in Paris. An anonymous 1841 portrait of Verdi's mistress, Giuseppina Strepponi, shows her with a single white camellia pinned to her décolletage and a cluster worn in her hair—an effect even more striking now as an uncanny prefiguration of her lover's most famous heroine. Camellias have no scent, which is why the consumptive Marie is said to have favored them, but in fact she loved all flowers—even those as heavily scented as hyacinths. A bill from the florist Ragonot, dated 9 November 1843, confirms this:

		F
	Vendu à Madame Dupleci [*sic*] d'une part	3
	9 pots de fleurs	15
16	2 grappe de fleurs	6
23	4 Camellia monté	12
30	2 grappe de Camellia	6
23 décembre	2 Camellia blancs monté	5
2 janvier 1844	1 Bouquet à la mains	15
	1 fleur de Camellia impérialiste	3
5 février	2 fleurs de Camellia monté	4
8	1 Bouquet à la main et	
	4 fleurs de Camellia monté	20
11	5 azaleas	15
12	2 Rose du Roy	16
	1 Bruere [Bruyère-heather]	3
	1 pot de yacinthe de Hollande	2
14	1 Bouquet à la main	20
	2 grappes de Camellia	8
	9 pot de yacinthe de Hollande	16
Total		184 f.
Sur le quele [*sic*] J'ai Reçu 20 Reste du		164 f.

Worth noting is the red "camellia impérialiste" bought on January 2. In the novel, Marguerite takes a single bloom from a bouquet of red camellias and places it in Armand's buttonhole, telling him that he may see her again when her camellias are white again. It is her way of alluding to the fact that she will be indisposed for the next five days of the month.

La dame aux camélias may have been a title given to Marie by one of the Opéra's usherettes, by her florist, or by Dumas fils himself. He always insisted that any portraits painted during Marie's lifetime that showed her wearing a camellia were apocryphal or retouched, since the whole idea of associating her with the flower belonged to him alone. Mme Judith echoed this: "It was

Dumas' invention to give her a taste exclusively for camellias." In fact, this was not the case. An earlier Lady of the Camellias, almost certainly using Marie as a model, had appeared two years before the novel came out. George Sand's *Isidora* was serialized in *La Revue Indépendante* in the spring of 1845 and published in book form in 1846. A woman of simple elegance and aristocratic manners describes herself as *"la dame aux camélias."* She reveals that she is consumptive, has known poverty and misery, but now that she is wealthy finds herself filled with self-reproach. George Sand never refers to Marie by name, but in a 1853 preface, as if describing a Mme Judith–type encounter, she gives a brief, enigmatic depiction of "a very beautiful person, extraordinarily intelligent, who came several times to pour forth her heart at my feet." This, she says, took place in Paris in 1845. And with several friends and acquaintances in common, it is more than likely that the two women had met.

———

No camellias were ordered for the night Marie appeared incognito at one of the season's Opéra balls, but a bill from Geslin, dated 21 January 1844, details the hire of a velvet mask with satin fringe for four francs. This formed part of a domino outfit—a half-mask and hooded black cloak—which was required dress for women at these balls. That Saturday night, Marie would have been among a black flood of people surging into the brilliantly lit grand salon of the Opéra. It was "one immense Belshazzar's hall," in the words of Lord Beaconsfield, who had been in Paris at Carnival time the year before and witnessed a sight that amazed him:

> Between three and four thousand *devils* dancing and masquerading beyond fancy. . . . The grand galoppe, five hundred figures whirling like a witches' sabbath, truly infernal. The contrast, too, between the bright fantastic scene below

and the boxes filled with ladies in black dominoes and masks, very striking, and made the scene altogether Eblisian. Fancy me walking about in such dissolute devilry . . .

An emancipated woman like Marie would have felt exhilarated by the domino disguise, which not only licensed a reversal of protocol between the sexes but allowed couples to speak their minds. In an Opéra ball scene in Sand's novel, the narrator is scandalized at first by Isidora's candor, but her "supple, fertile spirit and feverish eloquence" begin to captivate him. He learns that she is the famous Parisian courtesan, and she speaks freely about women of her kind and about the men who feign to love them but in fact feel nothing but contempt. With the laws of the masked ball permitting bolder emotional games, Marie made clear her own awareness of male duplicity in a note she wrote to a potential (anonymous) lover whom she had just met.

> *Your conversation tonight interested me but is there any truth in what a man tells a woman he desires at an Opera ball? And yet, if you have been sincere, I will prove to you that I am no less frank than you. I had made you promise not to try to contact me until the Ball next Saturday. But see how feeble I am! I am retracting this resolution: I will wait for you at home tomorrow at 4 o'clock, provided that you give me proof that your words can be trusted.*

It was after an Opéra ball—so, during the Carnival months of January or February 1844—that Marie appears to have met the man on whom Armand Duval is most closely modeled. A colorful account of the night exists written by the journalist Henri de Pené, under the pseudonym Mané. A woman in domino disguise had intrigued their group of friends throughout the evening, and, impatient to discover her identity, they invited her for supper. She seemed hesitant to accept and asked to see the guest list, which was persuasive enough for her to agree to join them. Pené continues, "When we were installed in one of the salons of the restaurant where so many infatuations are tied and untied, she removed her mask, and we saw that we had played a good hand." He noticed that one member of their party appeared to interest her more than any other. "I heard the first words of her conversation with Edouard P. a sentence that has remained engraved in my memory: 'Monsieur, I have often seen you on horseback in the Bois de Boulogne, and your mount seems to delight in carrying a cavalier such as you.'" Dining on prawns, lobster, and shrimp, Marie declared that she would drink nothing but pink champagne, and watched Edouard uncorking the bottles himself. The beautiful grace which he brought to this simple action won him the heart of Marie, who was already firmly disposed in his favor.

Count Edouard de Perregaux was an ex-cavalier and member of the Jockey Club, and his father had been Napoleon's chamberlain. Count Alphonse de Perregaux had died in the summer of 1841, leaving his two sons a fortune, but much of Edouard's share had been lavished on the actress Alice Ozy, whom he had stolen from the king's youngest son. In September 1841, when the nineteen-year-old Duke d'Aumale left Paris to fight in the North African campaign, Edouard made his move. One night after a performance at the Variétés, Alice found a fabulous carriage and pair waiting at the stage door—a first glimpse of what was in store for her. Aumale was a dashing war hero, also heir to a vast sum, but as a minor, his allowance and army income were negligible: Alice Ozy allowed herself to be driven away.

A couple of years later, the talk of Paris was an incident at the Chantilly races in May 1843, when the horses pulling her carriage bolted toward a lake. *Le Siècle* reported that "Mlle A.O. with long *anglaises,* diamonds, sapphires, rubies" had been rescued with seconds to spare by the Duke de Nemours, who ran to her aid. "That evening there was almost a heated incident between P. and d'A. because the former had found the other established, without ceremony, next to his favorite." By the summer, however, Ozy had shed both her young adorers and, having decided that influence was more seductive than money, begun an affair with Théophile Gautier, who had written a role especially for her in his vaudeville *A Voyage in Spain* (premiered at the Variétés in September). The Liste des Etrangers in the resort town of Spa that August records Edouard de Perregaux staying at the Hôtel de Flandre: he was alone and free.

It is hardly surprising that Marie targeted the count for herself. Prospects apart, Ned Perregaux was a sympathetic young man—honest, kind, attentive, and loyal to his numerous friends. With his hair combed forward and curling on his brow, he was also extremely good-looking, his lips girlishly full, his large eyes fringed with thick, black lashes. "I kiss your blue eyes a thousand times," Marie writes in one of several surviving notes to Ned, telling him in another that she is "all yours from the heart." She had given him the privileged position of *amant de cœur,* and yet these notes are completely different in mood from her one surviving letter to Agénor de Guiche. That was written by a girl smitten by first love, but the Perregaux correspondence—sometimes just a few lines hastily scribbled to arrange a meeting—are from a dispassionate courtesan. Marie is the one in control, and she comes across as a woman determined not to give up her independence—nor, for that matter, her other lovers. She opens her door to Ned at specific hours (as in "This evening, at six o'clock"), and for only small portions of her time. He receives his "orders," just as Armand does in the novel, although—mindful of her suitor's title—Marie is far more courteous than Marguerite at the start of the relationship.

Marguerite to Armand: "Tonight at the Vaudeville. Come during the third interval."

Marie to Edouard: "It will give me great pleasure, dear

Edouard, if you would like to see me this evening (Vaudeville Theatre [box] No 27)."

Elated by the prospect of their first rendezvous, Armand cannot stop himself from seeking out Marguerite before the prearranged hour. He gazes at her promenading in her carriage in the Champs-Elysées, and goes early to the Vaudeville to see her arrive. But when he catches sight of the "count de G." sitting in the back of her box, a chill cuts through his heart. Just before the third interval, however, she turns and says two words to her companion, who leaves the box. Marguerite then beckons to Armand to join her.

The beginning of Ned's affair with Marie coincided almost exactly with Agénor de Guiche's return from London. For just over a year, between September 1842 and December 1843, Agénor's name appears in social columns of *The Times*—at the Champagne Stakes of Doncaster Races, at the Polish Ball with his father, at a reception for the Duke of Bordeaux, and at gatherings of the French mission to China, the first sign of him embarking on his future career as a diplomat. Vienne recounts that when his exile was due to end, "Grandon" Guiche sent Marie a letter saying he wanted to see her as soon as he returned. He was graciously received, and during the course of their meeting she told him that she might have to sell her stable of horses. Forty-eight hours later, she discovered a little purse in her apartment, which contained tens of thousands of francs. Guiche, however, soon went back to his philandering ways, and in order to avoid rows and reconciliations, Marie decided to give him free rein, while still allowing him to call on her. This was, says a disapproving Vienne, "because of his princely generosity."

In the novel, Armand tries to convince himself that "M. de G." is no threat: he and Marguerite have a history together, and he has been told that the count has always given her money. But when he receives a note saying, "Dear child, I am a little unwell. . . . I will go to bed early tonight, and not see you," his first thought is that Marguerite is deceiving him. He searches in vain for her on the Champs-Elysées and in all her favorite theaters, until finally, at eleven o'clock at night, he goes to her apartment. It is in darkness, and the concierge tells him that she has not yet returned. He remains in the street outside and at around midnight sees "G's" carriage pull up. The count enters the building, and, four hours later, he is still inside.

Receiving an almost identical excuse ("Imposssible to dine with you, I am not at all well"), Ned Perregaux would also have experienced searing pangs of suspicion. Marie absorbed his entire being, Vienne says. "It was folly, exultation, adoration. For him, she was not a woman, she was a divinity." Marie, on the other hand, could sign a note "Completely yours," and yet regard Ned as only part of her life. She knew that she made him suffer, but she had warned him about the rules: "I beg you not to forget the subject of my letter."

A courtesan reformed by love was key to the romantic tradition, but George Sand discredited this convention. Her Isidora (who owes her name to Molière's Greek slave and concubine) deplores the conditions that her lover tries to impose. "You accept the sinner provided that, from tomorrow, from today, she will pass into the position of a saint! Oh! There will always be pride and domination in a man." In this reluctance to be owned she speaks for Marie—and so does Marguerite, who tells Armand that she has never yet found a man able to love without distrust, without claiming his rights. "Men, instead of being satisfied with having obtained for so long what they once scarcely dared hope for, exact from their mistresses a full account of the present, the past, and even the future. As they get accustomed to her, they want to rule her, and the more ones gives them the more exacting they become."

For this reason alone, Marie would have felt little guilt about deceiving Ned. In what is probably another alibi note—"I lie to keep my teeth white" she once quipped—she uses a rendezvous with a woman friend as the reason for not seeing him.

> *How cross I am, my dear Edouard, not to have received your letter an hour earlier! Zélia wrote to ask if I could spend the evening with her; and having nothing better to do, I agreed. If you'd like to, we will dine together tomorrow; let me know if you can.*

There were times, though, when she did not even attempt to spare his feelings by dissimulation. The tone of a formal, impatient note written while planning a trip to Italy is not just insensitive, it is insulting:

> *My dear Edouard,*
> *Be good enough to return to the porter my papers which I badly need. I will be grateful if you would ask M. Breton {a jeweler} not to keep me waiting any longer for my jewels; because, as you know, I wish to leave as soon as possible, and I cannot do without them. . . . As you are not coming with me to Italy, I don't know why you have told people that you will come later to find me.*

Marie was able to establish a divide between love and "business," and she expected Ned to do the same. "Do you wish to do me harm?" she snapped after he had committed some breach of their arrangement. "You are well aware that this could be a disaster for my future, which you seem absolutely determined to make unhappy and unfortunate for me." In this respect she was a reincarnation of Manon Lescaut, whose love of luxury outweighs the tenderness she feels for her *amant de cœur,* des Grieux. It was a kinship Marie acknowledged and one that absorbed her to the point of obsession. She had read and reread *Manon Lescaut,* which moved her greatly, Gustave Claudin said. "After her death a copy of the novel was found with notes and observations written in her hand in the margins."

Apart from recognizing her alter ego in the perfidious Manon, Marie could see that Ned was a latter-day des Grieux—well born and willing to forfeit his reputation and his fortune for love. For both young men, their passion was a source of misery; des Grieux, "able to live only through Manon," and Perregaux, "living for no one but Marie." Unable to continue sharing her, he wrote on 23 April 1844 to the Ministry of War, outlining the reasons for his resignation from the army and requesting to be readmitted.

> *The grandson of Marechal Macdonald {Ned's late mother was Adele Macdonald}, I started my military career as a simple soldier and participated in the Constantine campaigns of 1836, 37, 38 and 39 in Africa. I'm requesting you . . . to allow me the possibility of returning to Africa—a favor which has been granted to several retired officers like me. . . . During the time I was in service I was never reproached for my military conduct, and I believe I fulfilled my duties well in the Spahis and in the 3rd regiment of Africa.*

Ned had not particularly distinguished himself as a brigadier in a corps of cavaliers stationed in Bone, although he was admired for his horsemanship, and family influence had seen him quickly promoted through the ranks. He was regarded by his superiors as immature and dissipated, one character note officially recording his "light conduct and insolency." A Bordeaux wine merchant issued a claim to the army for an outstanding sum of 3,630 francs for claret and eau de vie, and there were numerous other unpaid bills. He tells the maréchal that he had gone to Paris hoping to persuade his family to clear his debts, but they had refused to help, and consequently, he had felt that it was impossible to remain in his regiment. He left the Spahis in April 1841. In the reply to his letter he learns that his voluntary resignation has ruled out reentry into the French army but that he is still entitled to apply to join the Foreign Legion. This news did not reach him until June 11, and he decided not to take things any further. There was no need.

It was the dream of many eminent Parisians to own a summer house in a village near the city, and Bougival, still many years away from being the crowded resort painted by the Impressionists, was a tranquil idyll in the late spring of '44. Terraced gardens descended the hill to the Seine, where little red-roofed houses were spaced between the poplars and willows on the riverfront. Ned Perregaux had acquired one such property for Marie, feeling that there, he alone could possess her. But what had brought about her capitulation? A remark made by Marguerite is one explanation: "I have a sudden aspiration toward a calmer existence, which might recall my childhood." Despite all the hardships of her Normandy upbringing, Marie regarded the French countryside as a healing place, a redemptive alternative to her city life, and perhaps even a prelapsarian prelude to it. In this she would have been influenced by her reading. Her decision to leave Paris for Bougival corresponds exactly with Manon's summer in Chaillot, where she and des Grieux sequestered themselves in order to live "a simple, honest existence."

Even more persuasive would have been the idyllic notion of rural life expressed in two other novels she loved, Rousseau's *The New Héloïse* and Bernardin de Saint-Pierre's *Paul and Virginia*. Common to both is the theory of natural goodness—man is born virtuous, in a state of nature; vice comes from living among worldly society and artificial urban pressures. *Paul and Virginia* was displayed in every bookshop and regarded as a fashionable classic (Marie bought her copy for 3 francs 50). "To many devoted to salon and boudoir life it called for an about-face toward a wholesome frankness, simplicity and naturalness," its English translator wrote in 1841. The hero and heroine, two children of Nature, are unrelated but brought up as brother and sister, until, in their teens, they developed a devouring passion for each other.

In an interesting coincidence, the book's wild exotic setting is Mauritius, then known as the Île de France—the same name as the region in which Bougival is located.

Now Marie the actress could play a role—she addresses Ned in one of her notes as "dear little brother." But, just as *Paul and Virginia*'s cloying picture of an idealistic society based on love and innocence fails to convince ("Voluptuous Nature squanders her caresses upon two nurslings . . . lulls them to the murmur of the springs and smiles upon them in a thousand brilliant colours"), the Bougival episode, as depicted by both Dumas and Vienne, seems doomed. Dumas's lovers walk together by the river, drinking milk, Marguerite wearing a white dress and a straw hat. "We breathed together that true life which neither she nor I had ever known before," says Armand. "There were days when she ran in the garden, like a child of ten, after a butterfly or a dragonfly."

Vienne's version is even more fanciful:

> They gathered enormous bouquets of roses and honeysuckle to give each other, plucked the petals of marguerite daisies while exchanging kisses. They retired early to their bedroom; listened to the last couplet of birdsong in the leaves; hunted for their star in the blue firmament, making the nights longer than the days, they intoxicated themselves with their happiness, burning their blood at the devouring flame of voluptuous ardour.

There was a train link from Paris to nearby Saint-Germain-en-Laye, and, according to Vienne, visitors would come once or twice a week, providing a brief diversion from the couple's routine. On a fine day they might make an excursion in the neighborhood or to the Bois de Boulogne, and occasionally they went back to the city for an evening at the Opéra and supper at La Maison d'Or. Marie, who had known only frivolous, ephemeral pleasures, was proud and happy, he reports, to find that she was capable of devoting herself to one man. "*Nobody* had loved like this."

Over the next decades Bougival and its neighboring islands on the Seine would become a watering place as vibrant as Le Trouville or Deauville. Posters and caricatures show bathing belles diving off wooden platforms and hiding behind reeds to strip off their corsets and stockings. Strolling under the shade of parasols were the Second Empire's most celebrated *filles de joie,* while the quays and café-restaurants thronged with a mix of aristocrats, *jeunesse dorée,* and shopgirls with their *canotiers*—sinewy rowers in sleeveless white vests and straw boaters. Renoir painted the end of a lunch party on a canopied balcony of La Maison Fournaise and made several portraits of the owner's pretty daughter, also named Alphonsine. La Grenouillère had a floating restaurant festooned with lanterns and held a ball every Thursday night. On the Île Gautier, a casino would eventually be built and a dance hall made almost as famous as the Moulin Rouge by cancan stars Jane Avril and La Goulue. In the 1840s, however, only a few auberge-restaurants existed in Bougival, one of which, overlooking the Seine, is said to have been frequented by Marie.

Ned was the first to succumb to the pull of the beau monde. For a week in June, an exodus of Parisian dandies, society beauties, "women of little virtue and an abundance of *viveurs*" crowded the little town of Chantilly for the Prix du Jockey Club, the culmination of the season's horse races. As a laureate of Chantilly himself, winner of the coveted prize in 1842 with his horse Plover, he would have felt it was a huge sacrifice not to be present. Aware of this and tempted by the fun they would have, Marie said that she would be delighted to accompany him. The seven-day fete, with its marquees of amusements, grand ball, and climactic fireworks display, was an opportunity for her to meet old friends—or even future clients, since she knew this was still a possibility. Marie was singled out among the modish women on the lawns of Chantilly as the best dressed and most radiant. Ned had been mentioned the previous summer in *Le Siècle*'s account of a game to the death at the Reine-Blanche: "There were enormous bets and terrifying losses. . . . P. won ten or twelve million louis." This year was no different. He gambled addictively, squandering his winnings on Marie, who assumed that this source of funds was inexhaustible, that her lover still had his inheritance of a hundred thousand francs.

The return to Bougival was anticlimactic for them both. By now she was tiring of their solitary, monotonous existence and wanted some kind of diversion. She began pressing Ned to marry her. But, although she was well aware of her hold over him, Marie may not have realized the extent to which her lover valued his name and reputation. Intending to investigate her background, Ned set off for Nonant, where he had reserved a room at the Hôtel de La Poste. Marie may have told him that the owner's son was a friend, but Ned did not make himself known to Mme Vienne. Her suspicions were aroused by his enigmatic silence, and she ordered all the servants not to speak to him, to give only the vaguest answers regarding the information he wanted. The mayor's office delivered a copy of Marie's birth certificate to the inn, which confirmed her status as a minor without rights, and that same morning Ned paid a call on Agathe Boisard, who had raised Alphonsine between the ages of eight and eleven. Puzzled by the elegant stranger's attitude and questions, Agathe said very little, and Marette, the coachman who drove him there, said even less.

Delphine told Vienne that she did not receive a visit from her sister's lover, which was unlikely, given that his mission was to research her family—and, if the anonymous benefactor mentioned in Marie's undated letter was indeed Ned, then this was simply untrue.

It's a very agreeable surprise that this Monsieur has paid you a visit in my native country, to give me news and to have left you ten francs to buy a dress. Always address your letters to this Monsieur when you write, because I intend to leave soon for Baden, where he will have the kindness to pass them on.

Soon after, the couple left in a *chaise de poste* for Germany. They may also have visited Switzerland, where Ned had several relations. His grandfather Jean-Frédéric de Perregaux, founder of the Bank of France, had been brought up in Neufchâtel. An ancestor, Béatrice Perregaux, had heard about Edouard visiting the family at Domaine de Fontaine André, a restored Cistercian abbey. "But he kept Alphonsine out of sight and installed her for the duration of his stay in the nearby village of Saint-Blaise, at a hotel which still exists."

On their return to Bougival a shock awaited them. Several sheets of stamped official papers had been sent by the Perregaux family's notary outlining Ned's expenditure and warning that the family was taking legal measures to prevent his complete ruin. Pressed by Marie, he admitted that he no longer had an income and that he had been drawing on the last fragments of his property inheritance. He had less than fifteen thousand francs left. For Marie this would last about a month, and she saw that life together would not be possible. It was only a question of time.

At a similar turning point in *Manon Lescaut,* the practical-minded heroine tries to make des Grieux see sense:

> There's no one in the world whom I could love the way I do you; but don't you realize, my poor dear soul, that in the state to which we are reduced fidelity is a ridiculous virtue? Do you really believe that we can still be tender with each other when we don't even have bread to eat? . . . I adore you—you can count on that—but let me have a little time to arrange our fortunes.

Dumas's Marguerite, declaring that she could never behave as Manon does, secretly pawns her horses, diamonds, and cashmere shawls for love of Armand. And Marie? Vienne knew only too well. "She was a thousand times more likely to leave her lover—even her future husband—than renounce her luxurious habits and lifestyle." In this respect, she bore more than a faint resemblance to Cora Pearl, an English courtesan (the model for Zola's Nana) who readily abandoned a suitor when she had exhausted his fortune. And yet, there was still a reason to prolong the relationship. Ned may have reached the limit of his resources, but he did have a title, and by marrying him, Marie would become a countess. This became her only goal.

Realizing that he was on the point of losing her, Ned agreed to go ahead with the marriage and told the Perregaux family of his intentions—news that was greeted with shock and unhappiness. Appeals were made to his honor and to the affection he felt for those close to him, but these were as ineffective as the numerous promises and the proposition of an exceptionally advantageous alliance. One word or glance from Marie dispelled every argument and generous offer. One wonders, though, which member of the family had so opposed the match. Ned was an orphan (his young mother had died when he was seven), and his older brother, Alphonse, had made a less than brilliant marriage to a *bourgeoise,* the daughter of a Boulogne customs inspector. Their late father, for the last few years of his life, had lived openly with a "lady companion," a Mlle Delacombe, and so was clearly unrestrained by propriety. The most likely source of resistance is Ned's aunt, the Duchess de Raguse, one of the most feted women of the First Empire. The duchess was a fierce custodian of her father's fortune and was also defined by her craving for luxury and frivolity. Then there was the fact that in February of that year the Perregaux lawyers had been forced to pay a substantial sum to the old count's mistress, who had taken care of him during the course of his long illness. The day after his death, Mlle

Delacombe submitted a claim for 10,600 francs—three percent of the estate—which she said had been promised to her by the count. She won her suit, setting a legal precedent in *Delacombe v. Perregaux.*

It was decided to send a family representative to Nonant (almost certainly Ned's guardian, M. Delisle, whom Vienne calls "Monsieur B."). He stayed at the Hôtel de La Poste and announced that he was making inquiries about Alphonsine Plessis with a view to her marriage but did not reveal the name of her fiancé. He learned only that she was the child of poor parents and had been left to fend for herself. But there was something in particular that he and his ward wanted to investigate. Ned went back to Nonant, where his identity became known when a local jockey had recognized him. Having learned no more than on the first visit, he agreed to return for a third time with his guardian, staying in the village until they had obtained the information they were after. They employed as a postilion Roch Boisard, Marie's cousin. He and Alphonsine were the same age and for more than three years had slept under the same roof, exchanging childhood confidences. Roch not only knew which of the small tracks were suitable for carriages; he could have answered many questions for the Perregaux family. But Roch, too, had been warned by Mme Vienne and so listened to his passengers' conversation without saying a word.

> Their latest appearance in Nonant was practically an event, with everyone wondering about the significance of these mysterious trips. It was well known what they wanted, but why these subsequent visits when it would take 24 hours to find out all there was? . . . As the lover, [Ned] was received with a certain sympathy mixed with a strong dose of feminine curiosity. Monsieur B., on the other hand, was viewed with cold reserve. . . . The information in Nonant and Saint-Germain-de-Clairefeuille was as favorable as

could be hoped: no one, in effect, felt hostile toward this unhappy young girl who could not be blamed for her background. People had sympathetic memories of her well-loved mother, and almost nothing was known of Marie's Paris life. . . . The old nun Françoise Huzet who had taught her to read and prepared her for her First Communion was full of touching praise for her dear little Alphonsine and asked the two messieurs to pass on her affectionate memories.

This was not what they were there to hear. Clearly, they had got word of the iniquitous behavior of Marin Plessis. They asked to be driven to Exmes, which was the hometown of the depraved old man to whom the twelve-year-old Alphonsine had been sold by her father. They also went to Ginai, where Marin had met his miserable end. His reputation was the only dishonor they could bring to Marie, but with no evidence and hearing nothing else but favorable reports, the pair were forced to conclude "that poverty is no vice."

During the trip Ned, understandably afraid that his own financial crisis would drive Marie away, had appealed to his guardian for help. Monsieur B. seized on this opportunity for a pact, volunteering to prevent the liquidation of Ned's assets on condition that he give up the idea of marriage to Marie. He also guaranteed an annual income of eight thousand francs. On their return to Paris, not trusting his weak-willed charge to see this through, he went to Bougival to reason with Marie in person.

This moment—or rather, a romanticized version of it—is the turning point in the novel, play, and opera based on her life. In *The Lady of the Camellias*, it is Armand's father who implores the young courtesan to give up his son. He has a daughter, he tells her, "young, beautiful, pure as an angel," whose future would be ruined by the disgrace brought about by her brother's liaison. He asks Marguerite to martyr herself, and this act of charity, to which she ultimately assents, is conveyed with a quasi-religious sense of exultation—"I seemed to become transformed," she says. In *La Traviata,* the exchange becomes the duet "Pura siccome un angelo / Iddio mi die' una figlia" and one of the most moving scenes in opera, with the weeping Violetta vowing to make the sacrifice that will shatter her own happiness.

The facts were far more prosaic. Ned did once have a sister (named Adèle after their mother), but she died at the age of thirteen. There was no venerable old man to win Marie's respect, just a financial adviser, whom Vienne dismisses as an idiot. He was there to talk business, not to appeal to Marie's spiritual courage, and he outlined his ward's prospects in the grimmest terms. Edouard had borrowed money from all his friends, and although his resources were not completely exhausted, he had been reduced to the legal status of a minor by the ban now imposed on his spending. Marie remained inflexible. Assuming that written proof would convince her, Monsieur B. returned a second time with documents to back up his claims, saying the family would be taking legal action to prevent the marriage. This final threat was too much for Marie. Vienne describes her rising from her chair, and saying, "with a superb air of dignity and formality: 'If M. de [Perregaux] cannot marry without your consent, what are you afraid of? . . . Occupy yourself with M. de [Perregaux] and do not bother me. I believe I have the right to hope, Monsieur, that you will cease these visits which are useless for you and disagreeable for me.' He was insensitive enough to return a third time, but was not received."

If Marie comes across as ruthlessly self-serving, it should be argued in her defense that she was a woman of her time. This was the epoch of the fortune seeker, a world defined by self-indulgence, frivolity, and a febrile quest for excitement. (In George Sand's definition, the beau monde was "a free, blissful society . . . devoid of any ideal, reduced to the enjoyment of sensation.") But even a century earlier, Marie would still have been a creature of luxury and joy—it was why she identified so strongly with Manon, "as passionate for pleasure as her lover was for her." The Bougival sojourn had come to seem intolerable to her, a kind of interment. It was something her friend Albert Vandam had intuited and discussed with Dumas père, who said:

> At the beginning of the third act I was wondering how Alexandre would get his Marguerite back to town without lowering her in the estimation of the spectator. Because, if such a woman as he depicted was to remain true to nature—to *her* nature—and consequently able to stand the test of psychological analysis, she could not have borne more than two or three months of such retirement. That does not mean that she would have severed her connection with Armand Duval, but he would have become *"un plat dans le menu"* after a little while, nothing more. . . . Depend on it, that if, in real life and with such a woman . . . la belle Marguerite would have taken the "key of the street" on some pretext.

Dumas could not have been more astute. The hectic, urban life that Marie had renounced to please Ned now appeared more seductive than ever. She yearned for daily promenades in the Bois, the homage from admirers in her box at the theater, the excitement of first nights, stimulating conversation during midnight suppers at the Maison d'Or and Café de Paris. With summer reaching its end, she decided to reestablish herself in Paris, her sense of resignation that she had loved only superficially mixed with a degree of irritation that she had been misled into "an intoxication of false hopes."

In mid-August, Ned was listed on Spa's register of visitors as staying alone at the Hôtel au Prince de Liège, but two bills in Marie's keeping suggest that he had indeed remained *un plat dans le menu*. One, made out in his name and dated September 29, is for a haircut by Marie's coiffeur; another, of October 4, is from a grain merchant and addressed to "Mme la Comtesse Deperegaud" [*sic*]. Evidently, Marie had not yet given up her ambition.

Part Four

Marguerite

☙

ONE DAY TOWARD the end of 1844, Romain Vienne's concierge gave him a note, a characteristically terse single line from Marie, asking him to visit her the following evening. When he arrived she was waiting impatiently, saying that she wanted to have a long talk with him and had ordered dinner from Chez Voisin. They fell into conversation, but it was not long before Marie broke off to fetch something from the mantelpiece. It was a cameo of a young woman. With a tiny beribboned waist and light brown hair curling onto her shoulders, she was exceptionally small and delicate, with an oval face, neat little mouth, and melancholy, heavy-lidded eyes. Romain recognized her instantly as Marie's mother.

The portrait had been given to her by an Englishwoman who had visited earlier that week, saying that she was there on behalf of "Madame la baronne Anderson," for whom Marie Plessis had worked as a lady's maid after fleeing Nonant in 1828. Over two years Marie had become more of a companion than a servant to her employer, who could sympathize with her lasting sadness as she, too, had lost a child, a daughter who had died at the age of fifteen. While spending the summer months of 1830 on Lake Geneva, Marie became fatally ill, a cause Vienne attributes to her broken heart. As she was slipping away, she took Madame

Anderson's hand and begged her to find the two daughters she had left behind in Normandy.

This had seemed impossible, due to a series of errors of name and address, but more than a decade later, following her return from England, the baroness made a trip to Normandy and tracked down the elder sister. By then Delphine had become engaged to a local weaver named Constant Paquet (they married the following year), and so Marie became her primary concern. She had been shocked and saddened to learn of the girl's occupation but was determined to honor her pledge. "The baroness wants to meet you and get to know you," the woman said. "And if you are prepared to renounce your current life, and take the place of her own daughter, she will put an end to her mourning and start a new existence with you and for you. Her house will be yours . . . she will start an immediate fund to make provision for your future, and she will adopt you, as she promised your mother that she would." She then gave Marie the miniature, explaining that it was one of two portraits that the baroness had especially commissioned. "She kept one, and she begs you to accept the other as the first token of her affection." Exquisitely rendered in pale pastel crayon, it is so much in the style of miniatures by the portraitist Elisabeth Vigée-Lebrun, a favorite of Marie Antoinette, that it is tempting to wonder if it could be her work. Vigée-Lebrun claims in her memoirs to have been a friend of a Madame Anderson, whom she saw in London, and they may well have resumed contact during her travels to Geneva and Chamonix. Vienne, however, says that the miniature was painted by a man, "a gifted artist" whom the baroness met at the Chamonix baths.

To what extent can this story be believed? Vienne's is the only account of Marie's offer from the baroness, although Charles du Hays, whose mother was responsible for helping Marie Plessis to escape, confirms the existence of a wealthy English benefactress. In one version, while protecting the woman's identity by calling her "Lady B." du Hays alludes to the possibility of the loss of a child by saying that she found in her maid's situation "a great similarity with her own." (A subsequent version deletes this personal reference, saying instead that she regarded her duty to help Marie "as a work of charity," but names the baroness as "Lady Henriette [*sic*] Anderson Yorborough [*sic*]."

There was indeed a Lady Henrietta Anderson Yarborough, who would have been thirty-eight years old at the time of employing Marie Plessis, but she had died in 1813, at the age of twenty-five. The true identity of Marie's benefactress remains a mystery, and yet two pieces of evidence corroborate Vienne's narrative. One is a certificate recording the death in Châtelard, Montreux, of "Marie Louise Michelle Deshayes, wife of Duplessis [*sic*]"; the other is the miniature itself. Mounted as a gold medallion, it was passed on to Delphine and her descendants and is now on display in the Musée de la Dame aux Camélias in the Normandy town of Gacé.

Marie's news that night delighted Romain Vienne. They had had many conversations on the subject of her future during which he would express his concern about what would happen once her beauty and youth had faded. There were disturbing stories of wealthy kept women who had fallen into abject misery. Alexandre Parent-Duchâtelet cites one, describing a courtesan whose protector had once provided her with two to three thousand francs a week. "She was discovered twelve years later in a slum house on the rue de Macon, frequented by the scum and filth of the population." Not being part of Marie's world, Romain found it hard to understand her obsession with luxury since his own friends were professionals—doctors, journalists, colleagues from the Bourse—and in the rue Saint-Lazare lodgings that he shared with two actresses they had just one maid among them. Inevitably, his appeals to Marie's sense of reason resulted in a bantering exchange:

—Mr. Moralist, I'm waiting for you to scold me roundly, and criticize my extravagances.

—To what purpose? I'd be preaching in the desert.

—Oh but you're wrong. I always listen, and without displeasure, to your sermons because they're meant well. If I don't act on them it's because I don't have the strength to resist habits which have taken over from my more prudent impulses—but that doesn't prevent me from recognising the truth of what you're saying.

Marie had come to rely on the frankness and genuine devotion of her "severe, sincere friend" as a welcome contrast to the flattering vacuities of her admirers. Not only could she reminisce with Romain about her youth, family, and friends, she also valued his sane outlook on life, addressing him sometimes as Mr. Philosopher and once, when introducing him to Lola Montez, describing him as "a financier, a journalist, a man of letters . . . and above all a wise man." Nevertheless, his constant entreaties to prepare herself "for a more tranquil future" could be exasperating.

How obvious it is that you're a financier . . . you only talk to me about pension schemes! Next you'll be telling me that I should use the wealth I've acquired to establish an annuity. Well, think about it: if I sold my horses, my carriage, dismissed my staff, took on a modest apartment; reduced my expenditures to a minimum, the following day all my suitors would disappear. It's not our virtues that attract them but our faults, our extravagances, our opulence . . . and to renounce all this would be to lay down one's arms and serve for nothing. It's only with sumptuous clothes, jewels and horses that we can be assured of conquering the debauched adventurers, and above all the blasé old men for whom refinement and luxury are essential.

But this, Romain argued, was shortsighted. "Don't you ever feel a sense of human mortality? You're the victim of a life which comes at a terrifying cost . . . and your opulence is a lie. It's not yours alone, it belongs to another—or rather to others. . . . Look into your heart. Why is it that you want to see me so often? It's certainly not to receive my compliments."

It was clear that Marie needed Romain to force her to confront brutal facts. Although only twenty years old, she often found herself brooding about "the abyss and the horror that awaits those who grow old and lose their charm." After he left, she would spend hours in a state of melancholy contemplation, but come the evening, when she was surrounded by smiling adorers, her anxieties would vanish. "Your lecture is too somber, in fact I find it not harsh enough," she told him. "I take your estimation of my character seriously . . . and I know that the body quickly wears itself out in this métier. But when you're young and full of passion, you don't control your destiny the way you should, you live only for the moment."

Now, though, Marie was being given a real chance of redemption. She had felt profoundly moved by Mme Anderson's offer, but had asked for time to reflect. Different scenarios kept playing through her mind. She thought of the strain she would be under in becoming a surrogate for the baroness's beloved daughter, and she was convinced, as she pointed out to Romain, that her past would be revealed.

Imagine that I am her protégée, maid of honour, friend, companion, or what you will. . . . In a very short while her household, among whom no ill doing goes unnoticed, would have been informed that this young lady was none other than a well-known courtesan. . . . A fortnight later the baroness would find that her salon was deserted, that the women and young girls were no longer visiting her and only the men were turning up from time to time. The mansion would be blacklisted; the benefactress reproached for her indulgence and generosity toward a girl of light morals. . . . Do you think for a moment that she would renounce old friendships and put up with the mutiny of servants for my sake? What would happen is inevitable: she would not regret her fine act of charity, but she would turn against a protégée who, rather than compensating for her cruel loss, would bring nothing but discord. Instead of adopting her, she would let her return to her old ways.

There was also the fact that Paris was a city Marie adored. She told Romain that the stiff severity of society in London, where she would be required to live, had as much appeal for her as the foggy Thames air. "It would kill me quicker than any penal colony, because the calm of such an existence would not be a deliverance but the peace of the tomb. I have neither the energy nor the inclination to bury myself there at the age of twenty. It would expose me to too many physical and moral deprivations."

She had already made up her mind not to accept the baroness's offer when she went to visit her on the rue du Faubourg-Saint-Honoré, but she had not prepared herself for the emotional turmoil she went through. The warmth of Mme Anderson's greeting—a spontaneous, motherly embrace—was disarming enough, while Marie's plan to express her gratitude and repeat the arguments that she had outlined to Romain, "adding others more convincing and more conclusive," now seemed brutally calculating.

Warring sentiments shook my entire being: I trembled with joy and was overwhelmed with distress. My refusal made me suffer horribly. . . . The dear woman was sadly affected, and when she spoke to me of her daughter, whom she said I resembled, she threw herself into my arms once again, and we both shed tears. How was I able to resist? I don't know.

I knew that I dared not visit her again, the intensity of my feelings had frightened me. . . . Our parting was cruel, and when I returned home my heart was broken. I went to the Bois hoping to rid myself of the somber reflections which had overwhelmed my spirit, but I saw only Mme Anderson, and heard only her tender appeals. . . . I went to the theater . . . but found I was infuriated by the chatter and intrusive compliments; and so finally I went home and barricaded the door. I waited until daylight for sleep.

But of all the reasons that had influenced Marie's decision, she had not told Romain the most decisive of all. She now had no need of a wealthy patroness: Count von Stackelberg had come back into her life.

———

There is no way of knowing how long Stackelberg had stayed away, but the death of his twenty-three-year-old daughter, Elena, in February 1843—the third daughter he had lost in three years—may well have driven him to Marie for consolation. An account published in *Gil Blas* claims that when Stackelberg, ever possessive, visited her at rue d'Antin, one of the first questions he asked was what had become of her portrait by Olivier. "Have you given it to your monsieur Duval?" he is quoted as saying—a reference not to Ned Perregaux but to Agénor de Guiche. During the young duke's exile in England, Marie is supposed to have hung the painting in his apartment—a touching attempt to sustain a presence in his life. But, according to the article, Agénor still felt great tenderness toward her, and after his return to Paris was "so impatient to make love to his beauty" that he went to call on her in the morning. What followed could be a scene by Feydeau. "Everything was calm . . . Ding! The bell rang. . . . It's the count! Quick, there—behind this curtain!" When Stackelberg interrogated Marie about the Olivier, it was her maid—"the most alert of soubrettes"—who came to the rescue, whispering that she would run to Agénor's apartment to fetch it. Fifteen minutes later it was back in rue d'Antin, hanging between an unfinished portrait of Marie and a framed print of her look-alike, the plaintive black-haired Marix, in a reproduction of *Mignon aspirant au ciel*. "The count immediately went on his knees swearing never to forgive himself for his unworthy and unjustified suspicions."

If this incident really happened, then Stackelberg's way of making amends was to set Marie up in even greater splendor. On 1 October 1844, at a cost of eight hundred francs a quarter, she began renting an apartment at 11, boulevard de la Madeleine, today's number 15. Situated on the ground floor, it was not large but was unusually light with five windows onto the boulevard and more overlooking a courtyard at the back. Redecoration went on for several months while Marie continued living on rue d'Antin (15 January 1845 is the date of her last rent bill there—a more moderate sum of 540 francs). She had erected an unusual trellis of gold wood interlaced with flowering plants to cover the length of the entrance hall, and the salon had also been designed to give an impression "of brilliance, of freshness and lively colors." This was achieved by daylight filtering through handmade lace curtains, Venetian mirrors on the walls, and more flowering plants, including camellias, planted in *jardinières* around the room. At night an antique chandelier gave a rich opulence and gravity to the room, enhanced by the cerise damask curtains and matching wallpaper, while perfume pans and scented candles produced a musky ambiance. To Marie's actress friend Mme Judith, the Louis XV interior was as grand as a palace or museum. "There were sofas covered in Beauvais tapestries, small rosewood tables displaying Clodion pottery, divine Riesener trinkets with copperware chiseled by Gouthière [*sic*]. She showed me each room with the passion of a connoisseuse."

Predictably, Marie's bedroom created the most impact. With

caryatids on every foot and four posts sculpted with vines, the Boule bed was her stage, raised on a platform and curtained with sumptuous pink silk drapes. The adjoining *cabinet de toilette* was also a courtesan's natural habitat, its dressing table a jumble of lace, bows, ribbons, embossed vases, crystal bottles of scents and lotions, brushes and combs of ivory and silver. To one awestruck young admirer, it was "an arsenal of the most elegant coquetterie . . . a profane little altar consecrating the cult of feminine beauty."

A Boucher-like boudoir element had infiltrated elsewhere, and even the sofas were "softened with a snow-covering of embroidered muslin," a profusion of pink satin, lace, braid, tassels, and gilded furniture was painted with flights of birds and garlands of flowers. It was not to everyone's liking. One observer ridiculed Marie's ornate rosewood furniture and her collection of porcelain figurines and platters painted with sentimental bucolic scenes. Signed and extremely valuable, many of these pieces would have been given as gifts and did not necessarily reflect Marie's own taste. Mme Judith recalled her burst of laughter as she pointed to a Sèvres biscuit container showing a drunken bacchante being teased by a faun, while in the Dumas novel, Marguerite finds a Saxe statuette of a shepherd holding a bird in a cage "hideous" and wants to give it to her maid.

Only the dining room was austerely masculine with dark walls of Córdoba leather, plain Henri II cabinets, and sculpted oak bookshelves with folding glass doors encompassing her extensive library. Here Marie began to play the role of hostess, running up huge accounts for feasts *au domicile* from nearby restaurants such as Chez Voisin and La Maison d'Or. There is little chance that Stackelberg was present at the dinners he funded. Marie was his private obsession, and like the duke of the novel, he would have gone out of his way to avoid large, high-spirited gatherings. (Marguerite's old duke arrived one day for a rendezvous *à deux* only to find that he had interrupted a luncheon party for fifteen, "his entrance greeted by a burst of laughter.") During this period, Stackelberg's extravagance knew no limits. His Christmas gift to Marie was a diamond ring priced at 4,364 francs. "I had a hard time reining him back," she told Mme Judith. But was this just largesse with no return? One report suggests not. "She particularly owed her fortune of several years to the little services she delivered," claimed an article in *Le Corsaire*: "Marie Duplessis played the role of a Russian secret policeman for the benefit of [Czar] Nicolas."

If Marie was being used by Stackelberg as a spy, she was not alone. "I do not positively assert that [the courtesan] Esther Guimont had a direct and clearly defined mission of espionage," wrote Albert Vandam. "But several of her letters . . . prove beyond a doubt that at least on one occasion she was engaged in very delicate negotiations on behalf of the Government with certain journalists of the Opposition; while her salon during the middle of the forties was looked upon in the light of a political centre." Marie herself would have been party to topical intrigues, as two new young admirers, Baron de Plancy and Henri de Contades, were both embarking on ministerial careers, while Agénor de Guiche was now deeply embroiled in foreign affairs. Not only had he come under the wing of Prince Friedrich Schwarzenberg (a protégé of Metternich and soon to be Austria's prime minister) but he was also growing very close to the future Napoleon III. The title Stackelberg had once held of Secret Adviser would have given credibility to this theory were it not for the fact that the Secret Council (*Tainii Soviet*) for which he had worked was a largely honorific body in the czarist era—the equivalent of the Privy Council. Now seventy-eight years of age and long retired from diplomatic duties, he seems as unlikely to have been involved in state espionage as Marie was to have been an informant. Whereas the politically powerful Esther Guimont had reveled in her access to "a thousand plots, clandestine adventures and secret machinations," Marie made it known that government figures, however eminent, "interested her far less than gens du monde, artists, and writers."

A more plausible motivation for Stackelberg's excessive indulgence of Marie may have been guilt. During the past few months, her resemblance to his daughters had only increased as she began to reveal alarming signs of tuberculosis, the disease that had killed all three. Could he have been a latent carrier? The cause of tuberculosis would not be discovered until 1882, but even though it was not considered contagious, Stackelberg, being Russian and innately superstitious, must have felt himself jinxed.

A bill for nightwear, including a cashmere nightdress and three bonnets, suggests that Marie may have been experiencing night fevers as early as March 1844, though Romain Vienne was made aware of her symptoms only at the end of that year. "They came on with immense speed as she led an impossible life of parties, balls, dinners and every sort of pleasure without any kind of break." Certainly by autumn she almost always had a temperature and suffered from appalling insomnia. A chemist's account details the remedies to which she resorted: laudanum, belladonna ointment, ether, leeches, opium patches, and—most poignant of all—an "elixir of long life."

To fill the hours after midnight Marie frequently called on her new neighbor, Clémence Prat, whose dressing room window looked directly onto hers. Once a courtesan herself, she was now a well-known procuress, a heavily built woman in her forties, who operated under the cover of a millinery business that she ran from her apartment. In the Dumas novel and play she is Prudence Duvernoy, so thinly disguised that everyone who knew of Clémence recognized her. She had made a brief, unsuccessful attempt at acting, and in an 1859 revival of *La dame aux camélias* she took on the role of Prudence, playing herself "with perfect mediocrity." To Marie she was a reminder of what Dumas fils called "the coming of old age, that first death of courtesans," a grim example of what happens to yesterday's kept women who still have expensive tastes.

Their friendship was based on mutual gain: Marie depended on her company, while Clémence relished the perks that no longer came her way, grateful to ride in Marie's carriage, borrow her cashmere shawls, and share her box at the theater. In a tellingly cynical portrayal, Marguerite tells Armand that women such as Prudence are companions rather than friends, adding that her ingratiation was always self-serving. When Prudence acted as go-between to squeeze extra cash from the old duke, she would ask also to borrow five hundred francs, which she did not return. "Or else she pays it off in hats which never get taken out of their boxes." Prudence cannot understand why Marguerite refuses to take on as her protector the wealthy "count de N.," an ardent young aristocrat, instead of the duke, "an insipid old man" who watches her every move. "She says he's too stupid," Prudence tells Armand, "Well, he may be stupid, but he could provide her with a good position, whereas the old duke will die one of these days."

This was presumably the young dandy scorned by Vienne as "an idiot . . . a badly brought up fop of deplorable ignorance." In his account, the "Baron de Ponval" first made contact with Marie on New Year's Day 1845, when among the gifts she received was a box delivered by a groom dressed in grand livery. Opening it, Marie found a dozen oranges, each wrapped in a thousand-franc note. The card, which read, "Hommage from M. le baron de Ponval to Mme Marie Duplessis," intrigued her, but she heard no more for a fortnight. On January 14, the eve of her birthday, the groom reappeared, this time bringing a casket containing a number of jewels and a note in which the baron asked to be received the following day.

Vienne, who met the young man, describes him as tall with reddish blond hair and the gaucherie of a grown-up schoolboy. A spoiled only son whose chief interests were hunting and fishing, he had been orphaned at twenty-five and was now squandering his parents' fortune. Marie took an instant dislike to him. Although gracious about the presents he had given her, complimenting him on his choices, she let him struggle to formulate his sentences and made it clear after only twenty minutes that their meeting was over. He, on the other hand, appeared enchanted by his visit, particularly since Marie had given him permission to return. But when, on this second occasion, he stammered out his wishes, she bluntly declared her own conditions:

> Monsieur le baron, I realise that mine is a sordid profession, but I must let you know that my favours cost a great deal of money. My protector must be extremely rich to cover my household expenses and satisfy my caprices. At the moment I have about thirty thousand francs of debts.

This was no deterrent. Stirred by the prospect of a chase, the fervent suitor redoubled his attentions—as Prudence put it, "He thinks he can get somewhere with her by visiting at eleven at night and sending her all the jewels she could ever want." In desperation, Marie arranged that her maid, Rose, would act one night as her replacement. All went according to plan, Vienne says, but then the joke rebounded: Ponval lured Rose away, "promising to make her a provisional baroness," yet gave no sign of giving up his pursuit of Marie.

In a version by Méjannes in *Gil Blas,* Ponval becomes the "marquis de G." (A possible model, if only because of the chime of his name, is the marquis de Grandval, who was also a Jockey Club member). "Marie Duplessis really did cast him aside, as Dumas wrote—even on the occasion when he brought her a tenth diamond ring." Méjannes then gives the following passage as an example of Marie's derision:

> —You're wasting your time, Marquis, take that away: I have forbidden you to return, and here you are again!

—But I saw the carriage of [Agénor de Guiche] downstairs. Can't mine just as well be in front of your door?

—Marquis, you imagine that giving me presents to the value of fifteen thousand francs allows you the right to become one of my intimate friends. And yet I know that you have an unhappy little mistress to whom you refuse five hundred francs a month. . . . Clotilde [Marie's new maid], show Monsieur the marquis to the door.

Some chroniclers of Marie's story have assumed that Dumas's doting young count is a caricature of Ned Perregaux. Now reduced to spending his money on necessities, Ned, according to Vienne, had become an encumbrance to Marie, but he certainly was not the Count de N. The fictional count, bombarding Marguerite with jewels, is an "imbecile" who infuriates her, whereas Marie was still fond of Ned. As Vienne says, "She had too big a heart to forget what he had thrown at her feet—everything that was left of his lavish inheritance." Her continuing affection is evident in the note she wrote on 25 February 1845. Although the favor she was asking could account for her endearments, she clearly preferred Ned's company to that of his profligate young rival, who had exasperated her in her box at the theater by his trivial remarks and braying laugh.

> *In great haste.*
> *My dearest Ned,*
> *This evening at the Variétés there will be an extraordinary performance in honor of Bouffé. It will start with* le Diner de Madelon, le Père Turlututu, Phèdre *by {sic—see notes} Audry {sic}, le Gamin de Paris, a bit of Sylphide, a quadrille of artists,—in all, a charming evening. You will give me great pleasure if you arrange a box for me. Let me know, my dear friend. I kiss your eyes a thousand million times, if you will allow me. Marie.*

———

The veteran actor Marie Bouffé had recently been taken on at the Variétés by Nestor Roqueplan—a significant coup, as Bouffé had made the fortune of the Théâtre du Gymnase. But as the actor's health was poor, and he did not think he could carry the repertory alone, he had suggested that Roqueplan engage as a second star the celebrated Virginie Déjazet. The gala that Marie was so keen to attend was as much a tribute to Déjazet as to Bouffé, an opportunity for the public to welcome her back to Paris after an absence of several years. "Her name on the posters was enough to attract the finest flowers of Parisian society," wrote one of her biographers.

By early evening on February 25, the Variétés was full to bursting, its auditorium ablaze with light from gas jets and the huge central chandelier, the buzz of anticipation exactly like that which Zola describes at the start of his novel *Nana:*

> Women were languidly fanning themselves, casting glances over the hustle and bustle; smart young men in low-cut waistcoats and with a gardenia in their button holes had stationed themselves beside the orchestra, peering through opera-glasses poised in their gloved fingertips. . . . In this first-night audience, always full of the same people, there were little private groups smilingly acknowledging each other, while the regular theatre-goers, still with their hats on, were exchanging waves and nods. . . . This was Paris: the Paris of literature, finance and pleasure; lots of journalists, a few authors, stockbrokers and more courtesans than respectable women; a strangely mixed bunch, comprising every kind of genius, tainted with every kind of vice.

It was much the same mix at Déjazet's debut. "Every member of the press, artists, theatre-lovers, gens du monde, students,

schoolchildren . . . everyone scrambling through the Variétés'
doors to pay homage to her." Renowned for roles *en travestie,*
Déjazet had a nondescript face but was adored by the public for her sparkling personality and exceptional range, which
spanned from grande dame to grisette, king to timid schoolboy.
"She spoke in all the jargons and dazzled with a thousand meta-
morphoses!" That night at the Variétés, appearing in her signature role in the vaudeville *Premières armes de Richelieu,* Déjazet
exceeded expectation.

In the audience was the actress's twenty-four-year-old son,
Eugène, who had grown up in an exceptionally free milieu (Virginie Déjazet's lovers included two members of the Café de Paris's
infamous *Souper des Douze*—the wealthy man-about-town Alfred
Tattet and his poet friend Félix Arvers). But, though spoiled
by his mother and avid for any kind of pleasure, Eugène was a
charming young man who had recently formed a close friendship
with an intelligent twenty-year-old whose upbringing had been
just as unconventional. This was Alexandre Dumas, the illegitimate son of the great writer, who was himself embarking on a
literary career and had been launched by his father into the easy
morality of the times—what Dumas fils called the paganism of
modern life.

He and Eugène had spent the day riding together in the forest of Saint-Germain-en-Laye and returned to the city in time
for an early supper and the theater. Sitting beside each other in
the stalls of the Variétés, they had a clear view of Marie, framed
in her box on the right of the stage. Alexandre could hardly take
his eyes off her.

She was alone there, or rather, she was the only person one
could see . . . exchanging smiles and glances with three or
four of our neighbours, leaning back, from time to time,
to chat with an invisible occupant of her box, who was no
other than the aged Russian Count S—. Marie Duplessis

was flashing signals to a fat woman with a freckled face and a flashy costume who was in one of the boxes of the higher tier opposite to her. This good lady, sitting beside a pale young girl who seemed restless and ill at ease, and whom she had presumably undertaken to "launch" in the world of gallantry, was a certain Clémence Pr—t, a milliner, whose establishment was in an apartment on the boulevard de la Madeleine, in the house adjoining that in which Marie Duplessis occupied the mezzanine floor. Eugène Déjazet knew Mme Pr—t, Mme Pr—t knew Marie Duplessis whom I was anxious to know.

It would not have been the first time that Alexandre had seen Marie. He was a familiar figure in the cafés and theaters of Paris and would have encountered Marie in her usual haunts. He had watched her arrive for her daily promenade on the Champs-Elysées in her small blue carriage drawn by two magnificent bays, noting how she maintained a mysterious discretion, unlike other kept women, whose aim was to be noticed. "She was almost always alone, and hid herself as much as she could." Like his narrator describing a sighting of Marguerite, he may have discovered her name after seeing her at the entrance of Susse on the place de la Bourse. Officially a stationery and art supply shop, it also sold knickknacks, silverware, bronzes, and paintings by contemporary artists—often at bargain prices. (Dumas père acquired a Delacroix at Susse for six hundred francs.) Fashionable Parisians rarely passed by without stopping to peer through the windows of Susse, although that day it was not the artworks Alexandre was eyeing but Marie.

She wore a muslin dress with full panels, a cashmere shawl embroidered at the corner with gold thread and silk flowers, a Leghorn straw hat and a single bracelet, one of those thick gold chains which were then just beginning to be fashionable. She got into her carriage and drove off. One of the shop assistants remained in the doorway with his eyes following the carriage of his elegant customer. I went up to him and asked him who she was.

Alexandre himself cut a striking figure. Swinging a cane with a golden knob, he was a quintessential dandy, swathed in a dark cashmere shawl and wearing a white cravat, black trousers hemmed with silk, and a quilted London waistcoat of impeccable cut. Such chic came at a cost, and by the age of twenty he owed debts tens of thousands of francs. Forced to pay his creditors himself, Alexandre turned to journalism, writing articles at ten centimes a line in voguish magazines, including *Sylphide* and *Paris Elégant*. He may, in fact, have been the new correspondent for *Paris Elégant*'s "Chronique de la mode," a fashion column published in serial form. The narrative in the issues of 10 February to 20 March 1845 is a spoof portrait of a lovely young courtesan named Sylphide, who bears more than a passing resemblance to Marie Duplessis. She is "as discreet as a woman of good family," and she wears a ravishing garland on her head of violets and pink camellias. She first appears at an Opéra ball accompanied by a young lion and a Russian diplomat, her box having been obtained that morning from the director of the Opéra himself. Her passion for shopping takes her to modish boutiques like the couturière Camille, and Mayer, where elegant Parisians, Marie among them, bought their gloves. En route, she encounters various well-dressed women, one wearing a white cashmere shawl "embroidered with white braid and threads of gold; its fringes long and thick in gold and white silk." The columns are signed "Marie," but when Sylphide arrives at an atelier on the boulevard Bonne-Nouvelle, the author plants a clue. The shop, which sold musical instruments, was Chez Alexandre, but its full title was MM. Alexandre Père et Fils—"a name which my readers will no doubt already have guessed."

In recent weeks, Dumas father and son had become closer than ever before. Their tropical ancestry (Alexandre fils's great-grandmother was a Haitian slave girl) had produced the same swarthy complexion and striking features, Dumas père taking great pride in his handsome son, with his curly hair and melting creole eyes. He saw himself as a friend and accomplice of his son, whose company he relished. "I know of no two characters more diametrically opposed . . . which yet harmonize better. To be sure, each of us finds plenty of enjoyment away from the other; but I think the best times are those we spend together. . . . He uses all his wit to make fun of me and loves me with all his heart."

This had not always been the case. Until he was eight, when his father finally acknowledged him, Alexandre's family had been his mother. At the age of thirty, Catherine Labay, a blond, pale-skinned seamstress, had begun an affair with Dumas, then a twenty-two-year-old bureaucrat with literary ambitions, who lived in rooms across the landing. When she gave birth to their son in 1824, Dumas installed them both in a little apartment in Passy but visited only rarely. Alexandre's earliest memories were of playing under the table while his mother sewed to scrape out a living. In 1831, after his first theatrical success, Dumas decided to take on material responsibility for his son and allowed him to use his name. He wanted Alexandre to benefit from the kind of education he himself had never had and sent the seven-year-old to an expensive boarding school—but still he kept away, absorbed by his writing and numerous female conquests.

Alexandre's attitude to his father's mistresses had always been hostile, but Dumas's marriage to the portly actress Ida Ferrier in 1840 caused a serious breach between them. The couple had settled in Florence, and a brief respite came three years later when Dumas returned alone to Paris. Father and son established a rapport for the first time, and the eighteen-year-old discovered his eminent father to be a big child, exuberantly identifying with his own youth and curiosity. "We went together into the pleasures of the world—of *all* worlds." At a masked ball in Montparnasse, they danced all night with such abandon that when they got home Alexandre had to split the seams of his father's tight, sweat-drenched breeches to get them off. Encouraging the rumor that they passed on their women to each other, he would jokingly rebuke Dumas père in front of friends for giving him cast-off mistresses to sleep with and new boots to break in. "What are you complaining about?" retorted the other. "It proves you have a narrow foot and a thick prick!"

Their complicity was destroyed by Mme Dumas rejoining her husband, and when relations reached crisis point, Alexandre fled, spending several months in Marseille, staying with one of his father's friends, poet and librettist Joseph Méry. With his passion for gambling and patronage of the sleazy cafés of the port, Méry was a wayward influence yet inspirational at the same time. He was the city's librarian and more cultured than anyone Alexandre had ever known, capable of singing his way through Rossini's *Otello* or *Guillaume Tell* from beginning to end (Méry did not believe he had the right to admire something he did not know by heart). Directing his protégé to the museum's paintings by Ingres, Puget, and Rubens, Méry also took him to the ancient town of Pomponiana and encouraged him to act on his dreams. While reclining in the shade of a palm tree in Hyères, the two recited their poems to each other. Méry responded to Alexandre's first attempts at verse with enthusiasm and astonished his young friend with his own rich creativity. Méry's literary renown had earned him such respect locally that he was virtually invincible—as Alexandre had been relieved to discover. "If you have spent a little too much time by the side of one of these charming Marseillaise grisettes with their little bonnet and little feet whose brother or fiancé waits for you at the corner of the rue du Vieux-Quartier you have nothing to fear if you are with Méry—because Joseph Méry is the viceroy of Marseille."

Under Méry's guidance Alexandre became involved with an actress, a relationship he hoped would continue when they both returned to Paris, but she wrote to end it, saying that he was too poor to keep her. When he took this to heart and stayed away, his seeming indifference reignited her interest, as he reported to Méry in a letter dated 18 October 1844: "She gave me to understand that although she was living with another, whom she regarded in the light of a husband, serving him only for money, she would be only too delighted to continue going to bed with her Marseille friends. . . . Now I am no longer very sad. I am working." What cheered him up even further was the news of his father's estrangement from Ida Ferrier, who had run off with an Italian nobleman. With his stepmother off the premises, Alexandre spent as much time as he could at his father's rented house in Saint-Germain-en-Laye, where Dumas, feeling isolated in the countryside, was always delighted to see him.

On one such day, Alexandre encountered Eugène Déjazet and accompanied him to the Variétés. Observing that his friend was inflamed with infatuation at the sight of Marie, Eugène arranged an introduction. "[He] went over to talk to Mme Pr—t, who was a born go-between for such purposes, and it was agreed that we should go round to her flat after the play was over, and that if the count said good-bye to Marie Duplessis at the door, instead of going in with her, she would allow us to pay her a short visit."

The rest of the evening, as related in the novel, was exactly what happened. Marguerite and her companion leave the theater early, disappearing in a phaeton drawn by two superb horses, which the old duke drives himself. Meanwhile, Armand and "Gaston R." have joined Prudence in her box, and the three also leave before the performance is over, taking a hackney cab to her apartment. As Prudence shows them around her shop she chatters away answering Armand's questions about Marguerite's lovers. "I never see anyone stay when I go, but I couldn't say no one comes after I've left," she says, mentioning the Count de N., who is often there, and the old duke, who will not leave her alone. When she hears Marguerite's voice, she goes into her *cabinet de toilette* and opens the window. "I've been calling you for ten minutes," Marguerite says imperiously, ordering Prudence to come right away because the Count de N. has not left and is boring her to death. The two young men follow Prudence to Marie's front door, lurking behind, as she tells Marguerite that she has two visitors who would like to meet her.

On hearing the famous names of Déjazet and Dumas, Marie would certainly have welcomed the pair, but Marguerite's eagerness to see Gaston and Armand, who were just another couple of handsome young lions, is due solely to her hope that they would drive away the besotted Count de N. "Try to be more amusing than him," Prudence whispers, "or else—I know Marguerite—she'll take it out on me." When they go into the drawing room, they see Marguerite sitting at the piano, struggling to master a piece by Weber, while the young man leans on the mantelpiece watching her. "I remember exactly his features and eminent name," Dumas *fils* later wrote. "He was someone I had met several times in *le monde*, who put up with the whims of Marie Duplessis with the most amiable and elegant courtesy." Count de N., as Marguerite had planned, announces he is leaving.

—Goodbye, my dear Count, must you go so soon?

—Yes, I fear I bore you.

—You do not bore me today more than any other day.

Armand flinches at Marguerite's cruelty but can't help admiring her behavior. "This proof of disinterest in not accepting an elegant, rich young man ready to ruin himself for her excused, in my eyes, all the faults of her past."

With Dumas's assurance that his account of that night was absolutely exact, we are given a fascinatingly impartial picture of Marie. In this scene Marguerite is a pitiless, petulant diva, who flings a piano score across the room in a tantrum of frustration and reveals harsh peasant roots beneath her discreet, aristocratic veneer. By 1 a.m., when the atmosphere and conversation have disintegrated into debauchery, she is tipsy and as raucous as a street porter. Gaston is amused by her bawdiness, but Armand is saddened to hear profanities coming from the lips of "this beautiful creature of twenty." When she starts to sing a squalid song, he is embarrassed and asks her to stop.

—Oh, how chaste you are! she smiles taking his hand.
—It's not for me, it's for you.

She waves her hand as if to say, "Oh, it's a long time since I was concerned about chastity."

With each glass of champagne Marguerite's cheeks get more flushed, and a cough, light at first, becomes troublesome enough to force her head against the back of her chair and make her support her chest with both hands. Toward the end of supper she is seized by an even more violent coughing fit, turns purple, shuts her eyes in pain, and brings a handkerchief to her lips. Seeing it stained with blood, she gets up and runs into her dressing room. Ignoring Prudence, who says that this happened every day and that she would soon be back, Armand goes after her.

In just this way, Alexandre followed Marie. It was, he wrote, "the same supper, the same animation, the same sudden indisposition of Marie Duplessis. . . . Of those who were at supper I was the only one to be concerned when she left the table." In a room lit by a single candle, he saw her lying on a sofa, deathly pale, her dress undone and one hand resting on her heart. She was struggling to get her breath back, and beside her was a silver bowl half full of water, which she had used as a spittoon. It was marbled with strands of blood. Alexandre sat down next to her. "I was not able to hide my emotion. I cried on kissing her hand."

At the turn of the twentieth century, when Sarah Bernhardt played this scene onstage, anyone in the audience with medical knowledge was appalled. The tuberculosis germ was now known to be transmitted by sputum droplets expelled through coughing, and the saliva was considered life-threatening. Invalids using spittoons were told never to leave them uncovered, and an article in *Le Monde* warned that spitting into handkerchiefs and letting them dry on beds or pillows "is likely to coat these (as well as the room's occupants) with bacilli." In 1898 the physician Joseph Grancher delivered a lengthy report singling out contagious spittle for his attack. "We know . . . that the *tuberculeux* is dangerous and that we must be protected from him."

Marie's era, however, was a time of "romantic medicine," when the profession still used a patient's individual temperament to explain the cause of the illness. In fact, René-Théophile-Hyacinthe Laënnec, who invented the stethoscope, attributed the cause of pulmonary consumption to "sorrowful passions." Romantic literature and art exploited this notion with images of the frail, consumptive heroine whose beauty was enhanced by the disease's wasting effect on the body. Marguerite Gautier, with her slender frame, pallid face, and eyes half circled by bluish shadows, became one of many idealized stereotypes. Dumas fils was partially responsible, but the responsive youth in Marie's boudoir did not have his literary future in mind and was genuinely overcome by her condition.

An early experience of intense misery had left Alexandre with a great capacity for compassion. When he was a small child, his mother had said, "You don't have a father . . . that doesn't mean that your father is dead: it means that a lot of people will despise and insult you." At the Pension Saint-Victor, the most renowned and least disciplined private boarding school in Paris, he had been persecuted by his peers, who called him "bastard," interrupted his sleep with surprise nocturnal attacks, and covered his exercise books with obscene drawings labeled with his mother's name. He said nothing but began to suffer from heart palpitations and nervous crises that went on for several years. The opening of his autobiographical novel *L'affaire Clemenceau* (1867) helped him to exorcise memories of this torment, but he never lost his conviction that on a basic level, human beings were cruel. Feeling he had a mission, Dumas fils became a writer "fired with proselytizing," in the words of English writer Edmund Gosse. "His great father, *le père prodigue,* had been all for self. Alexandre would be all for others."

His dissipated life, first in Paris with his father and then in Marseille with Méry, had fortified his sympathy for fallen women. In an 1872 pamphlet, *Homme-Femme,* he uses the term *feminist,* its earliest recorded use. It could describe his younger self. In a long diatribe in *The Lady of the Camellias,* he recalls seeing a girl being arrested in the street, still clasping the baby from which she was about to be separated, an image that filled him with as much dismay as the discovery of another victim, who had been led into a life of vice by her own mother. By the time Alexandre met Marie he was consumed by sympathy for courtesans. He was only twenty years old but had an intuitive knowledge of female psychology, and unlike most men, was indulgent about a woman's frailties. In Marie he saw great sadness behind the veil of feverish ebullience, and he sensed that the wanton behavior he had witnessed was her way of forgetting who she was. The dialogue that follows between Armand and Marguerite replicates almost word for word their own exchange.

> —You are killing yourself, Madame. I would like to be your friend, your guardian, so that I could prevent you from doing such harm to yourself.
> —Ah it's not worth you alarming yourself, she said bitterly. Look how the others aren't bothering. It's because they know

there's nothing that can be done about my illness. . . . If I took care of myself as I should I would die. What keeps me going is the pace of this life that I lead. . . . Love me like a friend and nothing more. Come and see me. We will laugh, we will chat. You have a good heart, you have a need to be loved. You are too young and too sensitive to live in our world. Get yourself a married woman.

But the tall, broad-shouldered young poet exuding kindness and sympathy was too engaging to turn away. "Adet," as Marie called him (from the French pronunciation of his initials), found himself being favored more and more in the coming weeks. He was sometimes invited into her box at the theater, and eventually allowed to spend the whole night. "One morning I left at eight, and a day came when I was permitted to leave at midday." He became known as Marie Duplessis's new *amant de cœur*—a situation that posed no threat to Agénor de Guiche, then in the midst of an affair with Rachel, but that devastated Ned Perregaux. In a letter dated March 1845, Ned reapplied to join the Foreign Legion. Thanks to three endorsements from well-connected friends of his family, his application was accepted this time, but the authorities could find no trace of him. Vienne says he vanished from Paris for four months.

Alexandre was exactly the same age as Marie. Like two children, they seized the chance to have fun together, roaming the dark alleys of the Champs-Elysées and making excursions outside Paris. A favorite outing was to stables owned by a man named Ravelet, who bought horses from the garrison of Saint-Germain—cast-off horses that kicked, reared, and bolted—and charged thirty sous an hour for vertiginous rides. "He was famous among our generation," Dumas fils wrote to his publisher, recounting how the nags were soon corrected of the vices that had expelled them from the regiment.

It did not matter if they were saddled for women or for men. Provided with their cavaliers they were whipped into action . . . helped by youth and laughter. . . . Happy times! This maison Ravelet was, you can imagine, a place for rendezvous. . . . Ravelet saw his jades ridden by all the pretty girls of the Parisian world of gallantry, including Marie Duplessis . . . whose impetuous nature reveled in these rides at top speed.

They often went walking together by the Rond-point des Roses and the terrace beyond Ravelet's property in Saint-Germain-en-Laye. This was close to Villa Médicis, the house that Dumas père was renting, but Alexandre did not take Marie to visit his father. "As soon as a woman takes my arm," he once told him, "the first thing she does is to lift her skirt to stop it getting dirty, and the second is to ask me when she can meet you."

Alexandre Dumas père was in his heyday and one of the best known and most affectionately regarded public figures in Paris. The moment he appeared in a theater or concert hall, the entire audience would rise to its feet. Journalist Hippolyte de Villemessant recalled, "Everyone turned to look at the illustrious novelist, whose tall figure dominated the crowd and who, smiling right and left at his friends and even at strangers, progressed only slowly towards his seat in the stalls, detained as he was by all the hands held out for him to shake on the way." This fascination was due as much to Dumas's charisma and notoriety as a womanizer as to his fame as a writer. His Caribbean ancestry also intrigued both men and women, "He benefited from the myth, already current, of the superior sexual prowess of men of African extraction," as one biographer put it.

Across the Channel, another national treasure, Charles Dickens, would, at forty-five, inspire the love of an eighteen-year-old actress, Ellen Ternan, the secret of his final years. For Marie, the idea of becoming the mistress of the forty-three-year-old French literary titan had equal appeal, and she had already made the first approach. Unattached and fabulously wealthy, Dumas père was an irresistible life force whose joie de vivre infected everyone around him. "It was absolutely impossible to be dull in his society," remarked Albert Vandam. He also had the power to make things happen. Another reason Alexandre fils's Marseille actress gave for ending their affair was that it might jeopardize her career by "causing problems" with his father. Perhaps suspecting that he was once again being used as a link and knowing of Marie's own ambition to go on the stage, Alexandre went out of his way to keep her to himself.

A section of his poem collected in his book *Sins of Youth* is addressed to "M.D." and describes the spring evenings they spent together. Marie was swaddled in winter clothes, sitting close to the fire, staring dreamily at the flames, or playing the piano while Alexandre listened. She was, he wrote, "always ready for love" and seemed to find a release through sex for her incessant insomnia.

> Do you remember the nights when burning with desire,
> Your frantic body writhing beneath kisses,
> You found the sleep you longed for
> In the warm afterglow . . .

Like Marguerite, whose eyes Dumas fils describes as flickering intermittently with flashes of desire, Marie could not hide her innate sensuality. But while the young writer championed a woman's right to feel unbridled passions, the moralistic, mature Dumas fils was implacably censorious. The narrator of *L'affaire Clemenceau,* published nineteen years after *The Lady of the Camellias,* is shocked when he discovers his lovely young wife, Iza, swimming naked in an icy river. She had asked him to bring her a large sheet and some hot milk in a silver basin, and when he prudishly rushes to cover her, she insists on drinking the milk first, swallowing it in long, slow gulps. "Then she threw herself into his arms, offering her red lips tinted with milk."

Iza's craving for new experiences is regarded in the novel as dangerous, the first sign of nymphomania. "Such is the woman you married," the husband is told. "You have naively developed her natural sensuality." Unable to remember the names of the men she has slept with, she admits that she is ill—a response that was standard at the time. Sexual appetite in a woman was seen as a symptom of disease or insanity, and tuberculosis was believed to set into motion a biochemical process that heightened a patient's libido. A Dr. C. Cabanes, writing about famous victims of the virus, including Marie and Rachel, entitles his book *Poitrinaires et grandes amoureuses* (*Consumptives and Great Lovers*). Alexandre was unsure whether Marie's love of sex was intrinsic to her nature "or else an effect of her state of health"— whatever the case, Dumas père was convinced that his son had toned down his portrayal.

He was not bound to let the public know that the frequent recurrence of these erotic episodes, always with a different partner, constitutes a disease which is as well known to specialists as the disease of drunkenness, and for which it is impossible to find a cure. Messalina, Catherine II, and thousands of women have suffered from it. When they happen to be born in such exalted stations as these two, they buy men; when they happen to be born in a lowly station and are attractive, they sell themselves; when they are ugly and repulsive they sink to the lowest depths of degradation, or end in the padded cells of a madhouse, where no man dares come near them. Nine times out of ten the malady is hereditary, and I am certain that if we could trace the genealogy of Alphonsine Plessis, we should find the taint either on the father's side or on the mother's—probably on the former's, but more probably still on both.

Dumas may have formed this opinion from boulevard gossip, from what his son had told him, or from an incident he described in his newspaper, *Le Mousquetaire.* He recalled walking along one of the passages at the Théâtre-Français when the door of a box opened and someone caught hold of his coattails. It was Alexandre.

—So it's you, is it? Good evening, dear boy.

—Come in here, Father.

—You're not alone?

—All the more reason. Shut your eyes, put your head through the door. Don't be afraid, nothing unpleasant will happen to you.

—True enough. I had hardly shut my eyes, hardly put my head through the door, than I felt upon my mouth the pressure of a pair of trembling, feverish, burning lips. I opened my eyes. An adorable young woman of twenty or twenty-two, was alone there with Alexandre, and had just bestowed on me that far from daughterly caress. I recognized her from having seen her more than once. . . .

—So it's you, dear child, I said, gently releasing myself from her arms.

—Yes, it appears that I have to take you by force.

—Why do you think that?

—Oh! I know that it is not your reputation, but why are you being so cruel to me? I have written twice suggesting a meeting at the Opera Ball.

—In front of the clock at two in the morning.

—So you did receive my letters.

—Certainly I received them.

—So why did you not come then?

—Because I thought your letters were addressed to Alexandre.

—To Alexandre Dumas, yes.

—But to Alexandre Dumas fils.

—Oh come now! Alexandre is Dumas fils; but you are most certainly not Dumas père, and you will never be.

—Thank you for the compliment, my lovely lady.

—So why didn't you come?

—Because at one or two in the morning in front of the clock there are only energetic twenty- or thirty-year-olds, or imbeciles of forty or fifty. As I have turned forty I would naturally be classed in the second category by observers, and that would be humiliating.

—I don't see why.

—Let me explain. A beautiful girl like you does not suggest lovers' meetings to men of my age unless she has need of them. What can I do for you? I offer you my protection without any question of love in return. . . .

—Well then, said Marie with a charming smile, her long black lashes veiling her eyes. We will come and see you, won't we, Monsieur.

—Whenever you wish, Mademoiselle.

And I bowed to her as I might have bowed to a duchess. The door closed behind me and I was back again in the passage. That was the only time I ever kissed Marie Duplessis: it was the last time I ever saw her. I waited for Alexandre and the lovely courtesan to visit me. A few days later Alexandre came alone.

—Well? I said to him.

—Ah, yes, you mean Marie?

—Why haven't you brought her?

The flirtatious exchange at the theater was reason enough, but Alexandre admitted that their fling was over. They had parted, he writes in *Sins of Youth,* as a result of a quarrel. "Why? I don't know: Over nothing! The suspicion of an unknown lover." It was an Englishman, he told his father.

—I hope you weren't in love.
—No. What I feel for her is compassion.

They discussed Marie's tuberculosis, Alexandre saying the fatal outcome was still not certain but would soon be confirmed. "With the life she leads things will move fast from probability to certainty." After that, Dumas claimed, they never spoke about her again, although years later, after a particularly moving performance of the play, Alexandre felt obliged to confess to his father that Armand had loved Marguerite that night with a passion he never felt for Marie.

Father and son began living together in Saint-Germain-en-Laye, "more closely bound to the other by ties of affection than to any other soul, his mother excepted in the young man's case." Marie, meanwhile, was missing the company of her *bel ami.* She had an Englishman, a generous, horse-mad aristocrat whom Méjannes calls "Lord A.," but he was of no consequence. She valued friendships with passion and wanted to keep Alexandre in her life.

> *Dear Adet,*
> *Why have you not let me know how you are? And why are you not talking frankly to me? I believe that you should regard me as a friend, so I'm hoping for a word from you, and I kiss you tenderly as a mistress, or as a friend. It's your choice. . . . Whatever the case I will always be your devoted . . . Marie.*

Only Romain, among her male friends, was consistently loyal and reliable. Like Alexandre, he was convinced that her wild lifestyle was hastening her end and asked which doctor was taking care of her. "I have three," she told him, "two French and a Prussian. You'd approve of the first two as they prescribe rest, country air, nutritious diet, Bordeaux wine and meals at regular intervals all of which is perfect, but impossible for me. As for the Prussian, I believe, quite frankly, that he's poisoning me. He's saturating me with a drug to which he gives some diabolic name, probably so that I won't know what it really is."

One of the French doctors Marie first consulted was Pierre Louis, a specialist in consumption who was researching the difference in occurrence in the two sexes. Another was Pierre Manec, who had also written a study of the disease and is regarded by anesthetists today as a pioneer, having performed major operations using the first ether inhalers. The German, David Ferdinand Koreff, was a controversial character. He had been personal physician to the king of Prussia and was a practitioner of magnetism (a belief in the existence of an indefinable, fluctuating current of energy in the human body with healing powers). The French medical community branded him as a mountebank, but his lively mind made him a valuable guest in Parisian salons, where he recruited most of his patients. Women in particular were drawn to Koreff, whose conversational ease and understanding of their foibles inspired confidence. "He always had a number of little remedies, anodynes and secrets on conserving beauty and youth," remarked the romantic novelist Countess Dash. And there was something about Koreff's physical charisma—his all-black clothes, combined with his unconventional doctrines—that gave him an air of necromancy, of being able to work miracles. "One often hears it said that he has saved the life of such and such a person," Madame de Bawr reported to the Duchess de Dino (both well-known women of letters), voicing the general view that Koreff was optimistic against all odds. The physician's popularity collapsed as a result of a lawsuit in which he demanded an absurdly high back payment of fees from one of his aristocratic clients. The beau monde's doors closed, and Koreff was denounced for his obsession with money and celebrity. "He is no longer received," Balzac wrote to a friend. "I no longer greet him, and hardly respond when he speaks to me."

Marie, however, liked Koreff and often invited him to her soirées, although she was far less appreciative of his professional skills. "I am continually agitated, I have heart palpitations, headaches and my cough gets worse instead of better," she complained to Romain, who, deeply suspicious of Koreff's infamous reputation, had the contents of Marie's vial of medicine analyzed by a chemist. The solution contained strychnine, of which Koreff had instructed Marie to take a centigram a day. This, in Romain's view, branded him unequivocally as an "abominable charlatan," although in fact poison was an accepted form of treatment. Eight decades later, an article in *The British Medical Journal* confirmed the efficacy of strychnine in tubercular patients—"It always improves the appetite and general condition . . . and acts as a general tonic and nervine stimulant"—while Marie's own Dr. Manec administered arsenic in the treatment of cancer— a rudimentary form of chemotherapy. Manec also prescribed a paste of arsenous acid mixed with black mercury sulfide to relieve coughs and mucus irritability in consumptives.

By June 1845, Koreff, who was traveling in Germany, had stopped treating Marie, and bills confirm that her summer was spent in Paris. In July, her account at Kuher, a saddler on rue Tronchet, reached a staggering 2,390 francs—the result of a splurge on new buckles, halters, stirrups, snaffle bridles, girths, a chain-mail breastpiece, and an embossed leather crown. As reimbursement for a dinner she had hosted for Lord A., he had promised to import a saddle horse for her from London, but it never arrived. Seeing how ill she was, he abandoned the idea of a horse and instead sent her an enormous rosewood trunk, one meter high by two meters long, full of chocolates, each wrapped in a hundred-franc note. Lord A.'s dealer, however, Tony Montel, who doted on Marie, is said to have made a gift to her of a magnificent pair of thoroughbreds. Catching sight of her galloping *en amazone* (sidesaddle) in the Bois de Boulogne, Gustave du Puynode, author of a long homage to her in verse, suggested that a pawing, prancing thoroughbred excited her far more than any lover.

In the woods, in early morning, see how it arches its back,
When, on its sensitive flank, her grey boot spurs it on.
Fearless amazon, ah! How beautiful she was when she
    rode in the Bois!
The dust flew up to the sky! Every stone became a
    jewel . . .
O Marie! Where are you heading as you trample the wild
    thyme?

Marie might have been spending rapturous days on horseback, but her nights seem to have been relatively tranquil. Receipts from Chez Voisin and La Maison d'Or show that a number of meals were delivered to boulevard de la Madeleine, the dishes themselves revealing a healthy appetite. One night she dined alone on a pigeon with peas, mashed potatoes, a salad, and a bottle of eau de Seltz; on another she ordered supper for two— trout with prawns, partridges, a dessert of vanilla *bavaroises,* a bottle of Bordeaux, and a bottle of champagne. She indulged her sweet tooth with cakes from Rollet the pâtissier, glacéed fruit from Boissier, and on one occasion sent for twelve biscuits, macaroons, and maraschino liqueur.

This last bill is dated 30 August 1845, the very night on which Alexandre is supposed to have written his famous *lettre de rupture:*

My very dear Marie.
I am neither rich enough to love you as I would like, nor poor enough to be loved as you would like. So let's both forget, you a

name which must be a little indifferent to you, me a happiness
which has become impossible. It is useless to tell you how sad this
makes me, because you already know how much I love you. So
farewell. You have too much heart not to understand the motive of
my letter and too much spirit to not pardon me for it. A thousand
memories.

A. D.

30 August midnight

Forty years later, intending to make an extravagant gesture
of thanks to Marguerite Gautier's most eloquent interpreter,
Dumas fils sent a rare illustrated edition of his novel to Sarah
Bernhardt. "What makes this one unique," he told her, "is the
signed letter which you will find on the 212th page, and which
slightly resembles the letter printed there.

"[It] was written by the real Armand Duval . . . the only palpable thing remaining of this story. It seems to me to be yours
by right, because it is you who have given youth and life to the
deceased."

Dumas fils always maintained that he had bought the letter back from a Parisian dealer of autographs, but this is highly
suspect. Marie's private correspondence was not put up for sale
(no letter from any other friend or lover has ever come to light),
and papers that were included in a posthumous auction of her
belongings, such as the bills she kept in a Moroccan leather box,
were all marked with a notary's squiggled initials. The letter
from "AD" has no such distinctive squiggle. Was it written by
Alexandre and never sent to Marie, or was it replicated later by
the author with posterity in mind? Whatever the case, there was
no novelistic symmetry to the end of their affair. By September, Alexandre had taken up with a Vaudeville actress, Anaïs
Liévenne, for whom he rented an apartment in his name, but
Marie still kept in touch. Dumas père's new play, *Mousquetaires,*
was soon to open at Théâtre L'Ambigu-Comique, and she asked

Alexandre to use his influence to get her a good seat. "It was 7 October 1845," he wrote. "I remember the date exactly because that was the day which I broke up with Marie Duplessis . . . and I broke up with her because of not being able to procure a box in the gallery."

In fact, the premiere was on October 27, and Marie must have managed to secure herself a ticket, as she was spotted in the foyer by the critic Jules Janin. "She walked on the muddy floor as if she was traversing the boulevards on a rainy day, raising her dress intuitively . . . The whole of her appearance was in keeping with her young and lithesome form; and her face, of a beautiful oval shape, rather pale, corresponded with the charm she diffused around her, like an indescribable perfume." Alexandre was there himself in a box with his father, but neither he nor Dumas père was on Marie's mind. Among the noisy crowd in the second interval she had seen a man with a beautiful, noble face and mane of long hair whom she recognized instantly as Franz Liszt. He had been a little surprised when she approached him, although he had noticed her too, "very much astonished at seeing such a marvel in such a place." When the three solemn knocks of the prompter resounded through the theater, calling the spectators and critics back into the auditorium, Marie and Liszt remained behind. Sitting in front of the greenroom fire, they talked throughout the whole of the third act, each equally captivated by the other. The pianist's plan to stay in Paris "for a week at the most" was about to be dramatically extended.

Part Five

The Countess

AT THIRTY-FOUR, FRANZ LISZT was a European sensation, a romantic icon with the long hair and charisma of a 1960s rock star. His genius as a pianist produced what Heinrich Heine called "a delirium unparalleled in the annals of furore," and when he dropped his gloves after a concert that year, they were seized by women in the audience, torn into fragments, and shared among them. Not that Lisztomania was a female passion only. "We were like men in love, men obsessed," exclaimed one young Russian. "We'd never heard anything like it." But if Liszt had reached the apogee of his career as a performer, his private life was bleak.

A decade earlier, he had fallen in love with thirty-year-old Countess Marie d'Agoult, author, intellectual, and rebellious wife of a French nobleman. Her affair with Liszt was as volatile as it was intense, their exchange of lofty ideas regarded as a blueprint for the grand passion. Mother of his three illegitimate children, d'Agoult sacrificed wealth and respectability for her younger lover—something she never let him forget. She was a joyless, brooding personality who became increasingly resentful and critical of Liszt's success. Dismissing his astonishing virtuosity as mere tricks, she accused him of seeking publicity and invitations to grand salons and never ceased regarding him as an incorrigible philanderer. Her "Don Juan parvenu" did his best to be conciliatory. "I have always been susceptible to physical temptations, you to those of the heart and intellect," Liszt admitted in one letter, while pointing out in another that his merciless touring schedules scarcely gave him time to lead the "orgiastic" life of which he was accused. In the spring of 1845, things finally came to an end. There had been newspaper reports about Liszt's liaison in Dresden with the scandalous Lola Montez, and Marie d'Agoult, after years of alternating threats and pleas, decided that this was the ultimate insult. She would be his mistress, but not *one* of his mistresses, she famously declared. As hostilities spiraled, their children (aged ten, eight, and six) became weapons of war. "If she tries to take Cosima by force," Liszt remarked, "I will retaliate in full by taking the three children to Germany where she will have no hold over them." Fortunately, his mother—an unassuming, warmhearted woman—gave her grandchildren a home in Paris, where they found the love and stability that had been missing from their lives.

As for Liszt himself, the breakup with Marie d'Agoult, compounded by the strain he incurred during a disastrous music festival in August, had led him to the point of collapse. To celebrate the unveiling of the Beethoven monument in Bonn for the seventy-fifth anniversary of the composer's birth, the event had been arranged almost single-handedly by Liszt. But instead of being credited as its moving spirit, he found himself criticized for using it as an opportunity for self-promotion. He had written a new cantata for the festival, and so strong were the currents against him that, as a German student observed, "People were hoping his work would fail." He did, however, have one staunch advocate. Jules Janin, drama critic of the *Journal des Débats,* was almost alone among journalists in recognizing Liszt as a great artist rather than an "acrobat of the piano"—or, as the Lisztophobes would have it, a "pretentious strummer." On August 10, Janin wrote a letter to his wife, describing the pressures Liszt was facing.

A chubby, teenage Marie in a Parisian theater in her phase
as a lorette, not yet able to afford a box of her own, and with no
signature corsage and bouquet of camellias. The watercolor is
by Camille Roqueplan, her friend Nestor's brother.

(*Above, left*) Nestor Roqueplan, the quintessential Parisian
dandy, whose domain was the fashionable cafés and
restaurants of the boulevard des Italiens. Former editor-
in-chief of *Le Figaro* and then director of the Théâtre
des Variétés, he more or less discovered Marie on the
Pont-Neuf, when she was still a waif without a sou, and
remained a friend.

(*Above, right*) One of ten pen-and-ink drawings by Viset
of intimate scenes from the demimonde (illustrating *Une
Courtisane Romantique* by Johannes Gros).

The Paris Opéra's infamous Foyer de la danse—an erotic marketplace for ballerinas and their wealthy admirers—painted by Eugène Lami. The elegant male habitués included figures from Marie's circle: the Opéra's director Dr. Louis Véron, poet Alfred de Musset, man-about-town Fernand de Montguyon, and Nestor Roqueplan. The legendary Romantic ballerina Fanny Elssler is pictured in the center, and on the right, lounging against an ornate pillar, is Monsieur Lautour-Mézeray. He was known to his friends as l'Homme au Camélia because of the white camellia he always wore—a habit Marie may well have copied.

(Left) A summer night at La Grand Chaumière, the favorite haunt of students and their grisette girlfriends on boulevard du Montparnasse. A couple head off through the hornbeams for a romantic tryst while at the rotunda in the background other youngsters dance wild versions of the polka, quadrille, and cancan.

(Below) Eugène Lami's painting *A Box at the Opera*—a larger version of the box Marie ordered for most first nights, when she attracted almost as much attention as the artists onstage.

An imagined rendering of Marie and an admirer in her opera box— the frontispiece to a memoir by her Normandy confidant Romain Vienne.

Lola Montez, the famous courtesan and acquaintance of Marie's, who was also part of the inner circle of the Café de Paris set, here in her favorite Spanish guise, c. 1847. Lithograph by J. G. Middleton.

Die Allee der Bereiche der Klosterwiese, one of the fashionable promenades in Baden-Baden, where Marie met Count Gustav von Stackelberg and discovered her passion for horseriding.

Marie's first love, Duke Agénor de Guiche, the eldest son of the Duke and Duchess de Gramont, who helped to mold the country girl into a model of Parisian style and manners. The portrait is by Agénor's uncle Count d'Orsay, the celebrated dandy and friend of Dickens's.

The doting Ned Perregaux, model for Dumas's Armand, who defied his family by marrying Marie in an English registry office in 1846.

Marie's most indulgent protector, Count von Stackelberg, *seated far right,* as Russia's special envoy at the Congress of Vienna in 1814–15. Engraving by Jean Godefroy.

Alexandre Dumas fils, whose 1848 novel *La dame aux camélias* and sensational play of the same name immortalized Marie. Exactly the same age, they were lovers for a short time in 1845.

A self-portrait by Count Olympe Aguado, a pioneer of French photography. He was only eighteen when he became Marie's lover, and he remained a loyal friend until the end.

The most famous pianist of his time, Franz Liszt was thirty-four and a romantic icon when he met Marie in 1845. He always said he was inspired by her enigmatic quality.

A painting of Marie by the twenty-one-year-old artist Charles Chaplin in 1846, just months before her death.

A miniature of Alphonsine's mother, the melancholy Marie Plessis, painted by an unknown artist in the style of Vigée-Lebrun, shortly before her early death in 1830. The pendant is on display in the Musée de la Dame aux Camélias, in the Normandy town of Gacé.

Found among Marie's things at her death: the skeleton of the once-stuffed green lizard given by Gypsies to Alphonsine on her way to Paris. Believing it would bring her luck, she kept it with her always.

Marie's tomb at Cimitière de Montmartre

Pretty young Marietta Piccolomini (1834–1899) was the first Violetta to make a triumph of *La Traviata,* and to launch it in Paris and London.

The original Marguerite Gautier, Eugénie Doche, a young Irish actress with something of a louche reputation herself. She made her debut in the role at the Théâtre des Variétés on February 2, 1852.

Sarah Bernhardt as Marguerite in 1884. It was a role she inhabited with complete authenticity and is said to have played a total of three thousand times.

The Italian actress Eleonora Duse, the only one to rival Bernhardt's interpretation of Marguerite. Pictured here at the Théâtre des Variétés in 1898.

(*Above*) Greta Garbo playing opposite Robert Taylor in the 1936 film *Camille,* directed by George Cukor. Giving not only the definitive screen performance, Garbo also comes closest to embodying the real Marie.

(*Right*) Maria Callas, considered the greatest Violetta, who identified with the heroine to the point of obsession. Photographed by Houston Rogers in the famous 1955 Visconti production at La Scala, Milan.

Margot Fonteyn and
Rudolf Nureyev
rehearsing one of the
rapturous duets from
Marguerite and Armand,
the 1963 ballet created
by Frederick Ashton as
a showpiece for the two
stars.

Isabelle Huppert as
Alphonsine in Mauro
Bolognini's 1981 movie
Lady of the Camelias.

Sultry Anna Netrebko, the superb Violetta of our time, in Willy Decker's production first staged in Salzburg in 2005.

Tamara Rojo and Sergei Polunin as Marguerite and Armand—the most exciting and affecting interpreters of Ashton's ballet since Fonteyn and Nureyev. Their performance at the Royal Opera House in February 2013 was Rojo's farewell to the Covent Garden stage.

You can imagine that it is impossible for him to be more businesslike, more occupied, preoccupied, captured, taken, recaptured, pulled this way and that. He has built the concert hall [seating an audience of 3,000], filled it with musicians, organized the program, housed the visitors. No one addresses anyone but him, he is agitated beyond belief. No sleep, too much coffee, tobacco . . .

When Liszt first saw Janin, quietly reading Horace's *Odes,* he fell into his arms. Liszt may have been a demigod for several days, but he badly needed moral support. "One can see that he is perturbed," continued Janin, who was right to be concerned: soon after the festival ended, Liszt was confined to bed with jaundice and complete exhaustion.

He arrived in Paris on the morning of October 25, staying with his mother and children on the rue Louis-le-Grand, and by midday he was at Jules Janin's house. "Very happy to see me. . . . His complexion still a touch yellow." Liszt was counting on Janin's help with a French translation of his cantata, and they shut themselves up to start work immediately. Janin had disliked the original German text—"Pompous nonsense," he told his wife. But having felt that he was being asked the impossible, Janin managed to come up with a libretto in two days that pleased both men. By way of celebration, he invited Liszt to accompany him to the premiere of the new Dumas play.

The Ambigu-Comique was filled to capacity that night, not with the usual elegant first-night audience but with the kind of crowd attracted by popular spectacles like *The Three Musketeers,* a melodrama lasting six hours. "There were more caps than hats with feathers, and more threadbare overcoats than new suits," wrote Janin. Marie's appearance created an extraordinary effect. "It seemed as if she illumined all these burlesque, uncultivated beings with a glance of her lovely eyes. She came into the room and moved, her head erect, through the astonished rabble."

Liszt's own version, told to his Hungarian compatriot the journalist Janka Wohl, was that "a very conspicuous young woman" had walked past them during an interval and stared intently at him.

—She has taken a fancy to you, Janin said.

—What an idea! exclaimed Liszt, who was disarmed, all the same, by the young woman's attention.

—Do you know her?

—No. Who is she? Liszt asked.

—That is Madame Duplessis. She'll take possession of you— mark my words.

Marie knew Liszt by sight because she had been at one of the concerts he gave in Paris, in either the spring or early summer of 1844. Intrigued to see if this passionate, demonic genius lived up to his rapturous acclaim, she had found herself so moved by his performance that she was inspired to start learning the instru-- ment herself. She rented a piano and began buying increasingly challenging scores of popular tunes like "The Blue Danube" and Weber's "Invitation to the Waltz," the piece that Dumas fils's novel describes Marguerite trying and failing to master. One passage in particular always defeated her—"the third part with all the sharps"—and sometimes she would practice it until the early hours of the morning. Instructing Armand's friend Gaston to play it for her, Marguerite intently follows each note on the page, softly humming along and silently moving her fingers on the top of the piano. "Re, mi, re, do, re, fa, mi, re. That's what I can never do," she sighs. "Invitation to the Waltz" was a favorite in Liszt's repertory, and if Marie had heard his version, the memory would have made mockery of her own workaday attempts. His music transcended the piano, which seemed to vanish before people's eyes, giving the audience the sensation that he was calling up mysterious living forms—"as if the air were peopled with spirits," as one spectator put it. This was Marie's experience too. The first words she spoke to Liszt was that his playing had "set [her] dreaming."

He had been at a table by the fire with Janin when she came over and sat beside them. "We were very much surprised for neither he nor I had ever spoken to her," Janin writes, noting how her familiarity soon gave way to an element of hauteur "as if [Liszt] had been presented to her at a levee in London, or at a party given by the Duchess of Sutherland." Visibly shivering, Marie had drawn near the flames, her feet almost touching the logs, allowing a glimpse of the embroidered folds of her petticoat. As she and Liszt fell into conversation, Janin observed her closely, admiring everything he saw.

> The curls of her black hair; her gloved hand, which made you think you were looking at a picture; her handkerchief marvelously trimmed with costly lace; whilst in her ears shone two pearls from the East which a queen would envy. All these beautiful objects were as natural to her as if she had been born amidst silks and velvet, beneath some gilded ceiling of the grand faubourgs with a crown upon her head, and a crowd of flatterers at her feet.

He was supposed to be reviewing the play for the *Journal des Débats* but, sitting with Liszt in the foyer, was reduced to listening to the cries of bravo and stomping of feet heard throughout the six hours. Guilt may have been the cause of Janin's bad temper—"I am convinced that the lady thought me grumpy and perfectly absurd"—or else the fact that Marie hardly addressed a word to him, except once or twice out of politeness. But it was hardly surprising that the enormously rotund, white-haired, whiskery Janin held no allure for her. It was Liszt who had captivated her, and they talked as if they were alone together throughout the whole of the third act.

On first hearing Liszt's vibrant, original conversation, Marie d'Agoult had felt a new world opening up. It was an impression Marie Duplessis must have shared. The pianist's itinerant life had led him to all of Europe's landmarks and museums, giving him an exotic air of having knowledge in reserve, of horizons far beyond the narrow Parisian beau monde. His initial exchange with Marie d'Agoult had been serious, she said. "We embarked at once upon elevated subjects . . . talked of the destiny of mankind, of its sadness and incertitude, of the soul and of God. . . . Nothing of coquetry or of gallantry was blended with our intimacy." In the Ambigu foyer with Marie, on the other hand, Liszt ran through the usual gossip and fashionable small talk, almost certainly laughing about their mutual acquaintance Lola Montez, who had ambushed him in Bonn. Claiming to be there as his guest and undaunted by the fact she was completely ignored by Liszt, Lola had then gate-crashed the international banquet and created an uproar by springing up onto a table strewn with bottles and glasses—a performance that almost eclipsed everything that had gone before it.

Liszt was adept at talking to women, moving from topic to topic, frivolous at one moment, erudite the next. And he clearly drew the best out of Marie, as both men were struck by her intelligence, tact, and common sense. Liszt, Janin says, totally abandoned himself to her, "listening with uninterrupted attention to her beautiful language, so full of ideas, and, at the same time, so eloquent and pensive." He kept asking questions, trying to discover more about this exceptional young woman, who lacked all protocol yet was full of dignity.

The next day a mutual friend offered to take Liszt to Marie's house. This was her Prussian doctor, David Koreff, whose patients also included Marie d'Agoult and Liszt's mother. Koreff was often used as a go-between, according to Flaubert's friend Maxime du Camp: "If a salonnière wanted to invite an artist or writer of renown she turned to Koreff to make the introduction."

A highly sought after guest in his own right, Koreff would far rather have been celebrated as a poet, translator, and librettist than as a physician. Marie had not been treated by Koreff for several months, but she continued to invite him to boulevard de la Madeleine, knowing that few grand soirées were given without him. She was no doubt also aware that Marie d'Agoult had set a high precedent for Liszt. In her salon in the Hôtel de France, George Sand had been introduced to Chopin, an encounter that marked the start of their ten-year affair, and the countess prided herself on her skillful mix of guests, telling Liszt, "Koreff said the other day that I will soon have a circle such as Paris has never seen."

It was not unknown for a demimondaine to establish a distinguished salon. The Second Empire courtesan known as La Païva, also a mistress of Agénor de Guiche, had married into the aristocracy despite being born in a Moscow ghetto and held court in the most opulent private house in Paris. Guests at the Hôtel Païva included Gautier and Delacroix, who, though disturbed by its overwhelming luxury, rarely refused an invitation. A combination of money and willpower had allowed La Païva to surround herself with some of the great men of her time, although, to her chagrin, she never gained recognition in French society. Marie, too, had no opportunity to learn the art of entertaining from the celebrated *salonnières* of the day, but her presence at dinners given by friends like Roger de Beauvoir and Nestor Roqueplan would have taught her everything she needed to know. An intimate gathering at Roqueplan's sumptuous apartment on the rue Le Peletier was a blueprint of how to receive. His guests—five or six like-minded men and a cluster of decorative women—would move from the crimson, damask-lined drawing room, where they had been surrounded by Louis XIII furniture, paintings, and sculptures, to the oblong dining room hung with antique Gobelin tapestries. A discreet, white-haired butler served each course—a menu that rarely changed: consommé, fish, roast meat, salad, cheese, and dessert. Roqueplan detested the "abominable inventions and falsifications of modern cuisine" and would tolerate only simple, provincial cooking. But if the cuisine hardly varied, the ingredients were sourced from the best merchants in Les Halles, just as the single wine on offer was "such that old vignerons would drink at the wedding of their only daughter." Two years earlier Marie's dinners had been frivolous, decadent occasions, but now, by assembling brilliant performers at her table and serving choice dishes from La Maison d'Or, she had achieved the renown she coveted. "The Lady of the Camellias had her own salon where others of her kind had no more than a dressing room," wrote an admiring Arsène Houssaye.

Liszt was certainly satisfied. "All the best people of Paris were there," he told Janka Wohl, who mentions the presence of writers and artists and singles out the Duke of Ossuna, a member of one of the oldest and richest families in Spain. "Liszt went there often after this." Drawn to strong-willed, independent women, he had been unfazed by Marie's making the first move (Marie d'Agoult had also been the instigator of their affair). Nor was he under any illusions about the origin of her wealth and position. "I am not partial as a rule to Marions de Lorme or Manons Lescaut," he told Wohl, "but Marie Duplessis was an exception. . . . I maintain that she was unique of her kind." He knew that she was ill, because Koreff had confided poignant details about her suffering, and Marie herself could not have been more frank. "I shall not live," she told Liszt, an avowal that affected him greatly (he had lost a brother to consumption). He found himself forming "a somber and elegiac attachment" for "Mariette," as he called her, while at the same time being enchanted by her joie de vivre and childish abandon. "[She] was certainly the most perfect incarnation of Woman who has ever existed."

Apart from Koreff, whom Liszt acknowledged as the one who helped him to appreciate her in a more profound way, his liaison with Marie was known to few. He met the young Dumas at one of her soirées and would later admire his fictional depiction of Marie, telling Wohl that Dumas completely understood her and could create her again with great ease. Nestor Roqueplan was aware of the situation, as he includes "the illustrious pianist L." among Marie's lovers. The fact that Liszt was still alive in 1887, when Vienne's memoir was published, may explain why he gives no hint of a romance, saying only that Liszt went twice to Marie's salon. Very probably, this was a relationship that Marie kept to herself, though Liszt could not help confiding his feelings to Marie d'Agoult. "I have never told you how strangely attached to this delightful creature I became during my last visit to Paris," he wrote. "Hers was a truly delightful nature in which practices commonly held to be corrupting (and rightly so, perhaps) never touched her soul."

In late January 1846 he was to embark on the most arduous tour of his life, traveling for eighteen months through northern France, Austria, Romania, Hungary, Transylvania, Russia, and Turkey. After that, he planned to abandon the concert platform altogether and settle in Weimar, where he had been appointed director of court music. The current duke, Carl Alexander, emulating the Renaissance-style patronage of his grandfather, wanted to reestablish the city as a haven for artists and intellectuals, and Liszt had ambitions of his own for Weimar. While concentrating on composing and conducting, he intended to create a workshop environment to convert audiences to "difficult" music. He had felt engulfed recently, not only by his impossibly demanding performing schedules but also by his spiraling dissipation—what he called "excitements . . . leading to disgust and remorse."

Marie, too, had reached a point of satiety. "I shan't be able to hold on to this life which I don't know how not to lead and which I can equally no longer endure," she told Liszt, seeing him as someone who could deliver her from this vortex of her own. "Take me, take me anywhere you like," she pleaded. "I shan't bother you. I sleep all day. In the evening you can let me go to the theater, and at night you can do with me what you will." Weimar was where she wanted to be, but Liszt pointed out that there would be certain inconveniences. What he must have thought, but did not say, was that in this anachronistic little duchy, a woman with Marie's past would be an embarrassment to him—almost certainly not received at court, perhaps even shunned by the townspeople. Nor was he willing to consider marriage an option. As he remarked to novelist Fanny Lewald, "I know I am easiest to get on with when I keep my freedom, and that it's risky to tie me down, to a person or a place."

The reason he gave Marie, however, was that Weimar would be dull and provincial after Paris and that she would soon regret her decision. Marie made clear that she did not agree, but she was given no choice. Liszt suggested that they meet the following summer in Pest and then travel together to Constantinople, where he was to spend most of June 1847. The site of Byzantium, source of spiritual philosophy, saturated with fable and mystery, was a place of wonder to Liszt. "I want to breathe in perfume, exchange coal smoke for the gentle whiff of the narghile. In short, I long for the East," he had exclaimed to Marie d'Agoult. It was somewhere he had planned to take her, too, at the height of their romance, and she can only have felt a stab of regret in learning of Liszt's arrangement with Marie Duplessis. "That was the only reasonably possible journey I could get her to undertake," he told her, "the prospect of which delighted her."

As a farewell to Paris, Liszt had arranged for his cantata to be premiered—not at the Opéra or Conservatoire, as might be expected, but at Jules Janin's house on the rue de Vaugirard. For Marie, this was a cruel blow. The guests were a mix of Parisian elite—musicians, Chopin among them, writers, lawyers, artists, and actors. Rose-Chérie, soon to be cast as the eponymous heroine of Janin's stage adaptation *Clarisse Harlow,* was there engulfed by admirers, but Marie, who was the same age, much prettier, and an intimate friend of Liszt, had not been invited. "You would have looked in vain in the very highest circles for a woman who was more beautiful and in more complete harmony with her jewelry, her dress, and her conversation" are Janin's words. He was one of Marie's greatest champions, but not when it came to having her in his home. In two published volumes, *735 Letters to His Wife*, Janin never once mentions Marie's name, and in his preface to the 1850 edition of *La dame aux camélias*, recounting the Ambigu meeting, she is not "Madame Duplessis," the femme fatale he described to Liszt, but "the unknown lady."

Liszt left Paris immediately after Janin's soirée and would not see his children for another eight years. If he stayed in touch with Marie on tour, no letters have been discovered. However, in the archives of Pleyel et Cie, a vertical piano costing 1,400 francs was billed to a "M{onsieur} Duplessis" in July 1846. Was this a memento from Liszt? It would have been a characteristic gesture (he made a gift of a Streicher piano to his friend Prince Lichnowsky), and one befitting a lover considered by Roqueplan to be "as generous with Marie as a Russian prince en passage."

The second time Jules Janin saw Marie was at a grand benefit at the Opéra. The door of one of the boxes was pulled open, and he glimpsed her inside with a bouquet in her hand. "Her beautiful hair was delightfully intermingled with flowers and diamonds . . . her arms and bosom were bare, though she wore a necklace and bracelets of emeralds." Janin remembered this as the autumn of 1846, but it was more likely to have been the gala held in honor of the opera singer Paul Barroilhet on Sunday, 10 February 1846, in which the performers he mentions (actors Rachel, Virginie Déjazet, and Bouffé and ballerina Carlotta Grisi) all appeared. Later in the evening, the Opéra's first tenor, Gilbert Duprez, took the stage, and Janin looked across the auditorium at Marie to see her reaction. Duprez was famous for his high C delivered from the chest, but the physical strain required to produce this sound (variously described as the shriek of a capon being strangled or a cry of the soul) had hardened his voice. The deterioration, which was first noticed as early as 1838, had increased over the following decade and would force the singer into early retirement in 1849. On this particular evening, it was clear to the cognescenti, though not yet to the public, Janin says, that Duprez was well past his prime. "Only a few amateurs amongst the most attentive part of the audience noticed the artist's fatigue and his exhaustion. This was in spite of his skill—because he still made great efforts to deceive himself." Marie appeared to be one of Duprez's shrewder critics. After listening for the first few minutes she was obviously unimpressed and picked up her opera glasses to turn them on the audience instead.

> Indiscriminately, she looked here and there, without bestowing more attention on one than on another, as if indifferent to all, while everyone repaid her attention by a smile, a rapid gesture, or a sharp and quick glance. Lastly, as if by chance, she directed her opera-glasses on the most renowned female members of the Parisian upper classes, and there was suddenly in her attitude an indescribable air of resignation and humility, which was painful to behold. But if, on the other hand, her glance happened to alight on any of those women of doubtful reputation and charming face, who occupy the best stalls of the theatre on grand occasions, she turned her head away with bitterness.
>
> The gentleman who accompanied her this time was a handsome young man . . . proud of this beauty, and not sorry to increase his own importance by showing that she was really his. But he seemed to be irritating her with those signs of attention so dear to a young creature when they come from the man she loves, and so disagreeable when they are addressed to a mind otherwise occupied. She listened to him without hearing him; she looked at

him without seeing him. What did he say? The lady had not heard him; but she endeavoured to answer, and the few words she uttered, and which contained no meaning, fatigued her. . . . At the conclusion of the opera the beautiful creature left: the performance was scarcely half over; she wanted to leave at once and return home, when many people still had three hours of pleasure before them, amidst the sound of music and underneath the flaming chandeliers.

I saw her leave her box and wrap herself up in a cloak lined with costly ermine. Her companion appeared out of temper, and, as he could no longer show her off, did not care whether she felt cold or not. I even recollect I helped lift her cloak on her shoulders, which were very white, and then she looked at me, without recognizing me, with a gentle mournful smile, which she transferred to the tall young man, who at that moment was engaged in paying the box-keeper, and in making her change a five-franc piece. "Keep it all, Madame," she said to the woman, bowing to her politely. I saw her come down the grand staircase, her white dress standing out against the red cloak, with a handkerchief over her head and fastened under her chin; the lace fell slightly over her eyes, but what did that matter? The lady had played her part, her day's work was finished, and she no longer thought of appearing attractive. No doubt that evening she left the young man at her door.

If this was in February, then Marie's escort was almost certainly Ned Perregaux. She had not undergone a sudden change of heart (Janin's observation of her inattentiveness rings true), but she had good reason to seek his company. Now that she had reached the age of consent, she was more determined than ever to marry him. Toward the end of January she had applied for a passport, having convinced Ned that they should have the ceremony in England, where the Perregauxs' consent would not be required. Incapable of refusing Marie anything, he had agreed, while reminding her that the marriage would be invalid in France. What he did not know—but Marie did, according to Vienne—was that annulling it would require the intervention of a French tribunal. Vienne felt that she was sure Ned's family would not go that far for fear of scandal, and he was convinced that the sale of their Bougival house for forty thousand francs provided the funds for the journey to London.

They were married at Kensington registry office on 21 February 1846 in the presence of two witnesses, F. Ferry and H. Blackwell. The certificate, written in English, confirms the groom to be "Edward de Perregaux, 29 years, bachelor; son of Alphonse de Perregaux. Rank or profession of father: Count." The bride is "Alphonsine Plessis, 22 years. Father's name: Jean Plessis. Rank: Gentleman." Their residence is given as 37 Brompton Row, Kensington.

Apart from this document there is no information about their trip. There was a program of French plays at the St. James's Theatre and a new opera of *Don Quixote* at the Theatre Royal, Drury Lane, but if Ned and Marie were in the audience or at any fashionable London event that week, their names do not appear in the society columns, and there is no announcement of their marriage in *The Times*. Méjannes, who knew about the secret Kensington ceremony, claimed that after their wedding Perregaux did not see his wife again, although a chilly, formal note from Marie suggests otherwise.

> *My dear Edouard,*
> *In everything that you wrote to me I see only one thing to which you wish me to respond, here it is: you want me to tell you in writing that you are free to do whatever seems fitting. I told you that myself yesterday, I'm repeating this to you and signing,*
> *Marie Duplessis*

What had caused their acrimonious falling-out can only be guessed. The most obvious motive for Marie's determination to become a countess was to make herself respectable for a life in Weimar with Liszt. Could Ned have discovered this? Vienne sheds no light on the cause of the rupture, saying only that the couple continued to see each other after returning to Paris, but their marriage had made them no closer. "Marie did not receive or hope for more from [Ned]. . . . It was not the status of having a husband that was important to her, it was the title. This astute young girl attached no importance of her own to such trifles, but she knew, from what she had observed, that it is with pomp and finery that one dazzles in this world."

In the case of Marie d'Agoult, a countess in her own right, with a husband she had not divorced, there had been no need for subterfuge. She and Liszt had lived openly together with a romantic disdain for bourgeois conventions. Of humble birth—Liszt's mother had been a chambermaid—he was impressed by nobility and eager to aggrandize himself. When it was mistakenly suggested that he might have been of aristocratic descent, Liszt went out of his way to search for documents to prove it and wrote to Marie d'Agoult for advice on the design of a coat of arms. Marie was unlikely to have been aware of this, but as she wanted so badly to be with Liszt in Weimar, her manipulation of Ned seems as logical as it was callous. On the other hand, her ambition to be a countess had long predated her meeting with Liszt. In 1844 she had described herself to a trader as "Mme la Comtesse Deperegaud" [*sic*] and in the well-known miniature painted around this time by society portraitist Edouard Vienot, she wears the diadem of a countess. "Having noble pretensions," as Johannes Gros remarked, "was the great vanity of her life."

Within weeks of her return to Paris, Marie was flaunting her new status. She was not brazen enough to use the Perregaux name, but there were bills made out to "Madame la Comtesse du Plessis," and a heraldic crest, which she had designed herself, was printed on a panel of her carriage and on her linen, silver, and china. She had copied the central motif of the Perregaux arms (three chevrons of sand on a badge with a crown above it) but replaced the supports of two bears with a lion and a unicorn. She seems to have known the tapestry *La dame à la licorne,* in which a tame unicorn gazes at its reflection in a mirror, because she borrowed the idea, substituting a lizard. This was Marie's private joke. It was inspired by the stuffed green lizard given to her by Gypsies en route to Paris, which she kept in a shagreen box. If the unicorn represents purity and the lizard temptation, then the pairing of the two aptly symbolizes her own dual nature.

The Ornais historian Robert du Mesnil du Buisson, who made the *Dame à la licorne* link, also discovered a portrait he believed to be of Marie in a local château. It shows a pensive young girl sitting at a table. Her cheek is inclining on her left hand, where her wedding ring is ostentatiously displayed, and her other hand rests on a folded letter, next to which is a stamp of a coat of arms and an ink block. The painting is unsigned, and research by the current owners of Château Le Logis in Fels revealed that the dates do not correspond, so it could not be a painting of the real Lady of the Camellias. Nevertheless, it can still be seen as a potent image of Marie at this time, and the likeness to her is striking: the same oval face, parted black hair, straight nose, black eyes, heavy brows, and curly, Leonardo mouth. As if sensitive to the cold, she wears a heavily padded silk gown over her lacy top—a solitary and melancholy young bride.

Before she fell ill, Marie's religious feelings had been vague and sentimental—a mix, Vienne says, of spiritualism and mysticism with sudden fears and superstitions. Mme Judith thought it no coincidence that Marie's apartment almost directly faced the church of La Madeleine, as if she wanted to be protected by the saint who had traded on her beauty before giving herself to God.

Did Marie take comfort from Marochetti's High Altar, a marble figure of Mary Magdalene borne heavenward by three powerful angels? Vienne noted how she had developed a strange attraction to her patron saint and was attending mass at La Madeleine more and more frequently. She had recently bought a tapestry-covered prie-dieu, and her rosary was said to have been blessed by Pope Leo XII. Arriving at boulevard de la Madeleine on one of his visits that winter, Romain was warned by Clotilde to be quiet, and through Marie's open bedroom door he saw that she was kneeling on her prie-dieu. When she came into the salon some minutes later to greet him, she thanked him for not interrupting her. "When I pray I find a real sense of relief."

Vienne says that for several months after her marriage, Marie took on no new protector, turning down all propositions out of gratitude for what Ned had done for her. Her debts, amounting to nearly thirty thousand francs, bear this out: 1,449 francs owed for linen, 250 to her vet, 225 for unpaid laundry bills . . . and she made nineteen transactions at the Mont-de-Piété to pawn jewels and other valuables in return for cash. In April she was sued by her lingerie merchant and could not pay the rent of her stable, yet she gave no outward sign of any change in her circumstances. In the early afternoon of April 25, her carriage was spotted among a procession on the boulevard des Invalides, the starting point for demimondaines, aristocrats, and ordinary Parisians in a crush of cabs, chariots, phaetons, and landaus en route to Croix de Berny races. "I can see her now," writes Charles du Hays, "pale and distressed, all dressed in white, in her faded green landau borne along at full trot by four splendid white horses." Marie's main reason for being there was to watch the steeplechase of gentleman riders performing feats of horsemanship over hedges and ditches in the great meadow. One of the two chosen to represent France, displaying more courage than good fortune, was a mud-spattered Ned Perregaux.

By May 1846 she had taken on a wealthy new lover—

eighteen-year-old Count Olympe Aguado de las Marismas, whose father, the late marquis, had left a legacy estimated at between 35 million and 65 million francs. The first nineteenth-century banker to acquire a Bordeaux château, Château Margaux, the Marquis de las Marismas also owned an immense and important art collection and was close both to the imperial court and to renowned artists and musicians of his era. (Rossini composed a cantata for Olympe's baptism.) Wanting to link the two great Spanish families of Aguado and Montijo, he had ambitions for Olympe to marry Eugénie, later empress consort of France, but he died in 1842, when his son was still an adolescent. Having inherited his father's passion for art as well as his fortune, Olympe studied drawing at Henry IV College before entering le beau monde, becoming an habitué of the *foyer de la danse* and a member of the Jockey Club. With his theatrical black beard, hair combed forward, and hefty build, he was not especially good-looking but was highly sought after by women. "Thanks to his opulence, he had a number of mistresses on the go, without counting those in reserve," says Vienne, who disguises the young count as Gaston de Morenas and evidently approved of his easygoing character and kind heart. Olympe had made clear to Marie from the start, Vienne maintains, that he did not want a long, complicated relationship, but, at the same time, he realized that she was too special to be just a passing fling. Olympe was loyal, sweet-natured, and generous, and Marie had complete confidence in him, acquiescing to demands she would refuse any other lover.

To illustrate this, Vienne presents a scene in which the dialogue is invented, as he was not there, but the story itself is convincing and could have been passed on to him by Marie or Olympe. A group of women in a sumptuous drawing room are discussing the lovely young girl they have often seen in her box at the theater. Propriety forbids them to invite her to their salon, and they cannot visit hers. "I wish I could talk to her incognito," says one, "so that I could see for myself whether she deserves the praise lavished on her by men." Aware that Marie Duplessis is "not unknown" to Olympe, they ask him to think up a pretext for them to meet her. Her work for charity might be the answer, he says, as she had always been discreetly generous to the needy—especially to girls of ill repute. The women each pledge between five hundred and one thousand francs, and Olympe makes them promise that if he brings the courtesan to see them, they will ask no personal questions. He then pays a visit to Marie, telling her that he has organized a collection for orphaned girls, and asks for her cooperation. She immediately reaches for her purse, but Olympe says that he needs more from her than a donation: he wants her to take on the role of patroness and collect funds from the women of the grands faubourgs herself. Marie is shocked—"I'll be chased away by their valets"—but Olympe vows to be her escort, reassuring her that any injurious remarks would have to be made in his presence. "Anyone else would have failed in this proposal," writes Vienne, "but [Olympe] occupied an exceptional place in Marie's esteem."

On the day of the rendezvous, everyone present was in on the secret. Marie was pale and trembling as she entered the room but gained confidence from the murmur of approval that greeted her arrival. She had dressed with simple, almost severe elegance, and as the women chatted to her on all manner of subjects, they were struck by her dignity, tact, and eloquence. "She's enchanting," the hostess whispered to Olympe, remarking how unfortunate it was that a woman so distinguished should be lost to society. She was, indeed, a fine girl, he replied, and it was through no fault of her own that she had been thrown into a life of vice. "You must pity her and not condemn her." When Marie took around the collection box, only one woman was frosty toward her. Vienne calls her the Countess de la Brosse, but she is very likely to have been Valentine Delessert, whose eighteen-year-old son, Edouard, was one of Olympe's closest friends. Wife of Gabriel Delessert, the prefect of police, she was hardly a model of convention herself, being mistress for ten years of Prosper Mérimée, the author of *Carmen*. But what either irked or embarrassed her was that she knew her own son was infatuated with Marie. A protégé of Mérimée, who helped him with his first attempts at writing, Edouard Delessert was a painter, archaeologist, and soon to be (along with Olympe) one of France's first photographers. "A delicious young man," wrote an acquaintance, "of a grand culture and chivalrous heart . . . he had read everything, seen everything, knew everything." Marie would undoubtedly have enjoyed Edouard's company, but she asked Olympe to discourage him from pursuing her. She could not face another young man's declaration of undying passion, she told him, but her real reason, according to Vienne, was the respect she felt for Edouard's mother. Because Mme Delessert had been gracious enough to receive her, she felt it would be tasteless to accept the attentions of her son.

It was Olympe who introduced Marie to Aguado's personal physician, Casimir Davaine. A precursor of Louis Pasteur in discovering the role of microbes in infectious diseases, Davaine would like to have concentrated on scientific research but was too generous with the time he devoted to his patients. (He was with the Aguados in Spain when the marquis collapsed during a meal and never recovered.) A nature lover, he believed that health is the principal element of happiness, and he suggested to Marie that she should to go for a rest cure to the countryside. Heeding his advice, she went back to Normandy, staying with her great-uncle Louis Mesnil, now a widower, in La Trouillère. Living nearby with her new husband, Constant Paquet, a weaver, was Delphine, whose modest, respectable life Marie could not help envying. "She has done a thousand times better by staying in the village," she would remark to Romain. "How much happier she is. . . . And how misguided I was to have tried to persuade her to live a life like mine!" And yet, when Clotilde arrived after little more than a fortnight, saying that she was wanted back in Paris, Marie needed no persuasion to return.

Olympe planned to take her on a tour of the German spas, but first they were to travel to Brussels for the social event of the summer. This was the inauguration of the Great Northern Railway, launching a new line from Paris whose significance for a new era of European travel was greeted with excitement (Berlioz had composed a cantata in celebration). "Over there is the Ocean and the Mediterranean, behind is England . . . the world and Paris at the center of the universe!" exclaimed Jules Janin, one of numerous journalists covering the occasion. Assembling a spectacular wardrobe for the trip but more susceptible than ever to feverish chills, even in June, Marie had ordered a selection of furs from Révillon to be delivered to her on deposit—coats of ermine, sable, and wolf. Vienne says that the couple left in a *chaise de poste* "without having said goodbye to anyone," but in fact the cortege bound for Brussels traveled from Paris by train. At four in the morning on Saturday, June 13, three thousand people set off on the journey, although only three hundred would attend the grand soirée the following evening. It was an impressive gathering, according to Janin, a "moving mass of nations"— the royalty and nobility of Belgium, France, Germany, Spain, and Flanders—uniformed men decked with medals, dowagers displaying ancient jewels, and Europe's most elegant women. Marie, although more pallid than usual, stood out among them all, writes Janin.

> She had gained admission to the ball in spite of her reputation, favored by her dazzling beauty. . . . A flattering frisson greeted her as she passed along, and even those who knew her identity bowed; while she, calm and dignified as ever, accepted this homage as though it were her due. . . .

More than one prince stopped to gaze at her, and she knew exactly the meaning of their looks: "I think you are very splendid, and I'm sorry I have to let you go."

That evening she was leaning on the arm of a stranger, as fair as a German, and as sedate as an Englishman, over-dressed, with clothes fitting him too tightly, who was walking quite erect, and believing that he was committing one of those acts of derring-do, which men regret to their dying day. This gentleman's demeanour displeased the sensitive girl on his arm; she felt it with that sixth sense within her, and she became haughtier, for her shrewd instinct told her that the more this man was ashamed of what he had done, the more insolent she should show herself to be, and con-temptuously trample under foot the remorse of the timid youth.

This was the young blond man named Prince Paul by Vienne. "He had regular features, eyes pale and lustreless; thick, sensual lips—a physique that altogether lacked expression. There was a touch of English haughtiness in his attitude and of Teutonic stiffness in his manners, which was unsympathetic. . . . On first acquaintance one judged him unfavorably." Vienne describes him as being very close to Liszt, but, if so, he was not known to Janin, who watched Marie punish the "Anglo-German" for his reservations about her. At the end of a long, well-lit corridor, she caught sight of someone she knew—"a friend without any pre-tensions . . . one of our own acquaintances, an artist, a painter." Clearly, this was Olympe Aguado. "Ah, here you are!" she said to him; "give me your arm, and let us have a dance." Abandoning her companion, she began a Strauss waltz.

She danced marvellously . . . scarcely touching the ground with her light feet, now bounding, then pausing, keeping her eyes fixed on those of her partner. A circle formed round her; everyone tried to be brushed by her beautiful hair, which followed the movement of the rapid waltz, and everyone strove to be grazed by her light dress, exhaling such delicate perfumes.

From Brussels Marie went on to Spa, where the doctors insisted that she must rest more to restore her health. For a few days she did as she was told, going for walks or reading quietly under the trees. She wrote a letter while she was there to her horse dealer, Tony, who had become extremely attached to her.

Dear friend, don't be too resentful about my negligence in writing to you, and please don't think that it is due to forgetfulness or indifference towards you. I am very happy about your friendship, but you know, that among my numerous faults, laziness is not the last on the list.

You must understand that my long country walks do not encourage me to write stylishly, and far from accusing me, you should appreciate the tremendous effort I am making to overcome the sleepiness that overwhelms me.

Goodbye, dear Tony, no more, otherwise I am afraid of boring you, so goodbye, with a thousand good wishes,
Marie Duplessis.

A thousand thanks for your sympathy towards me. Dear, do not sell my carriage.
Soon, I will have the pleasure of seeing you, at least I hope so.
MD

But her good intentions were in vain. She was seen by day on horseback, recklessly clearing high hedges, and spending most of her evening hours in the casino. "In Spa no other fever is known than ball fever, no other remedies but those of talking, dancing, music and the excitement of gambling," writes Janin, who, needless to say, was there himself, noting Marie's every move.

> Our fair friend was welcomed with an eagerness somewhat rare in this rather prudish village. . . . Soon she became the lioness of this beautiful spot, and the life and spirit of every party and ball. She made the orchestra play her favorite tunes; and when night came, when a little sleep would have done her so much good, she terrified the most intrepid gamblers by the heaps of gold she piled up before her, and lost at a single stake, as indifferent to gain as she was to loss.

In his book *Consumptives and Great Lovers,* Dr. Cabanes sees this kind of euphoria as a symptom of the disease. He quotes a remark made by the eighteenth-century *salonnière* Julie de Lespinasse, in a letter to a friend, "I do not know if it is my ill health," she wrote, "but I have never been so pressed to live."

Marie's frenzied routine was not appreciated by Olympe, who had left Paris to relax and be reinvigorated by the mountains and panoramas. The count was happiest when he was somewhere wild and rustic, Vienne says, and his sketches capture his passion for nature—poetic studies of landscapes flooded with sunlight, trees reflected in water, woods casting mysterious shadows—the tranquil, topographical scenes that would define his pioneering photographs a decade later. But despite his own inclinations he understood the reason for Marie's fast living and put two hundred thousand francs at her disposal. In three weeks she had lost half, according to Vienne, only to win most of it back again. "Losses left her indifferent, gain only gave her mediocre satisfaction," he says, echoing Janin's remark.

Either with or without Olympe, Marie then traveled to Baden-Baden, staying once again at the Hôtel de l'Europe, before moving on to Biebrich, Koblenz, Wiesbaden, and Ems. And then, suddenly, it was all too much. Her philosophy of carpe diem, of squeezing pleasure out of every second, seemed pathetically superficial now that death loomed so close. What she began to crave was some kind of spiritual redemption—her own *Traviata* moment of reconciliation and atonement. Feeling ashamed of her treatment of Ned Perregaux, she wrote him a farewell letter.

> *Pardon me, my dear Edouard, I kneel to you in begging your forgiveness. If you love me enough for this I ask of you only two words, my pardon and your friendship. Write to me, poste restante at Ems, duchy of Nassau. I am alone here and very ill. So, dear Edouard, quickly, your forgiveness.*
> *Adieu.*

———

By mid-September, Marie was back in Paris, trying out all manner of remedies, each offering a touch of hope. She ordered packets of sulfate of quinine, almond milk, a lichen tisane, a syrup of asparagus spears, and bottles of asses' milk (an ancient Arabic cure for diarrhea). Nothing, though, could relieve her insomnia, and she would pace her apartment throughout the night, talking to a yellow-and-blue parrot perched on her shoulder or to the dogs she adored—spaniels Duchesse and Chéri, and Dache, a magnificent hunter. Sometimes she was seen on her balcony above the boulevard, her head draped in a cashmere shawl, her thin frame lost in a copious white dressing gown. "When the night was pitch black, it was like seeing an apparition." Marie's neighbor Clémence Prat was a rare visitor, always making some excuse for her absence, as Marie was no longer of use to her.

Tuberculosis in its final stages is anything but romantic, with the dying incapacitated by paroxysmal coughs, chills, and night sweats, visibly wasting away as the disease spreads to other organs of the body. Almost all Marie's friends had abandoned her, and watching Paris life go on in the street below her window, she felt as solitary as Marguerite. "I saw some faces I knew. They passed rapidly, joyous and carefree, but not one lifted his eyes to my window."

Her affair with Olympe was over. They had made a pact to part on their return to Paris, while remaining good friends. He told Marie that he wanted to keep his freedom and have only casual liaisons, but this was not the case. In 1846, Olympe became deeply involved with a countess married to an Englishman, a Mrs. Adrian Hope, who remained his mistress for the next five years. When Romain visited Marie, she was in tears over Olympe, whom she said she had come to love without his knowing it. Olympe, though, was true to his word about their friendship. He remained as generous as ever, and he went out of his way to spend time with her.

Over the next few months, Marie's most frequent visitors were her doctors, although they could only helplessly watch her die. Dr. Manec of La Salpêtrière saw her thirty-nine times between mid-September and November, while Dr. Davaine, who had become her main consultant, went eighty-four times during the same period. One of her notes to him has survived—a couple of lines scribbled on her white writing paper with its blue coat of arms:

Monday 10 o'clock

Mon cher Monsieur,
Be kind enough to come and see me today 28 September at 3 o'clock. Mille amitiés. Marie Duplessis.

With his kind, pinkish face, white curly hair, and steel-rimmed spectacles on a chain, Davaine was a comforting presence. Marie gave him her miniature by Edouard Vienot, the portrait that best captures her demure appeal, showing her long black *anglaises* and signature corsage of a white camellia. In the opera, Violetta gives Alfredo one such medallion to pass on to his future wife. It is a gesture heavy with sentiment and self-abnegation ("Tell her it's the gift of one who from heaven, amongst the angels, prays always for her and for you"). The gift to Davaine, on the other hand, was characteristic of Marie—gracious and practical. It was to show gratitude for the fact that he would accept only a token fee.

Davaine must have decided to seek advice on Marie's treatment from King Louis-Philippe's personal consultant Auguste-François Chomel (a descendant of Jean-Baptiste Chomel, Louis XIV's doctor). She had four consultations with Chomel, who is cosignatory with Davaine on three elaborate prescriptions:

THE UNDERSIGNED DOCTORS ARE OF THE OPINION THAT
MADAME DUPLESSIS SHOULD:
Every evening massage her armpits with a pomade of potassium iodide one part to ten, the size of a hazel-nut.
Continue with the same alternating liquids with a solution of *Fucus crispus.*
She should return to the asses' milk sweetened with syrup of fern.
As an aid to sleep, she should take in the evening a mixture of equal parts of sweet milk of almonds and bitter milk of almonds, each of sixty grams. To this milk of almonds should be added 2–5 grams of extract of opium.
To moderate her sweating every day in the first spoonful of soup she should put 1 or 2 grams of soft extract of cinchona wrapped in a piece of wafer.
The diet consists of soup or bouillon of rice, fresh eggs à la coque or boiled, white fish grilled or steamed, poultry, vegetables lightly boiled, bread containing very little wheat, a compote of fruits, of jams, hot chocolate for lunch. To be drunk with meals, eau de Bussang mixed with a 6th of wine.
She should go out whenever the mildness of the weather

permits, between noon and three o'clock. She should not go out at all in the morning or evening until further notice. She should lie on horsehair in preference to wool. She should speak little, and never in a loud voice.

THE UNDERSIGNED PHYSICIANS ARE OF THE OPINION THAT MME DUPLESSIS SHOULD:

Take in the morning of every day an enema prepared with a solution of starch in which is dissolved a little vinegar, 30 grams of sulfate of quinine and she should hold this in for as long as possible.

She should replace the decoction of *Fucus crispus* with Tussilage sweetened with syrup of marshmallow.

To ease her cough at night she should take 10 grams of syrup de Karabé and repeat when needed.

At times when the cough is most persistent she should also try inhaling the steam of an infusion of poppy flowers.

Build up her strength with good, substantial food.

Continue to drink the same amount of asses' milk sweetened with syrup of Tolu.

Continue to drink eau de Bussang.

9 NOVEMBER 1846. DAVAINE; CHOMEL

THE UNDERSIGNED PHYSICIANS MAKE THE FOLLOWING SUGGESTIONS:

Use as a tisane the Swiss Vulnéraire, continue the enemas of quinine and syrup of Karabé.

Try using Icelandic lichen.

Continue the same diet and the same hygienic precautions.

19 NOVEMBER 1846. DAVAINE; CHOMEL

"How distressing it is to read the prescriptions made in 1846 by Davaine and Chomel to the unfortunate Lady of the Camellias," said Georges Daremberg in his 1905 study of tuberculosis.

"The care of consumptives by the grand physicians who practiced their art in the middle of this century was ridiculous. The two celebrities have the good idea of prescribing asses' milk for their beautiful patient, but they cannot resist recommending that she sweeten the precious nourishment with syrup of tolu [an aromatic balsam obtained from a South American tree] or of maidenhair: an excellent way of suppressing the appetite and inciting disgust." Daremberg also ridicules Chomel's mentor, the eminent specialist Réne Laënnec. Believing that sea air had a therapeutic effect on tubercular patients, Laënnec had advocated the use of seaweed inhalers in hospital wards. Daremberg called this artificial atmosphere disastrous, as only fresh air can help consumptives to get well. Marie was in the hands of the greatest practitioners of nineteenth-century French medicine, but, working in the dark, they were powerless to cure her.

The morphine was making her act bizarrely. Romain Vienne had not seen her for two months, as he had been in Nonant in the late summer of 1846 following his mother's death, and when he went to boulevard de la Madeleine in October, he was deeply disturbed by her deterioration. Marie was in bed and very frail, leaning back on her pillow, although some color came into her cheeks as she chattered away. She insisted that she was well enough to get up and go out somewhere, but Romain made her stay in bed by promising to spend a couple of hours with her. Her mood darkened when she started to complain about the lovers and friends who had abandoned her, embarrassing him by her revelations and recriminations. "I had never seen Marie like this—she who was so sweet and good, who never had a bad word for anyone." Understanding that she was overwrought, even delirious, he did all he could to calm her, telling her that her grievances were no more than hallucinations produced by the drugs she was taking. "This had the opposite effect to what I'd hoped. She ranted more and more."

Stranger still was the hostility Marie was showing toward

Ned Perregaux, whom she said she hated more than she had ever loved. "I don't want him ever to set foot here; if [Clotilde] opens my door to him I will chase him away." The writer Charles Matharel de Fiennes confirms this. "She developed a great aversion toward the count P. whom she did not wish to see again." Matharel de Fiennes tries to explain it as "a caprice of the dying," and Vienne is no wiser, convinced only that the rupture was final. On 30 July 1846 Ned had asked once again to be admitted to the Foreign Legion, but when the ministry tried to contact him a fortnight later, he was not to be found at his address, number 25, rue de la Ville-l'Evêque. "He is said to have gone to the countryside." This suggests that Marie's note begging his forgiveness had not reached him, though by early September he was back in Paris. On the other hand, Ned may simply not have felt ready or inclined to pardon her.

Distressed by what he was hearing, Romain rose from his seat as if to leave, which had the effect of forcing Marie to regain her composure. They moved on to mundane topics, discussing a field that she and her sister had inherited from their grandfather: Delphine wanted to sell it, Marie to buy her out. Romain would be able to act as go-between, as he was returning to Nonant to put his mother's affairs in order, but he promised to be back in Paris within a few months' time.

Marie's devoted staff were doing all they could to care for her; Clotilde was with her day and night. The concierge, Pierre Privé, had taken charge of the domestic finances (his wife cleaned the apartment every day for sixty francs a month). Unable to face another glass of asses' milk or eau de Bussang, Marie sent him out one night to buy a two-franc bottle of champagne and on another occasion a *cigare camphré*. Debts were mounting alarmingly, and, like Clotilde and Etienne, Marie's coachman, Privé had paid several hundred francs of his own money to keep the bailiffs at bay. This was proving a losing battle.

A young advocate named Henry Lumière, a recent graduate

from law school, was visited by a locksmith one day who sought his help in recovering an unpaid sum for work on an apartment on the boulevard de la Madeleine. "Although everything there is luxurious, indicating great wealth and opulence, my repeated requests have been ignored," he complained to Lumière, who then wrote to the *débitrice*, asking her to come to his office to discuss a matter that concerned her. After some time had passed he received a brief note written "in a fine, anglicised hand" on lightly perfumed paper:

> *Monsieur,*
> *You should be aware that the sick have sad privileges: suffering greatly at the moment, allow me to invoke them, in asking you to take the trouble to come and see me about the affair in question.*
> *MD*

The following day he went to Marie's apartment and was shown by Clotilde into her bedroom. The sight of the lovely invalid in her sumptuously draped bed—a "nest of pink silk"—disarmed Lumière, who found himself stammering out his reason for coming, while emphasizing that he was only executing his client's request. Marie, dressed in a peignoir of white cashmere edged with blue silk, explained that because of her illness she was without funds for the moment and asked if it might be possible to delay the payment. "She was so deliciously pretty, her plea so touching, that I was seduced and fascinated into agreeing. . . . I was rewarded with a gentle, gracious smile of thanks, and the offer of a little hand, practically diaphanous, which seemed to me to be burning with fever." Other creditors, he discovered, had been less indulgent and had called in bailiffs to intervene.

Another young man was equally charmed. Charles Chaplin was an art student at the Ecole des Beaux-Arts when he received word that a beautiful woman living in a splendid apartment on boulevard de la Madeleine wanted him to paint her. Although the name Marie Duplessis meant nothing to the unworldly twenty-one-year-old, who still lodged with his mother and siblings in rooms on the rue d'Enfer, he was delighted to have a commission. He had been asked to bring an example of his work, and, trying to think of something that would impress "such a noble person," he chose one of his religious paintings. When Marie saw it she burst out laughing, and she was still laughing when the humiliated young man got up to leave. Calling him back, she said that she would like him to go ahead with her portrait, and also asked him if he would copy a painting in the Louvre for her.

Preliminary sketches were done at Marie's apartment as she lay under covers on a chaise longue, attempting to smile between coughing fits. Sometimes she lacked the strength to receive Chaplin, but he would return the following day without complaint. "He worshipped this dying woman as much as one of those saints pictured in the old mass-books," writes Claude Vento in *Les peintres de la femme*. One unseasonably sunny day, Chaplin's subject, feeling better than usual, suggested that they go for a promenade in the Bois. The carriage was already waiting on the boulevard, and Marie, wearing blue velvet, her waist svelte in a tight-fitting coat, looked ravishing as she walked along holding her young escort's arm. She was soon recognized and beset by admirers who gathered round to greet her. Chaplin knew then that the woman who had sat for him was someone famous and suddenly felt intimidated, although it did not prevent him from finishing the painting.

The result is a truthful and not particularly flattering portrait of Marie. She wears no jewels and a plain, governessy dress, and yet the somber effect is softened by her almost beatific expression of serenity. It is not known what she thought of the painting, but she made sure that Chaplin, of whom she had grown fond, was amply rewarded. When the time came to be paid, and he blushingly hesitated about naming a price, Marie cut him short by saying, "Ask for 200 francs. . . . M de T. [Marie's horse dealer,

Tony] is rich enough to pay you." Chaplin was overwhelmed and could hardly believe that he was taking home ten louis that he had earned himself. As he was leaving, Marie called out, telling him not to forget the painting she wanted him to copy at the Louvre. Sadly, however, death was swifter than he was.

On December 11, Marie had her hair styled at home by the hairdresser Dezoutter, who fitted the crown of six white camellias delivered that day from her florist. (To complete the effect, she had also ordered a large *bouquet à la main* of white camellias, costing twenty francs.) She wanted to go one last time to the theater. Marguerite, too, had insisted on seeing a final performance. "Despite the burning fever which devoured me, I made them dress me. . . . Julie put on some rouge for me, without which I should have looked like a corpse." Marguerite goes to the Vaudeville, but Marie went to the Palais-Royal, to see the revue *La poudre de coton*. Taking its title from the discovery that year of the explosive known in English as guncotton, it was a satirical roundup of the year's inventions, fashions, new novels, plays both good and bad, and eccentric personalities (Le Bal Mabille's Céleste Mogador among them). For Marie the evening was a way of suspending reality and turning back the clock. The two-and-a-half-hour show was like gaining twelve months as she revisited the excitements and absurdities of Parisian life in 1846.

Act 1 had already started when she made her entrance, carried in the arms of Etienne and his son, Marie's stable lad, who had both dressed up to make an impact. "Two lackeys gold-laced in braided uniform from head to foot set her down in a stage box," wrote the young journalist Alfred Delvau. "She was no more than a shadow of a woman—white and diaphanous, with consumptive pallor and a large bouquet of white camellias." The account by Charles Matharel de Fiennes is more emotive still.

One believed on seeing this beautiful specter with inflamed eyes, covered with diamonds and enveloped in a flood of white satin and lace that Marie had risen from the grave to come and reproach this brilliant society of young fools and Ninons of the day for their abandon and their unfeeling forgetfulness. Then at the end of the performance when she left her box, supported by her maid, and followed by these people, a path was cleared for her, and more than two hundred young people, their eyes lowered, bowed in front of this Madeleine, who very soon would appear before God.

For centuries the Catholic ideology had associated the wasting away of youth and beauty with spiritual innocence—the redemptive suffering later embodied by the patron saint of tuberculosis, Thérèse Martin of Lisieux. In recent months Marie, too, had acquired a tragic, quasi-religious aura. Seeing her looking so pure and dignified in her carriage, Charles du Hays described her as a saint being transported up to heaven. (It was this sense of transfiguration captured by Sarah Bernhardt's Marguerite with "the halo of a saint" upon her forehead.) Marie was expecting to be forgiven for her past. "My heart lifts up toward heaven from where I trust will come truth and salvation," du Hays quotes her as saying. "I have remained pure amidst affections which have only inspired sadness in me." In the play, too, Marguerite's friend Nichette believes that even the erotic liaisons will somehow transmute and augment her deliverance. "Rest in peace," she whispers, kneeling by the bed. "You will be much pardoned because you have much loved."

Eros was giving way to Agape—but not just yet. There was to be one more outing. January was Carnival time in Paris, and Marie was determined to attend her last Opéra ball. "Her faded, still voluptuous grace" made the writer Paul de Saint-Victor think of a fallen flower trampled underfoot, and as he watched her throughout the evening, his feelings of pity were mixed with admiration.

She was already mortally ill. The pure whiteness of her skin had been melted like snow by the fire of her fever; the flush of exhaustion wasted her thin cheek, the light had extinguished in the huge black eyes, and there were circles beneath them. . . . [And yet] she had dressed herself that evening with a wild brilliance. She was wearing all the necklaces and diamonds from her jewel box, like the Roman empresses who envelop themselves in purple robes before they die. Sitting drowsily on a small sofa she fixed on the crowd her eyes opaque with disgrace and boredom, until a waltz tune brusquely revived her from this dismal slumber. It was one of those Viennese airs of a sentimental gaiety whose ethereal, distant melody strikes you as supernatural—like music from the spheres commanding you to follow it in the whirling intoxication of an embrace.

This stirring sound raised her from her seat and, as regal as a princess, she went over and put her hand on the arm of a young man, who was overwhelmed by this good fortune. She danced for a long time, with passion, with rapture, with a giddy and vertiginous ardor which caused a shudder in anyone who knew how little breath she had left.

Marie's pallor and the melancholic delirium of her dancing reminded Saint-Victor of "one of those dead bacchantes who, in Northern fables, waltz in moonlight on the grass of their tombs." They are the Wilis of the second act of *Giselle*—the ballet Gautier created from a Heinrich Heine story set in the Rhine Valley— vengeful spirits who dance the men who betrayed them to their death. But Marie was not seeking retribution: this was her swan song, her last waltz, and a farewell to the Paris she loved.

Then she went home to die. Her curtains were drawn day and night, with only lamps and candles casting a wan light in the rooms. Her doctors tried to get her to open the windows to let in fresh air and sunlight, but their pleas were in vain. It was a foreshadowing of the tomb.

On Marie's twenty-third birthday, January 15, the bailiffs forced their way into the apartment, citing the name of the law. As she lay in bed she could hear a monotonous voice making an inventory of contents and the sound of furniture being moved. Describing the scene in a letter to Armand, Marguerite's maid told of her despair:

> I wanted to use my last resources to put a stop to it, but the bailiff told me that there would be other seizures to follow. Since she must die, it is better to let everything go than to save it for her family, whom she has never cared to see, and who have never cared for her. . . . Yesterday we had absolutely no money. Plate, jewels, shawls, everything is in pawn; the rest is sold or seized.

In the novel it is the Count de G. who settles Marguerite's debts and gets the creditors to leave her in peace. Marie's benefactor, however, was not the Count de Guiche but Olympe Aguado. Writing under the pseudonym Grimm, Amédée Achard says that the count, whom he does not identify, still being a minor, could do nothing himself but rushed home to beg his mother's help. "His mother listened to him, and every other thought disappeared in the face of death. She told her lawyers to take care of the debts of Marie Duplessis. How many other virtuous grandes dames of the world would have accomplished such a noble action which she made appear so simple?" Hippolyte de Villemessant tells the same story in his memoirs, also paying tribute to the humane generosity of the marchioness. While not revealing the Aguado name, he calls them a family with a soul. "All the poor of Paris and of Spain knew that they would never find the door closed. . . . When the marchioness heard what her young son had to say, she blushed perhaps in thinking of the French aristocracy's reaction but without reproach or thought of her immorality, she paid the dying girl's debts."

Why had Marie not appealed to her "pseudo-father" for money, as Marguerite does in the novel? She had deeply offended Stackelberg, but, according to Roqueplan, he did return to Paris to see her before she died. In Marguerite's description of the encounter, two large tears rolled from the old man's eyes when he saw how pale she was, and he remained with her for several hours, hardly saying a word. "Since she got so ill the old duke has not returned," Marguerite's maid told Armand. "He said that the sight was too much for him." Stackelberg, who had now witnessed the dying of four young women he had loved, had far more reason to stay away. But for Marie's Etienne, his desertion was unforgivable. "He's a miserable old screw," he remarked to Vienne. "When you're eighty years old, what's the point of economizing? As soon as he realized that she was dying, he completely abandoned her."

Amédée Achard suggests another reason why Stackelberg might have stayed away. That summer in Dieppe when a steamer arrived from Brighton and the passengers alighted, a Russian called Gustave noticed an elegant young beauty promenading along the jetty. "Celebrated for more than a title," she had not been introduced to the Russian, but by that evening the pair were walking together by the sea.

———

Marie was vacillating between despair and the belief that she might recover. She had told Clotilde that she was leaving everything to her in gratitude for her loyalty, and she asked for a notary to be summoned so that she could make a will. "Why, Madame?" Clotilde said, humoring her. "You're going to get better . . . . If it was the end, and if you were really dying I would obey you . . . [but] I'm going to stay by your side. Then I will hear you say that you made a mistake and that in a few days you will be saved." Convinced of this herself, Marie got Clotilde to pawn some jewels (for 1,500 francs) to provide the rent for a depot where she could hide her most precious things. "Because they'll return in a few days to seize more, and this time they'll succeed. . . . I can't be allowed to die hungry, and I want to keep something for starting again, when I will be healed."

Ned Perregaux, still forbidden to enter the apartment, was so desperate to know how much time Marie had left that he begged Clotilde to smuggle out one of her flannel vests for a psychic to interpret. He took it to the twenty-year-old phenomenon Alexis Didier, who, given an object charged with personal association, could recount an individual's history, make a medical diagnosis from a distance, or predict events to come. Blindfolded, in a hypnotic trance, he could read messages in a sealed envelope or the pages of a closed book. His paranormal gift for "remote viewing" had enabled him to detail the contents of the French emperor's study; and when Céleste Mogador consulted him to identify the thief who robbed her lover, he described exactly where the woman lived. But Alexis's clairvoyance was more precise about the past and present than about the future. "Go quickly to her," he urged Ned. "She has no more than a few hours to live." In effect, this was inaccurate: Marie had two more days left.

It is this moment in the play and opera that provides a soaring *coup de théâtre*. As soon as Armand/Alfredo appears on her threshold, Marguerite/Violetta runs to the door and flings herself into his arms. They ask each other's forgiveness, and she tells him that she wants to live. Liszt had imagined himself in this role, confiding to Marie d'Agoult, "If I had happened to be in Paris when la Duplessis was ill, I would have had my quarter of an hour as Des Grieux and tried to save her at any price." But he was thousands of miles away, and of all those who had loved Marie, only Ned, "banned from the bedroom of her for whom he wept"—and Olympe—were faithful to the end. "Forty-eight hours before her death she still recognized one, the younger

[Olympe], and she took his hand. 'You've come to see me,' she whispered. 'Adieu, I'm going away now.' "

Like the novel's Marguerite, Marie was alone with her maid and a priest during her last hours—and she was very frightened. "Oh, I'm dying!" she cried, grabbing Clotilde's hand. "I want you to bury me yourself. Do not declare my death straight away so that I can stay here longer in my house." Fighting the inevitable, Marguerite utters a series of tortuous cries and sits upright in bed two or three times, "as if she would hold on to her life." Marie's behavior was even more disturbing. "When the death-rattle began she made the strangest exclamations," claims Charles Matharel de Fiennes. "This woman, who had never spoken of affairs of state, cried out three times, an hour before her death, a pronouncement baffling for this era, a prophetic cry which we will not reproduce because it is improbable even if certified as true." Armand had struggled to pry his hand out of Marguerite's when all was over, but it was Clotilde's hand that Marie squeezed so tightly "that it was almost impossible to disengage the hand of the living from that of the dead." Clotilde closed her eyes and kissed her on the forehead. It was a little before 3 a.m. on February 3. "Then I dressed her as she had asked me to do . . . and put her in her shroud."

That evening Clotilde answered the door to Romain Vienne, who had sent a note to Marie saying that he was back in Paris and would be calling around eight o'clock to see her. The creditors' representative, Nicolas Ridel, who was holding Marie's papers, had told Clotilde to expect him, saying, "It's likely that this monsieur will want to see the body, so do not close the coffin." Clotilde disliked Romain, who she felt should have visited more often and who, because he was just a friend, had never tipped her as a courtesan's lovers were expected to do. She had made no attempt to contact him in time to see Marie alive, nor to prepare him for the shock in store. He had hardly stepped into the apartment when she coldly announced, "Monsieur, Madame is dead."

—Come now, [Clotilde,] why this morbid joke?

—Unfortunately Monsieur, it's the sad truth. Follow me.

Stunned, Romain walked behind her, through the dining room and into Marie's candlelit bedroom, hung with black drapes, where a young priest was praying. To his right, under the window, was the coffin, raised on trestles. As Clotilde removed the cloth and lifted the lid, Romain felt a jolt of terror. "I'm not superstitious . . . but there is nothing more hideous than the sight of death."

Marie was swathed in lace—Alençon lace made in her native Normandy. "The tenderness and touching taste of her friend had adorned her so well!" Roqueplan writes. "Her hands held a bouquet of camellias, her favorite flower, in the midst of which was a crucifix. . . . Her coffin was filled with camellias. . . . The beauty of the dead girl was a new marvel." But not to Romain, who says nothing about camellias, only that Marie's body was already rigid when he removed the winding sheet.

With both hands I gently lifted her head, and after stroking her forehead and temples, I opened her lips and her half-closed eyelids. Her hair was loose and uncombed; I divided the long tresses into two and placed one on each side of her body, under her extended arms. Then I took her two icy hands in mine, which were burning, and examined them with such minute attention that [Clotilde] could not stop herself from shuddering; none of my actions escaped her. The priest, moved by an instinctive curiosity, got up to see what I was doing. Both of them, motionless and silent, looked at me with bewildered surprise. I asked [Clotilde] to fetch me a pair of scissors and continued my examination. While I was waiting a cloud suddenly passed in front of my eyes; a cold sweat broke out on my forehead; a terrifying emotion strangled me, and I felt I was going to faint.

He staggered into the dining room and collapsed into an armchair. When he came around Clotilde was standing in front of him with a pair of scissors, and he asked her to cut a lock of Marie's hair as he did not have the strength to do it himself. Romain then left the apartment as soon as he could, only to find Etienne waiting for him on the pavement. "I knew you were coming and I've been here since seven o clock," he said. "I am deeply sorry that I was not given your address: you could have consoled the dear lady in her last moments, and she could have confided her last wishes to you. But [Clotilde] did not want this. I believe I will not be telling you something you don't know if I say that she does not like you."

They went to a nearby café together, and Etienne described Marie's last months—"an impossible life of theatre, balls, la Maison d'Or, the Café Anglais. At the end she drank nothing but champagne." By December most of her close friends, Agénor de Guiche among them, had stopped coming to see her, but not a day went by, Etienne said, without Olympe visiting Marie. He told the story about her "birthday present" from the bailiffs and how the young count had prevented the seizure with a check for a thousand francs. But they returned a few days later, and this time Marie said, "There's no point, my friend. I am crushed by debts and my creditors are pursuing me relentlessly, which means that my end is near. . . . Let them ruin me to the point of destitution. If I don't die then I will learn from this lesson." Olympe had left in tears. Etienne then spoke of Stackelberg's desertion, and how Ned Perregaux had not been received for several months. "I don't understood why. . . . He loved her, despite everything, as much as in the beginning. . . . This morning, an hour after the death three men came into her bedroom. One of them—I don't have to name him—knelt by her bed, praying and sobbing. The two others [presumably Ned's guardian and lawyer] searched through all the drawers in all the chests; [Clotilde] helped them. They took letters and papers, but they did not find the important one they were looking for." It was a document "written in English"—Marie and Ned's marriage certificate.

Two days later, on the afternoon of February 5, Marie's funeral took place at La Madeleine. Parish archives record that the cosignatories on the death certificate were Frédéric Romain Vienne and Marie's concierge, Pierre Privé, who paid the ceremony cost of 1,354 francs. The church was still hung with black draperies from two earlier requiems that day, the decoration of a crown and silver initial *D* (the insignia of the deceased Count Ducamp de Bussy) assumed by *Le Siècle*'s obiturist to be Marie's own coat of arms.

In *Sins of Youth,* Dumas fils maintains that only two men followed Marie's coffin. He identifies them in his novel as the "Count de G., who came from London on purpose, and the old duke, who was supported by two footmen." Méjannes, however, who claimed to have attended Marie's funeral himself, says that there were four other men present—but not Guiche or Stack-elberg. These were: "Olympe A. Edouard D[elessert]. . . . Tony and Edouard P." Vienne provides yet another version. He noticed Guiche there as well as "a grand old man," who he did not think could be Stackelberg, as he had not been invited. In his account the congregation at La Madeleine comprised "a sympathetic, welcoming crowd"—a fact that can be documented, because chairs for a special mass at La Madeleine had to be paid for, and a receipt exists listing twenty of them.

The same people followed the hearse to Montmartre cemetery, Romain walking beside Ned, who was trying in vain to hold back his tears. Behind them, at a slight distance, came Olympe, also visibly moved, and then the other friends. "I saw several women crying on the tomb," said Romain. "They had come to say goodbye to the one who had been so good to them." He also saw the relative with whom Marie had first stayed in Paris, Mme Vital, who had not spoken to her distant cousin since throwing her out of her house, now loftily declaring that she had come to pardon her. Standing at the graveside, Ned Perregaux was growing even more distraught, oblivious to everything around him, his gait unstable, his features distorted. He seemed about to faint when he was handed the holy water sprinkler that the priest was passing around, and when the service was over, out of respect for his grief, the rest of the group left him alone by the grave.

————

Some days later, Delphine, wearing her usual rough serge clothes and clogs, arrived in Paris with her husband, Constant Paquet. They were there to claim their inheritance but were immediately faced with a barrage of unpaid bills and lawsuits. Dr. Koreff would be suing them, alleging (falsely) to have made 280 visits to Marie, and Ned Perregaux had already started legal proceedings. He was claiming back diamonds he had given Marie and a thoroughbred "of superb genealogy," which he said had only been loaned to the deceased. A vet had testified that the horse was the viscount's property, and jewelers had produced bills in his name, as well as receipts for the rental of her apartment, but Ned, capricious as ever, abandoned the suit after the court's first sitting.

When an emerald necklace and other jewels were reported missing, Clotilde was "hunted down" by the beneficiaries. Charles Matharel de Fiennes defended her in print, declaring that the dead girl had been buried with the rings and "a magnificent rosary" that her maid was accused of stealing. It was Romain who was most convinced of her guilt, and he went as far as reporting her to the police. He had taken on the role of adviser to the Paquets, suggesting that they go together to a marble cutter to arrange a headstone and escorting them to Montmartre cemetery. But when they reached the place where Marie had been buried a fortnight earlier, they discovered the earth leveled off: her grave had disappeared.

This was Ned Perregaux's doing. Distressed to find that Marie had been allocated a space for only five years, he had immediately arranged to buy a vault and two meters of ground with a concession for perpetuity. Moving a body from one grave to another required the permission of the deceased's family as well as the presence of the police. Dumas fils, who records this in the novel, has Armand leave Paris for a few days to seek the permission of Marguerite's sister. But as Marie's husband, albeit in English law, Ned was not obliged to contact Delphine and instead had acquired the consent of the prefect of police—Edouard Delessert's father.

In the novel, the gardener at Montmartre—who has been paid by Armand to keep Marguerite's grave covered with fresh white camellias—is convinced that the young man's motive for exhuming her body is more emotional than practical. "I would wager that he wants to change her grave simply in order to have one more look at her," he tells the narrator. "The first word he said to me when he came to the cemetery was: 'How can I see her again?'" This was Heathcliff's response after Cathy's burial in *Wuthering Heights* (coincidentally published at the end of that year). "I'll have her in my arms again!" he vows, casting aside his spade when it hits the coffin and scraping away the earth with his hands. He never sees her body but hears a sigh, and then another, close to his ear, which convinces him that Cathy's presence is still with him. "I relinquished my labour of agony, and felt consoled at once: unspeakably consoled." Armand, on the other hand, needs the horrible reality of the corpse itself to persuade him that Marguerite is lost to him forever. Taking pity on him, the narrator volunteers to accompany him to the cemetery.

> The police inspector was there already. We walked slowly in the direction of Marguerite's grave; the inspector in front. From time to time I felt my companion's arm tremble convulsively, as he shivered from head to feet. . . . When we reached the grave . . . two men were turning up the soil.

Armand leaned against a tree and watched. All his life seemed to pass from his eyes. Suddenly one of the two pick-axes struck against a stone. At the sound Armand recoiled, as at an electric shock, and seized my hand with such force as to give me pain. As the grave-diggers began emptying out the earth Armand watched, his eyes fixed and wide open, like the eyes of a madman, and a slight trembling of the cheeks and lips were the only signs of the violent nervous crisis he was suffering from. When the coffin was uncovered the inspector said to the grave-diggers: "Open it." They obeyed, as if it were the most natural thing in the world. The coffin was of oak and they began to unscrew the lid. The humidity of the earth had rusted the screws, and it was not without some difficulty that the lid was opened. A foul stench rose up. . . . "Oh my God, my God!" murmured Armand, turning paler than before. Even the grave-diggers drew back.

A great white shroud covered the corpse, closely out-lined some of its contours. This shroud was almost completely eaten away at one end, and left one of the feet visible . . . "Quick," said the inspector. Thereupon one of the men put out his hand, began to unwrap the shroud, and taking hold of it by one end suddenly laid bare the face of Marguerite. It was terrible to see; it is horrible to relate. The eyes were nothing but two holes, the lips had disappeared, vanished and the white teeth were tightly set. The black hair, long and dry, was pressed tightly about the forehead, and half veiled the green hollows of the cheeks; and yet I recognised in this face the joyous white and rose face that I had seen so often. Armand, unable to turn away his eyes, had put the handkerchief to his mouth and bit it. . . . I heard the inspector say to Duval, "Do you identify"? Yes," replied the young man in a dull voice. Then fasten it up and take it away, said the inspector. . . . Armand allows himself to be led away, guided like a child, only from time to time murmuring, "Did you see her eyes?"

Marie was now, as Liszt put it, "delivered up to sepulchral worms," lying beneath a tomb of white marble engraved with the words

Alphonsine Plessis

Born 15 January 1824

Died 3 February 1847.

De Profundis

On one side the initials *A* and *P* are entwined in an exact replica of the Perregaux script—a token consolation for Ned. Her destiny had come full circle, but this was not the end. "I've always felt that I'll come back to life," she told Clotilde, as if foreseeing the last words of Marguerite ("I am going to live!") and of Violetta (*"Ah! ma io ritorno a viver!"*). Her final wish could not have been more specific. "I want you to put a very weak bolt on my coffin," Marie implored. "This is the most important thing of all."

Postscript

On 18 February 1847, an advertisement in several leading Parisian journals gave notice of an auction the following week of "a rich and elegant property." Its entire contents were to come under the hammer, from kitchen utensils to objets d'art—even the horses, bridles, and saddles from its stables. Two hundred posters were erected around the city and eight hundred catalogues distributed, but what caught everyone's eye were the words in small print: "After the death of Mme Plessis boulevart [*sic*] de la Madeleine, no 11." It was this that caused such excitement. The public preview and four-day sale would provide the chance to explore a celebrated courtesan's domain; to examine not only Marie's furniture, ornaments, paintings, and books but her dresses, furs, jewels, cosmetic pots, and all the other glamorous accessories of her profession. Grandes dames, dandies, and demimondaines could talk of little else, and among others determined to attend were genuine collectors, enthralled by the rarity of certain items, as well as more unexpected figures. One of these was Charles Dickens.

Dickens had been in Paris at the time of Marie's death, renting number 48, rue de Courcelles, in the elegant Eighth Arrondissement. His incredulity at the public's response was compounded by a fascination of his own. Fallen women of all types intrigued him, and, according to his friend and biographer John Forster, it had crossed his mind to make Marie the subject of a book, feeling that her short life contained a powerfully moralistic story. He was aware of legends starting to circulate about her, from the romantic to the absurd, and he himself had already fictionalized her end. "The greatest medical practitioner in Paris was called to her bedside. 'What are your wishes?' he asked when he saw that she was lost. She replied, 'To see my mother,' and her mother came running, a simple Breton peasant, wearing the picturesque costume of her province; she knelt at the bed of her daughter, stayed there praying until Marie was dead." Dickens had heard it said that a broken heart had killed the young courtesan, but he was not convinced. "For my part, as a genteel Englishman, I am inclined to believe that she died of ennui and satiety. Satiety can kill just as effectively as hunger."

He and Forster had spent a fortnight together sightseeing, their itinerary taking in the usual attractions—the Louvre, Versailles, opera, theaters, and concerts—interspersed with "the gaudy and ghastly." Of far more interest to Dickens were their visits to the women's penitentiary of Saint-Lazare, to hospitals, prisons, cemeteries, and the morgue, all of which he observed "with a dreadful insatiability." The sale of Marie Duplessis's possessions would be another such excursion. Although not in Paris for the day of the preview, he was back in time for the sale itself, and in a letter to Count d'Orsay (who, as Agénor de Guiche's uncle, already knew all about Marie Duplessis), Dickens expressed his astonishment.

> Everyone whom the capital of France counts as illustrious was there. The women of the very grandest circles found themselves in the crowd, and this social elite was waiting, curious, moved, full of sympathy and tender emotions for a simple girl. . . . To see the admiration and the general tristesse, one could believe that it was some kind of heroine like a Jeanne of Arc.

Théophile Gautier also wrote of his amazement at the turn-out of *le tout Paris*. As he joined the jostling crowd, he noticed Marie's yellow-and-blue parrot looking for a few seeds in its empty container and stopped for a minute, touched by the sight. Another writer edging his way through each room, and even more affected by the poignancy of the experience, was Alexandre Dumas fils.

It had been more than a year since Alexandre had visited boulevard de la Madeleine, and as he sat at the table at which they had often dined together, he looked around, imagining that he could hear "each object speak." Marie's piano was silent, the flowers in the grand Chinese vases were dying, and yet her presence was palpable, her clocks still ticking. Following behind the inquisitive women, he found himself cynically noting their mixed expressions of awe and shame at being inside a courtesan's apartment. "This one was dead, so even the most virtuous among them could enter her bedroom. And if more excuses were needed, they could say they did not know whose sale it was." For Alexandre, it was seeing Marie's bed, enveloped in pink satin, that brought back the tenderest memories.

> For it is there, in the past, O my dear departed
> That we lay together when midnight came
> And, awake from then till dawn,
> We listened to the night hours pass
>
> I re-opened the pink satin curtains
> which shaded the morning sun
> and allowed in a single ray which hesitantly set
> its waking light upon your sleeping brow

At home that night, still shaken by the emotions of the day, Alexandre wrote his sentimental elegy "M.D." from which these lines are taken. "I cried when I wrote them and I cried on reading them," he told his father, admitting that they had given him the idea of writing a book about Marie.

—Well then, do it, replied Dumas père.

—Perhaps I will try.

There was much speculation that week about who would benefit from the proceeds of the sale. One account claimed that Marie Duplessis had made a will in which she bequeathed the profits to her niece, on condition that the young girl never let herself be corrupted by Paris. This, though, was another fable. Marie's niece, Zoë Adèle Paquet, had not yet been conceived. Delphine, Marie's sister, and her husband were the only inheritors, and were also responsible for settling her debts. These now amounted to nearly 21,000 francs, a sum easily covered by the sale's profit of 89,017 francs. Delphine had held back Marie's rosewood couch, her prayer book, the stuffed lizard, and the miniature of their mother, but virtually everything else was auctioned. At noon on Wednesday, February 24, Constant Paquet made the opening bid, on Delphine's behalf, paying sixty-five francs for eight cotton petticoats. He went on to buy a cashmere nightshirt and flannel vests and also secured some of Marie's most valuable possessions, including her chandelier and the bronze and porcelain candelabras given to her by Stackelberg.

Romain Vienne appeared to be equipping an apartment with his choice of lots: a stove, four firedogs, thirty-four pieces of glassware, cooking utensils, twenty-one pillowcases, a tablecloth and dish cloths. More curious was his purchase of six dresses, a set of perfume bottles, and a feather boa. "Did he intend to give the courtesan's gowns to his wife?" ventured a recent biographer, but Romain had no wife. What he knew was that Marie's dresses and boa would still be scented with her light l'Eau du Harem cologne—and that, for him, was reason enough to want to own them.

Postscript

Thursday's sale of jewels was the bounty of Marie's admirers, but apart from Tony, none of their names appears on the list of successful bidders. (Ned's aunt the Duchess de Raguse, on the other hand, spent a total of 1,740 francs, presumably claiming back the Perregaux diamonds.) Tony bought a jardinière, small table, rosewood desk, expensive water glass (forty francs), figurine of Diane and Endymion, and Marie's prie-dieu. At Saturday's auction of paintings and drawings he was the main bidder, buying costume designs and seven other drawings, including a Vidal for 860 francs. Marie's concierge, Pierre Privé, bought one portrait as a keepsake for three francs. On the fourth day, when the library of more than two hundred bound classics was auctioned, Eugène Sue was reported by Dickens to have acquired Marie's prayer book, but again, this is fiction. The final lots were an odd miscellany—oil containers, bottle racks, candlesticks, sconces, and—surely a grotesque oversight—Marie's enema-injecting apparatus. These *clysopompes* were bought by Gautier for twelve francs.

Gautier had written a long and effusive tribute to Marie in *La Presse,* and Romain Vienne, hoping that he could be persuaded to expand the article into a book, decided to pay him a visit. Vienne had been appointed by the Paquets as Marie's executor, and despite being responsible for destroying most of her private correspondence, he had taken it upon himself to find a biographer. At nine in the morning he arrived at the house once inhabited by Byron on the Champs-Elysées. "Théo," Vienne reports, was still in bed, but eventually appeared wearing pantaloons and sandals. Surrounded by cats of every color, he sat cross-legged on Oriental rugs "disguised as chairs, the Chinese way" (Gautier had bought two more rugs at Marie's sale). After talking for an hour, they went out for lunch, during which time Vienne provided "all the information he would need to write either the history of Marie Duplessis, or a novel drawing on the important episodes of her life." Gautier declined. He had been compromised enough, he said, by *Mademoiselle de Maupin,* his 1835 novel that borrowed the name and bisexuality of a notorious eighteenth-century cross-dressing adventuress.

By the early summer, Alexandre Dumas fils's book was well under way. He and an unnamed male companion had each taken a room at Le Cheval Blanc, an inn near his father's house in Saint-Germain-en-Laye. The next morning they decided to extend their stay in the country and go riding, and the friend volunteered to return to Paris to fetch suitable clothes and clean linen. When he was alone, Alexandre began thinking again of Marie and decided that the time had come to attempt his novel. On his return, the friend found him hard at work and became involved himself, making copies of the sheets as Alexandre completed them, on condition that he be given the original manuscript to keep.

Could this have been Ned Perregaux? In *The Lady of the Camellias,* Armand is complicit in the writing of the novel. "I feel obliged to recount this story to you," he tells the narrator. "You will be able to make a book from it which no-one will believe, but which will perhaps be interesting for you to do." No evidence exists of a collaboration between Ned and Alexandre—nor, in fact, a link of any kind, although they probably met at Marie's apartment and certainly frequented the same boulevard restaurants. But the explanation Dumas fils gives as to why the manuscript of his novel was not written in his own hand is so far-fetched that one can't help wondering if he had inherited his father's habit of appropriating other people's stories as his own. The friend, he says, took the original with him when he went on a trip to India. "Somewhere about the Cape of Good Hope there was such a hurricane that everything that could be spared was thrown into the sea to lighten the ship. The manuscript of *La dame aux camélias* was in one of the trunks tossed overboard."

If Ned Perregaux was a key source for the novel, then he was among several. Alexandre's eyewitness account of the sale had given him his opening; he had his own chapter of autobiography to incorporate, and his acquaintance with members of Marie's intimate circle, such as Agénor de Guiche, had provided him with other characters. It is the novel's Count de G. who "launched" Marguerite, whose photograph she keeps long after their affair is over, and whose commitment to her, like Agénor's to Marie, was "no more than an agreeable past-time." Alexandre was also well aware of the name of Agénor's famous ancestor, as Dumas père had cast Armand, Count de Guiche, in *The Man in the Iron Mask*. Brazenly factual, brilliantly observed, *La dame aux camélias* was completed in three or four weeks at Le Cheval Blanc. It was a remarkable achievement, but more than one contemporary has noted that it is more biography than novel. "It's a history," remarked Paul de Saint-Victor. "The intimate and secret history of Marie Duplessis."

The following February, exactly a year after Marie's death, revolution broke out in the streets of the city, and the government of Louis-Philippe fell. In these early days of the Second Republic of France, Marie's Paris became unrecognizable. "The habitués of the boulevard cafés were mostly National Guards," wrote Albert Vandam. "Our fillet of beef was brought to us by a corporal, and our coffee poured out by a sergeant. The patrons were no longer 'messieurs' but had already become 'citoyenes' [*sic*]." Pasted across billboards outside the Comédie-Francaise were strips of paper with the word RELACHE [NO PERFORMANCE] in large black letters. Déjazet and Bouffé were appearing in a mixed program at the Variétés, but the house, like the Gymnase, was almost empty. At Tortoni, the café au lait and hot chocolate had to be made with water because the delivery carts of milk could not pass through the barricades.

By the end of 1848, most of the activities had been crushed, but Bloody February had paralyzed commerce and industry, leaving France in economic crisis. At precisely this moment came news of the discovery of gold in California. The press published essays about the California climate, products, and history; companies were formed with alluring names such as La Fortune and L'Eldorado; a state lottery was organized with the aim of raising seven million francs to transport, free of charge, five thousand French emigrants to the New World. The writer chosen for the publicity brochure, *La loterie des lingots d'or,* was Alexandre Dumas fils. His father, now bankrupt and living in Brussels, had also cashed in on gold fever, with *Un Gil Blas en Californie,* a book plagiarized from an actual traveler's journal. From September 1849, and over the next few years, thousands of French émigrés poured in through the Golden Gate. The majority of these were bachelors of the intelligentsia—lawyers, doctors, bankers, architects, scholars, and journalists. "Acting on impulse," Romain Vienne, leaving on a frigate from Le Havre, was among them.

And what of the other men who had been close to Marie? Agénor de Guiche, as a lieutenant in the National Guard, had taken up arms to defend Paris against the insurgents. His gallantry earned him a Legion of Honor nomination, but he was struck off the list when he changed allegiance and became a partisan of Louis-Napoléon Bonaparte. By now, at twenty-nine, Agénor had decided that he was ready to settle down and make a good marriage. This, however, proved harder than he had anticipated. "The Faubourg St Germain withheld its daughters from such a weathercock," Elisabeth de Gramont wrote in a memoir of her grandfather. "He had to look for a wife in the mists of Scotland." Agénor brought back Emma MacKinnon, the daughter of a Tory MP, and married her later in 1848. A country girl with a passion for horses, she was strong and hardy, and never took to her bed except to bear their four children. One son was named Agénor and another Armand. In 1852, when Louis-Napoléon Bonaparte became emperor, he helped to advance his friend Agénor's political career by making him French ambassador in the increasingly influential posts of Cassel, Stuttgart, Turin, and Vienna. He succeeded as the tenth Duke de Gramont in 1855 and was appointed foreign minster in 1870. "Haughty with men and delightful with women," cultured and handsome, Agénor was the ideal diplomat but far less accomplished as a politician, and was held largely responsible for the disastrous 1870–71 war with Prussia. At the fall of the Empire, three-quarters ruined having spent his wife's fortune maintaining the splendor of his embassies, Agénor bought a modest house on the rue La Pérouse, in the center of Paris, where he lived until his death in 1880.

There is little trace of Ned Perregaux after Marie died. In March 1847, in a letter to Gautier, the actress Alice Ozy writes, "My dear count honoured me with his presence all day [but] I was very anxious that he had consumed a lot of hashish on leaving me: he wrote to me that evening saying that he had a horrible headache and was staying in bed." A footnote by the editor of the Gautier correspondence names the count as Edouard Perregaux. It seems perfectly reasonable that a bereft Ned would seek consolation in the company of his former mistress, and might want to escape reality with a mind-altering drug. His presence in Ozy's apartment, however, turns out to be a case of misidentification: the visitor with a penchant for hashish was Count Rostopchine, "an amiable and witty Russian." In December 1848 Ned renewed his request to join the Foreign Legion and a fortnight later received official permission—on condition that "Citoyen Perregaux" pay off all his debts. Yet again, he failed to take up the offer. After resigning from the Jockey Club in 1850, Ned moved to Chantilly, outside Paris, where he rented a furnished villa on the Grande-Rue and became an active participant in the town's prestigious races. According to Henri de Pené, he knew that he had been made a theatrical hero but refused ever to see a performance of *La dame aux camélias.* "And he has kept his word."

By February 1847, Liszt was in Kiev, where he met twenty-eight-year-old Princess Carolyne zu Sayn-Wittgenstein, a small, dark, reclusive woman with whom he settled in Weimar the following year. He had been immediately smitten by the "very extraordinary and distinguished" Carolyne, his companion until his death, but nevertheless, news of Marie's death had shaken him badly. "It was the last and only shock I have felt in years," he confessed to Marie d'Agoult in the spring of 1847. "It is useless to try to find an explanation for these contradictions of the human heart." Janka Wohl wrote of how, especially during the last years of Liszt's life, a melancholy note infiltrated his reminiscences. "He loved to lay stress on the chances he had missed, on the grand opportunities which he had spoilt for himself. He accentuated this idea with wonderful frankness and candour one evening when he was speaking of Madame Duplessis." Remembering how excited Marie had been by the prospect of a trip to Constantinople, Liszt told Wohl that not having taken her there was something he had always regretted.

Olympe Aguado had remained with his married mistress, Mrs. Adrian Hope, until her scandalous divorce in 1855, when their affair was made public. Five years later he married Bertha de Freystedt, former demoiselle of honor to Stéphanie de Beauharnais, Grand Duchess of Baden. They had two children, Louis and ravishing, cat-eyed Carmen, named after his mother, who lived with them in the sumptuous Hôtel Milon d'Inval at 18, place Vendôme. This was also where Olympe had his photographic studio. By the 1850s, having learned the daguerrotype technique from Gustave Le Gray, Olympe had become a founding member of the Société Française de Photographie. In 1854, he and his young friend Edouard Delessert invented the photographic visiting card, which caught on with the verve of an early Facebook. Later, Olympe became known for the tableaux vivants he staged with family and friends, dressing them up as fishermen in foul-weather oilcloths; poking fun at the pastimes of his grand milieu (*The Reader,* one of many Aguado photographs in the collection of Musée d'Orsay, shows him irreverently dozing off during one of the reading sessions that were a regular practice at court). Madame Aguado was always a game subject, whether disguised as a lace maker or as a duenna with keys hanging from her belt. Small and rotund, she has a plain, mannish face with several chins, but her warmth is visible as she sits playing cards and gazing mischievously at her son. With Emperor Napoléon III and Princess Eugénie among Olympe's regular sitters, he moved in a sphere that never could have included Marie. All the same, given his affection and loyalty, it is not fanciful to presume that had she lived just two more years, there would be photographs of Marie Duplessis among the Aguado archive.

Of all the men in Marie's life, there were two who never stopped loving her. Ned Perregaux, having inherited the authentic title of count after his brother's death in 1857, was a highly desirable bachelor, but he chose never to marry. He was living alone in Saint-Cyr, Inde-et-Loire, when on 30 May 1889, at the age of seventy-three, he died in the middle of the night. His body was discovered by two neighbors, a gardener and a farmer.

Romain Vienne was declared missing in Nonant, where reports of the ravages of cholera among émigrés in California had led villagers to suppose that he had fallen victim to the epidemic. The Ornaise writer Gustave Le Vavasseur wondered if Vienne had rekindled his medical knowledge in order to work toward finding a cure or whether, "with his inventive intelligence," he had made a fortune in the gold rush. In fact, Romain did not stay long in San Francisco, instead spending almost a decade on what he called "peregrinations" across America. When he finally returned to France in 1858, having almost forgotten his native language, he settled in Nonant and became a local racing journalist. Only in his final years was he able to exorcise what Le Vavasseur called "the phantom who had haunted him since he was a young man—that of the Dame aux Camélias." In 1862, at the age of forty-six, Romain finally married: his wife was twenty-three, Marie's own age when she died. Her name was Alphonsine.

A Note on Sources

The prime source as well as the inspiration for my book is Romain Vienne's *The Truth about the Lady of the Camellias,* and yet it is by no means definitive. "I know the complete list of Marie Duplessis's lovers and I intend to tell all," he declared to the editor of *L'Eclair* in 1886, the year he began writing the book (issue 10 April 1894). But there were several lovers whom Marie kept to herself. One was Alexandre Dumas fils, whose affair Vienne believed was pure invention. "He was bragging," he continued. "He never saw Marie. This beautiful girl, despite being known for her generous heart, would never have granted that writer a single kiss." Enough evidence exists to prove otherwise, and I can't help wondering if Vienne's exclusion of Dumas fils from his book was motivated by an element of revenge. He was obsessively proprietary about Marie, to the point of having visiting cards printed with the words *Friend of the Lady of the Camellias* under his name. Regarding himself as a man of letters, Vienne believed that he knew Marie better than anyone else in Paris. How galling, then, it must have been that a penniless young poet had made his name and fortune out of her. Nevertheless, he actively sought Dumas fils's approval by sending him a copy of his own work. The famous novelist eventually responded, and his description of Vienne as "a sympathetic and faithful historian of the model" would today be used as a jacket quotation (extract of a letter dated 1 April 1887, catalogue to Hôtel Drouot sale on 23 and 24 March 2009). But this must have been an early draft. In a preface in which Vienne describes being taken to a performance of the play after a decade of living abroad, he claims never to have read "a traitorous word" of *La dame aux camélias*. He left before the curtain rose.

Vienne himself, I feel certain, would have kept Marie's confidences to the grave, had it not been for the publication of two revealing articles. The first, by Charles du Hays, exposed "the bitter truth and secret sadness" of her childhood and was collected in a book published in 1885 (*L'ancien Merlerault: Récits chevalins d'un vieil éleveur*). The second, *"Les quartiers de la dame aux camélias,"* by Count de Contades, was a detailed, if erroneous, investigation into her genealogy and appeared at the end of that year in *Le Livre* (reprinted in Contades', *Portraits et fantaisies*). These clearly acted as a trigger. In an unpublished letter to Contades, a well-known Ornaise figure, Vienne announced his intention to write his own book, saying he had begun assembling reminiscences and jotting down notes.

"A hundred times I have felt inclined to write the story of Marie Duplessis. A hundred times I have been urged to do this. I was not able to decide for a number of reasons which do not have any place here. Now at last I am resigned. . . . The memory of Marie herself has been lost for too long under the fanciful pen of Dumas" (letter from the collection of Jean-Marie Choulet).

He was, he told Contades, the only person alive who knew all the particularities of the courtesan's life, but he promised to treat its "devilish details" with discretion. He was obliged for reasons of the narrative, he said, to give himself a leading role, although it vexed him to do this. When writing the book itself, Vienne also felt the need to explain his motives. Not only does the title attest to his monopoly on the truth, but he ends the memoir with a pedantic series of paragraphs intended to put the record straight. A remark made decades earlier (by Jules Janin), that Marie's love letters had been auctioned along with everything else, produced a tirade of protest from Vienne. He knew the whereabouts of a secret drawer, he declared, and had personally overseen the burning of all three hundred letters, apart from saving thirty—which must have been his own.

Romain Vienne was, in the words of a contemporary, "a real character" (*L'Eclair*, 10 April 1874). He studied medicine, read for the bar, became involved in politics, worked as a journalist and a financier, and joined Lamartine's revolutionary movement in 1848. He regarded himself primarily as a writer and in the Great Fire of San Francisco claimed to have lost ten volumes of work—"diverse poems, dramas and comedies, two libretti which Donizetti had commissioned, certain novels, etc." This, I believe, was wishful thinking, as Vienne was never prolific. His only other extant work is *Le berceau,* a collection of juvenilia, and *Système des bornes,* a political pamphlet. Another book, *Pages oubliés,* was advertised but never appeared.

The Truth about the Lady of the Camellias was published in 1887 by Paul Olendorff and reprinted eleven times that year. The daily journal *L'Estafette* had serialized it between 21 August and 5 October 1887, and although the first extracts were anonymous ("by a childhood friend"), Vienne was named in all the others. He had clearly expected his book to cause a stir because in an unpublished letter to Delphine, dated 21 October 1886, he urged her to wait until publication to sell her sister's portrait. "It will be the moment when everyone is talking about the true story of Marie Duplessis . . . and if you miss this opportunity you will never have another" (from the collection of Jean-Marie Choulet). He was mistaken. Marie's great champions, literary giants Jules Janin and Théophile Gautier, were no longer alive, and Vienne's memoir was not reviewed in any major publication. Then, almost a decade later, came a resurgence of interest in the real Lady of the Camellias. This had been initiated by the prestigious Parisian *Revue Encyclopédique,* which devoted the issue of 15 February 1896 to Marie, publishing previously unseen portraits and half a dozen of her notes to Ned Perregaux. A subsequent issue of 24 October 1896 contained a long, deferential article focusing on "A Friend and Biographer of the Dame aux Camélias" by Edmond Deschaumes. For Vienne, though, this accolade was too late. On 9 April 1894, he had died in Nonant, at the age of seventy-eight.

In 1898 came George Soreau's *La vie de la Dame aux Camélias,* which closely followed Vienne's account, even adopting his pseudonyms for Marie's lovers. Johannes Gros's exhaustively researched *Alexandre Dumas et Marie Duplessis* appeared in 1923, followed six years later by the even more thorough *Une Courtisane romantique, Marie Duplessis.* The punctilious Gros was maddened by Vienne's factual inaccuracies, lapses into fiction, and disguised dramatis personae, but his own books are completely without any linear narrative or sense of character. I decided to draw extensively on both. I used Gros as a bibliography, his invaluable footnotes with details of articles (not always correctly dated) leading me to obscure nineteenth-century journals, stored either as bound tomes or on microfilm in the Bibliothèque Nationale de France. Crucial too was his reprinting in *Une courtisane romantique* of the sale catalogue, with its list of successful bidders, as well as the long, detailed medical instructions by Marie's two doctors. Vienne I felt I could trust on everything to do with Marie's Normandy background, but I had to follow my instinct when it came to believing his account of her life in Paris.

The almost total absence of any personal correspondence (destroyed either by accident or intention) was a serious obstacle. Agénor de Guiche's papers were burned in a fire at his château, Mauvière; Perregaux family legend has it that Marie's letters to Ned, "tied with a pink ribbon," as well as his to her, tied in

blue, were thrown on the fire in 1915 by fifteen-year-old Claudine de Perregaux on the orders of her blind grandfather Frédéric
de Perregaux (Béatrice Perregaux in *Violetta and her Sisters,* edited
by Nicholas John). There are no references to Marie in Stackelberg's archive in Tallin, nor have any letters between Marie and
Liszt come to light. I found I had to be grateful for a fragment
of a letter quoted in an Hôtel Drouot catalogue or already published in a book. One important source for several unknown letters and documents was Jean-Marie Choulet's *Promenades à Paris
et en Normandie avec la dame aux camélias.* With its illustrations
of nineteenth-century Paris and photographs of the unchanged
villages of the Orne, Choulet's book is also a splendidly evocative
portrayal of Marie's two worlds. Essential, too, as a visual repre-
sentation of her life and afterlife, is Christine Issartel's *Les dames
aux camélias de l'histoire à la légende.*

Several articles contained fascinating new material. In
L'Entr'acte, Charles Matharel de Fiennes, a well-respected theater critic, defended Marie's maid in print after she had been
accused of stealing. In return, Clotilde gave him some extraordinarily vivid, intimate information about Marie's early life and
final days (published in two parts on 10 and 11 February 1852).
L'Intermédiaire des Chercheurs et Curieux, a nineteenth-century
news aggregate, picked up an item published without a date in
the Caen-based theatrical journal *Les Coulisses.* It was a conversation about Marie's upbringing between Delphine and a lawyer, pseudonymously named "Quivis," under the heading "The
Truth about la Dame aux Camélias" (the title Vienne later used
for his book). This gave rise to a "curious letter" published in
Les Coulisses on 8 November 1882 by one E. du Mesnil, whose
convincing account of Marie's ancestry provided me with a fresh
interpretation. (Both accounts appeared in *L'Intermédiaire des
Chercheurs et Curieux* on 10 September 1890).

Two unexpectedly valuable sources were a quirky book and a

single page of a sale catalogue. Docteur Lucien-Graux's *Les factures de la dame aux camélias* itemizes and discusses all the bills kept by Marie—a revealingly exact record of how she lived—and includes two previously unpublished letters. The Hôtel Drouot sale, *Théâtre et Spectacle,* on 28 June 2004 auctioned Jean Darnel's collection of Marie Duplessis's memorabilia (much of it now in the Frederick R. Koch Collection of the Beinecke Rare Book and Manuscript Library at Yale). The Furnishings category included 1842 receipts for Chinese vases, a clock, and candlesticks paid for by Stackelberg, which enabled me to date the beginning of his relationship with Marie. A rental bill was even more telling—the evidence I needed to challenge Dumas fils's account about the duration of his affair with Marie. As Lucien-Graux says, "Dates can speak."

Notes

INTRODUCTION

3   "For several days": Letter (written in French) by Dickens to Count d'Orsay, Paris, March 1847. Published in Robert du Pontavice de Heussey, *L'inimitable Boz: Etude historique et anecdotique sur la vie et l'oeuvre de Charles Dickens* (Paris: M. Quantin, 1889).

5   "I should have died": Quoted in Francis Gribble, *Dumas, Father and Son* (London: Eveleigh Nash & Grayson, 1930).

5   "It's original!" Alexandre Dumas fils, "Mémoires littéraires: L'odyssée de la dame aux camélias," *L'Illustré Soleil du Dimanche,* undated, from the collection of Jean Hournon.

6   "I was the son": Ibid.

6   "It's impossible": *Revue Illustrée,* 15 May 1896, from the collection of Jean Hournon.

6   "a young scamp": Horace de Viel-Castel, *Mémoires sur la règne de Napoléon III, 1852–1864* (Paris: Chez Tous les Libraires, 1883).

7   "This play is shameful": Ibid.

7   "pocket-handkerchiefs as a provision for a play": Henry James, *The Scenic Art: Notes on Acting and the Drama, 1872–1901* (London: Rupert Hart-Davis, 1949).

7   "It's the new theatre": Arsène Houssaye, "Souvenirs de jeunesse," Sonnet LXXI (Paris: Flammarion, 1896).

8   "He could see the end of one era": Henry James, *The Scenic Art.*

9   "desired, demanded and begged": in Peter Southwell-Sandor, *Verdi: His Life and Times* (London: Midas Books, 1978).

9   "It's a work which goes straight to my heart" Quoted in Choulet,

Promenades à Paris et en Normandie auec la dame aux camélias (Paris: Editions Charles Corlet, 1998).

10 "How could Violetta be in her condition": Quoted in Arianna Stassinopoulos, *Maria: Beyond the Callas Legend* (London: Weidenfeld & Nicolson, 1980).

10 "What is immensely striking": Quoted in Joanna Richardson, *The Courtesans: The Demi-Monde in 14th-Century France* (London: Weidenfeld & Nicolson, 1967).

11 "If only I had seen her Marguerite": Quoted in Guido Noccioli, *Duse on Tour, Diaries 1906–07* (Manchester: Manchester University Press, 1982).

12 "Nothing makes any difference": James, *The Scenic Art.*

12 "an old clown": Quoted in Justine Picardie, *Coco Chanel: The Legend and the Life* (New York: HarperCollins, 2010).

12 "She never touches but kisses" Quoted in Diana Souhami, *Greta & Cecil* (London: Jonathan Cape, 1994).

13 "old hack story": Frederick Ashton to author.

14 "a mysterious friend": Bernard Raffailli, in notes to Dumas fils, *La dame aux camélias* (Paris: Gallimard, 1975).

15 "No one had told them": Théodore de Bauville, *Mes souvenirs* (Paris: G. Charpentier, 1883).

16 "What rankles in me" and following analyses of Violetta: Quoted in Nicholas John, ed., *Violetta and Her Sisters: The Lady of the Camellias* (London: Faber & Faber, 1994).

17 "something of that vulnerability": Margot Fonteyn, *Autobiography* (London: W. H. Allen, 1975).

17 "Oh how I could have loved!": Julie Bernat Judith, *La vie d'une comédienne: Mémoires de Madame Judith de la Comédie-Française et souvenirs sur ses contemporains,* ed. Paul Gsell (Paris: J. Tallandrier, 1911).

17 Performance history has made this a love story: Isabelle Adjani played Marguerite at the age of forty-five; Fonteyn was forty-four to Nureyev's twenty-five; and in the most recent *Marguerite and Armand* partnership there are fifteen years between Tamara Rojo and twenty-three-year-old Sergei Polunin.

17 "far superior to the profession she practises": *Le Mousquetaire,* 23 March 1855.

17 "Without her knowing it": Franz Liszt and Marie d'Agoult, *Correspondence,* ed. Serge Gut and Jacqueline Bellas (Paris: Fayard, 2001). Letter to Marie d'Agoult, Iassy, 2 May or 2 June 1847. Frederick

Ashton always felt that the Piano Sonata in B Minor—the music he chose for *Marguerite and Armand* before learning of Liszt's affair with Marie—serendipitously fell into place after he discovered the context. "One doesn't know how much of the piece was Liszt's memory of her. It may not have been so, possibly not in the least. But you see it *could* have been." Ashton to David Daniel, November 1974.

PART ONE: ALPHONSINE
WAIF

22   "Continuously going up and down green humps": Theodore Reff, ed., *The Notebooks of Edgar Degas* (Oxford University Press, 1976).

26   "He was of an ideal beauty": Charles du Hays, *L'ancien Merlerault: Récits chevalins d'un vieil éleveur* (Paris: Morris Père et Fils, 1885).

27   "Marie Deshayes fell in love at first sight": Ibid.

27   The younger of their two daughters was Marie Louise Michelle Deshayes: The source of the error was the article *"Les quartiers de la dame aux camélias,"* written in 1887 by Count Gérard de Contades, president of the Historic and Archaeological Society of Orne. The Ornaise historian Robert du Mesnil du Buisson, himself a descendent of Anne du Mesnil, put the record straight, explaining that the confusion had arisen over the homonyme of Louis Deshayes (born 1761, son of Anne de Mesnil and Etienne Deshayes) and Louis Deshayes (born in 1765, son of Louis Deshayes and Françoise Riche). The correct family tree, which first appeared in the January–March 1982 edition of *Au Pays d'Argentelles: La Revue Culturelle de l'Orne,* is duplicated in Jean-Marie Choulet, *Promenades à Paris et en Normandie avec la dame aux camélias* (Paris: Editions Charles Corlet, 1998).

27   "Because the Count du H. was a gentleman": E. du Mesnil, *L'Intermédiaire des Chercheurs et Curieux,* 10 September 1890.

30   "After her recovery": Ibid.

32   It was Marie's aunt and uncle: An unpublished letter written by the well-known Ornaise writer Gustave Le Vavasseur claims that after selling his wife's possessions in the town square of Exmes, Marin took both girls to Paris—but this is a misapprehension: Delphine did not leave Normandy until after her sister had died. Beinecke Rare Book and Manuscript Library, Yale University.

34   "The immense convoy was watched": Imbert de Saint-Amand, *The Duchess of Berry and the Revolution of 1830* (London: Hutchinson, 1893).

36   "He made everyone tremble": Charles Matharel de Fiennes, *L'Entr'acte*, 10 and 11 February 1852.

39   Maison Fremin, the umbrella shop where she began work: Vienne misspells the owner Louis Fremin's name as Firmin.

40   a louche element to Gacé: Vienne claims that it was in Gacé that Alphonsine met the procuress whom Alexandre Dumas fils names Prudence in *La dame aux camélias*. But, as Vienne also calls her Prudence, rather than her real name, Clémence Prat, this may just be supposition on his part.

40   "the old swooning sweetness": Appendix to R.W.B. Lewis, *Edith Wharton: A Biography* (New York: Harper Collins, 1975).

41   Vienne, however, insists that it was Marin: Matharel de Fiennes, *L'Entr'acte*, 10 and 11 February 1852. Fiennes wrote with such insider knowledge about Alphonsine's early life that he must have been fed information by someone close to her—very probably her maid.

41   Alphonsine was given a stuffed green lizard: In a letter to the firm making an inventory of her dead sister's belongings, Delphine wrote, "Look carefully in my sister's peignoir, and, unless it's been stolen, you will find there a little box containing a green lizard." Charles du Hays, "The Ring and the Lizard," in *Récits du coin du feu: Autour du Merlerault* (Alençon, 1886).

41   "What do you expect?": Matharel de Fiennes, *L'Entr'acte*, 10 and 11 February 1852.

42   "child full of fear": Ibid.

42   "pay for her promiscuity": *Paris Elégant*, 1 March 1847.

42   "the most suspect places": Gustave Claudin, *Mes souvenirs: Les boulevards de 1840–1870* (Paris: Calmann Lévy, 1884).

43   "She was nibbling a green apple": Nestor Roqueplan, *Parisine* (Paris: J. Hetzel et Cie, 1868).

43   "Not only delicious, but sacred" Théodore de Banville, *Petites études, Paris vécu* (Paris: G. Charpentier, 1883).

43   "like a peasant" . . . "This made her": Roqueplan, *Parisine*.

GRISETTE

44   "Most of those without cavaliers left better accompanied": Anon., *Paris dansant; ou, Les filles d'Hérodiade* (Paris: J. Bréauté, 1845).

44 "Louise was one": Henri Murger, *Scènes de la vie de bohème* (Paris: Calmann Lévy, 1886).

46 "Jumps, fluttering": Anon., *Paris dansant*.

46 "A helter-skelter of bewildering dash": Quoted in David Price, *Cancan!* (London: Cygnus Arts, 1998).

47 "would recount": Murger, *Scènes de la vie de bohéme*.

48 "Since when have we eaten": Ibid.

48 "explosion of joy": "Un Inconnu," in *Paris Elégant*, 1 March 1847.

48 "one of those girls of the Latin Quarter": Roqueplan, *Parisine*.

49 "A dinner tempts her": Anon., *Paris dansant*.

49 "on anatomy, physiology": Anon., *La grisette à Paris et en province. Sa vie, ses moeurs, son caractère, ses joies, ses espérances, ses tribulations* (Paris: Renault, 1843).

49 "sparked a revolution": Matharel de Fiennes, *L'Entr'acte*, 10 and 11 February 1852.

50 "welcomed by two students": "Quivis" in *L'Intermédiaire des Chercheurs et Curieux*, 10 September 1890.

50 "Tired of this miserable life": Matharel de Fiennes, *L'Entr'acte*, 10 and 11 February 1852.

50 "lulling the dark city": Emile Zola, *The Belly of Paris*, trans. and ed. Brian Nelson (Oxford: Oxford University Press, 2007).

51 "They're virtuous": Quoted by Joëlle Guillais-Maury in Michèle Bordeaux et al., *Madame ou mademoiselle? Itinéraires de la solitude féminine, 19–20me siècle* (Paris: Montalban, 1984).

51 "the prettiest working girls": Roqueplan, *Parisine*.

52 "frisked about like fish": Quoted in Guillais-Maury in Bordeaux, *Madame ou mademoiselle?*

52 "It's the intimate hour of the Bois": Edmond Texier, *Tableau de Paris* (Paris: Paulin et Le Chevalier, 1852–53).

54 "Her hat is not much more": Ibid.

55 "ugly, improper": Nestor Roqueplan, *Regain: La vie parisienne* (Paris: Librairie Nouvelle, 1853).

56 As well as returning the money she owed: Charles du Hays gives a completely contrary account. It was when Alphonsine fell on hard times, he says, that she gave away her ring. "One of her companions, moved by pity, offered the poor Alphonsine nine francs—everything she possessed. Then poor Alphonsine, in a surge of gratitude, gave her friend this ring. . . . These nine francs bought bread for a few days." Matharel de Fiennes, *L'Entr'acte*, 10 and 11 February 1852.

LORETTE

57   "The lorette is a grisette": Bordeaux et al., *Madame ou mademoiselle?*

57   "The lorette sleeps in an acacia gondola": Anon., *Paris dansant.*

57   "The grisette gives, the lorette receives": Bordeaux et al., *Madame ou Mademoiselle?*

58   "to this aim one sacrifices everything": Anon., *Paris dansant.*

58   "At Chaumière the woman dances for pleasure" . . . "From these aquaintances": Ibid.

59   When she realized that Valory had abandoned her: This is presumably "le petit vicomte de L.," whom Prudence describes to Armand Duval in the novel of *La dame aux camélias*. He is forced to leave, she says, "because Marguerite almost ruined him." She cried when he left, and although she went as usual to the theater as if nothing had happened, she still kept a miniature of him.

60   "a true friend" . . . "I lack nothing": Letter quoted in Emile Henriot, *Portraits des femmes d'Héloïse à Katherine Mansfield* (Paris: Albin Michel, 1951).

61   There, a midwife was employed: Doubting the veracity of Vienne's account, a subsequent biographer, Georges Soreau, wrote to the mayor of Versailles asking if one Alphonsine Plessis had given birth to a child around 1841. The mayor, replying on 21 February 1898, claimed that there was no record of any such birth on the Etat Civil lists from 1833 to 1853—as indeed is the case. These lists and parish registers are now numerized and available online. Document, code 5MI131BIS-Commune ancienne paroisse Versailles Acte: TD-Dates: 1833–1842, pp. 92–467. We can see that eight Plessis children were born over this period, but none to a single mother named Alphonsine. It could well be that Vienne was mistaken and the child was born in a different parish or in Paris itself. But this is impossible to confirm as the city's registry acts before 1859 were among the Hôtel de Ville's eight million documents destroyed in the great fire of May 1871. However, even the skeptical Soreau came to conclude that Alphonsine had "very probably been a mother." He was assured of this by Mme Henriette Alexandre Dumas, the author's widow, who said that her husband had alluded more than once to the fact that the Lady of the Camellias had borne a child. And there are other endorsements: *L'Intermédiaire des Chercheurs et Curieux* of 10 September 1890, claims, "She had a child who was

recognised by his father, who favoured him in his will." While the most convincing evidence of all is a remark in a letter from Charles du Hays to Gérard de Contades. Helping with background research for the count's seminal article *"Les quartiers de la dame aux camélias,"* du Hays urges, "I beg you to not talk of her son." This was written in January 1885—two years before the publication of Romain Vienne's memoir.

61   "moderately pretty": *L'Intermédiaire des Chercheurs et Curieux,* 10 September 1890.

64   But the viscount's letters and payments had then stopped: Unconvinced by the viscount's claim, Vienne asked Alphonsine if she had requested the proof of a death certificate. She had not. But, once again, there are different accounts of what became of her son. *L'Intermédiaire des Chercheurs et Curieux* (10 September 1890) reports: "The child died, and la dame aux camélias inherited from her son." Charles du Hays told Count Gérard de Contades that a stranger, renowned in equestrian circles, arrived one day in his office who was not only "the image of Mlle Plessis" but also the right age to have been her son. Delphine also believed that she had seen Alphonsine's son as an adult. In 1869, she told Vienne, a young man in his late twenties had turned up at her home near Gacé. With exquisite politeness, he asked if he could see the portrait of her sister painted by Vidal. "He looked at it for a long time in silence, with visible emotion, not managing to hide the tears. . . . He then thanked her and greeted her graciously, leaving his card with the words: 'Judelet, employee of a business in Tours.'" "Good God—how like my sister he was!" Delphine exclaimed to her children, and the next morning she sent her eldest daughter to all the hotels of Gacé in an attempt to find him. To no avail. She also wrote to the mayor of Tours, sending him the business card and asking him for information, only to be told a week later that no person or business existed bearing this name.

64   "plush white hat": Docteur Lucien-Graux, *Les factures de la dame aux camélias* (Clichy: Paul Dupout, 1934).

65   "Our cousin Marie": In Charles A. Dolph, *The Real "Lady of the Camellias" and Other Women of Quality* (London: T. W. Laurie, 1927).

65   "Rare lorettes": Roqueplan, *Regain.*

66   "I felt myself tapped on the shoulder": Roqueplan, *Parisine.*

PART TWO: MARIE

70 "The Gs have retired": Benjamin Disraeli, *Letters* (University of Toronto Press, 1982).

70 A portrait of him as a student: Puzzlingly, both Nestor Roqueplan and Agénor's biographer, Constantin de Grunwald, describe the young duke as blond.

71 "absolutely without fortune": Dorothée Dino, *Chronique de 1831 à 1862 par la princesse Radziwill* (Paris: Librarie Plon, 1909).

71 "The Duke de G.": Column signed "Méjannes," *Gil Blas,* 18 October 1887.

71 "beautiful lion" . . . "On a day of mourning": Matharel de Fiennes, *L'Entr'acte,* 10 and 11 February 1852.

72 Barely disguised in his memoir: There are several inaccuracies in Vienne's account of "Tiche," who was twenty-two at the time, not "about thirty," but the description of him as a "beautiful man with an impressive moustache and superb black side whiskers" exactly mirrors the handsome figure in Count d'Orsay's portrait.

73 Aware that a sense of shame prevented Lili: In the 1921 silent film *Camille,* the bisexual movie star Alla Nazimova introduced a charged encounter with a trusting ingenue played by a pretty actress whom she was pursuing offscreen.

73 If their intimacy was a sapphic interlude: The practice of lesbianism by "tribades" was defined by Alexandre Parent-Duchâtelet, author of the renowned 1836 survey *Prostitution in 19th-Century Paris,* as "the basest degree of vice of which a human being is capable." Alexandre Parent-Duchâtelet, *La prostitution à Paris au XIXe siècle* (Paris: Editions du Seuil, 1981).

74 "Her presence produced": *Courrier de la Ville,* 20 May 1842.

75 "another person" . . . "the delirium of transformation": Stefan Zweig, *Post Office Girl,* trans. Joel Rotenberg. (London: Sort of Books, 2009).

76 "an oracle of fashion": Lady Blessington—whose lover was Ida de Gramont's brother the Count d'Orsay—gives an amusing account in her memoirs of the duchess taking her shopping. Her dress and bonnet, which she had always considered perfectly wearable, drew a contemptuous look from the couturier at Herbault, "the Temple" of Parisian fashion. "The Duchess, too quick-sighted not to observe his surprise, explained that I had been six years absent from Paris, and only arrived the night before from Italy." After proceeding to

another boutique to order lace jackets and morning dresses, the pair
returned to Lady Blessington's hotel, "my head filled with notions
of the importance of dressing à la mode . . . and my purse consider-
ably lightened." Countess of Blessington, *The Idler in France* (London: Henry Colburn, 1841).

76 "Who can explain": Matharel de Fiennes, *L'Entr'acte,* 10 and 11 February 1852.

77 "Someone you don't know": Letter dated 24 July 1842. Original
copy in the Frederick R. Koch Collection, Beinecke Rare Book and
Manuscript Library, Yale University.

77 "What should I do?": Quoted in Baron de Plancy, *Souvenirs et indiscrétions d'un disparu* (Paris: Paul Ollendorff, 1892).

77 "History of His Own Times": Quoted in R. R. Madden, *The Literary Life and Correspondence of the Countess of Blessingham* (London: T.
C. Newby, 1855), vol. 1.

78 "a modern Raoul de Courcy": Letter of 3 January 1845, in ibid.,
vol. 2.

78 "My dear Agénor": Frederick R. Koch Collection, Beinecke Rare
Book and Manuscript Library, Yale University.

79 "Adieu my darling angel, don't forget me too much, and think
sometimes of her": Instead of "celle" Marie writes "sel" [salt]—the
only conspicuous slip in her otherwise polished, if poorly punctu-
ated, French.

79 Like the two single Englishwomen: If Vienne is correct in saying that
Marie still lived in the rue d'Antin, then the address she gave in *Badeblatt* of "St Germain" was false (perhaps explained by a remark in a
book of Parisian mores that an "Honest Young Girl" would live only
in the faubourg Saint-Germain). More confusing is the address in her
passport, which is given as 28, rue Mont du Thabor: the Archives de
Paris provide no name of owner or lessee of the property but details
this only as "a boutique and other residences." It may, however, have
been Guiche's address—as claimed by the Count de Contades in an
article published in *Le Livre* (10 December 1885, no. 72).

81 But while she was in her element: On July 25, *Badeblatt* records
that the Marquis de Rodes was still at the Hôtel d'Angleterre, but
General Duke v. Skarzynsky had left Baden-Baden.

81 "Do not fear": Judith, *La vie d'une grande comédienne.*

82 "He has just rented" Letter of 21 December 1802, in Comte de Nesselrode, *Lettres et papiers, 1760–1850* (Paris: A. Lehure, 1904), vol. 2.

83 As special envoy for the czar: With his customary "tetchy" expression, Stackelberg is seated on the extreme right of Isabey's sepia drawing, seen remonstrating with a German confederate who is taking notes. The count's main aim was to unite Poland with Russia—which was successfully achieved.

84 "He's a unique character": Grande-Duchesse Hélène to Countess Charles de Nesselrode, 26 December 1828. Nesselrode, *Lettres et papiers*, vol. 7.

84 "The feelings of this father": *La dame aux camélias* (Paris: Collection Folio Classique, Gallimard, 1975).

85 "The count, in spite of his great age": Alexandre Dumas fils, *Théâtre complet*, vol. 3: *Notes* (Paris: Calmann Lévy, 1898).

85 "The essential fact": Francis Gribble, *Dumas Father and Son* (London: Eveleigh Nash & Grayson, 1930).

85 "they were taught not only to dance": Maria Czapska, *Une famille d'Europe centrale 1772–1914* (Paris: Plon, 1972).

86 "From this moment": Judith, *La vie d'une grande comédienne.*

86 Sporting chain-mail breastplates: From Lucien-Graux, *Les factures de la dame aux camélias.*

87 Still renting cheap lodgings: The platonic friendship that the novel's narrator forms with Sally Bowles, a bohemian English cabaret singer, is founded on the same blend of fondness, trust, and exasperation. She too openly confesses her noctural adventures until he protests, "If you go to bed with every single man in Berlin and come and tell me about it each time, you still won't convince me that you're *la Dame aux Camélias*—because, really and truly, you know, you aren't." Christopher Isherwood, *Goodbye to Berlin* (London: Hogarth Press, 1939).

87 Still addressing her as Alphonsine: A change of name was not unusual among women of the demimonde as a way of protecting the honor of their families, but Alphonsine's choice was a tribute to her late mother, Marie Plessis. Duplessis—or du Plessis—is a common name in Normandy, though the addition of a prefix may have been Agénor's idea (the mother of Armand de Guiche was a du Plessis—Françoise-Marguerite). It seems fitting in Marie's case that the original definition came from the language of courtly love and meant a "park of pleasure."

87 "Call it a project, a fantasy": Situated just outside the village of

Nonant-le-Pin, "Le Plessis" is now a working farm whose owners, M. and Mme Ruault, offer bed-and-breakfast accommodation.

88 could never confess his feelings: The English journalist Albert Vandam was someone else whose company she welcomed because he avoided flattering her. Albert Vandam, *An Englishman in Paris,* vol. 1 (New York: D. Appleton & Co., 1892).

88 "For some time": Judith, *La vie d'une grande comédienne.*

89 "like fits of madness": January 1821. Nesselrode, *Lettres et papiers,* vol. 6.

90 "a duchess could not have smiled differently": Dumas fils, *La dame aux camélias.*

90 "retired existence": Vandam, *An Englishman in Paris,* vol. 1.

91 "Mixing only with men of wealth and education": Parent-Duchâtelet, *La prostitution à Paris.*

PART THREE: THE LADY OF THE CAMELLIAS

95 "In novels": Arsène Houssaye, *Man about Paris,* trans. Henry Kepler (London: Victor Gollancz, 1972).

96 "the poem of Paris": Quoted in Philip Mansel, *Paris Between Empires: Monarchy and Revolution 1814–1852* (London: John Murray, 2001).

97 "culinary glory": Jacques Castelnau, *En remontant les grands boulevards* (Paris: Le Livre Contemporain, 1960).

98 "Nobody was tolerated": Claudin, *Mes souvenirs.*

99 "I gave in": Quoted in Joanna Richardson, *Rachel* (London: Max Reinhardt, 1956).

99 *"Le tout Paris"*: Jules Bertaut, *Le Boulevard* (Paris: Jules Tallandier, 1957).

99 "Alphonsine Plessis interests me very much": Quoted in Vandam, *An Englishman in Paris.*

99 "I wanted to know the refinements": Judith, *La vie d'une grande comédienne.*

100 "Whoever dares": Quoted in Arsène Houssaye, *La pécheresse* (Paris: M. Lévy Frères, 1863).

100 "friend of the Café de Paris band": Bertaut, *Le Boulevard.*

101 "without intellect, but with a rich instinct": Roqueplan, *Parisine.*

101 "but she talked nothing but nonsense": Houssaye, *Man about Paris.*

101 His main talent was as an observer: Vandam's anecdotal "Notes and

Recollections," entitled *An Englishman in Paris,* was first published anonymously in 1892 and then reprinted several times under his own name.

102 "something provoking and voluptuous": Claudin, *Mes souvenirs.*

102 "The Irish woman": Ibid.

102 Lola's phony Spanish look: The painter is likely to have been either Jean-Charles Olivier, a pupil of Delaroche, who exhibited at the Paris Salon from 1840 to 1848, or Louis-Camille d'Olivier, who specialized in portraits and whose work was shown at the Salon between 1848 and 1870.

103 "Only the large black eyes": Paul de Saint-Victor, *Le théâtre contemporain* (Paris: C. Lévy, 1889).

104 "a woman of unnerving contrasts": Jennifer Homans, *Apollo's Angels: A History of Ballet* (London: Granta, 2010).

104 "the devotion of the erotic Boulevard": Claudin, *Mes souvenirs.*

104 "Disciples of Eros": Roger de Beauvoir, *Voluptueux souvenirs; ou, Le Souper des Douze* (Paris: Romainville, no date).

105 "the most audacious": Castelnau, *En remontant les grands boulevards.*

105 "thrice rich": Preface to Roger de Beauvoir, *Les soupers de mon temps* (collection of Jean-Marie Choulet).

105 "not one had the verve of Roger de Beauvoir": Ibid.

105 "My dear Arvers": Quoted in Léon Séché, *Alfred de Musset: L'homme et l'oeuvre—Les camarades* (Paris: Société du Mercure de France, 1907).

106 "At first glance": Houssaye, *Man about Paris.*

109 "the consecration of Marie Duplessis": Johannes Gros, *Alexandre Dumas et Marie Duplessis* (Paris: Louis Conard, 1923).

110 "From the stage": *The Goncourt Journals, 1851–1870,* ed. Lewis Galantière (London: Cassell, 1937).

111 "All these girls wanted to be actresses": Houssaye, *Man about Paris.*

111 Marie studied for a short time: I'm indebted to Kristine Baril for finding the reference to Marie's link with Ricourt in Henry Morel, *Le pilori des communeux* (Paris: E. Lachaud, 1871). Ricourt studied painting with Géricault and Delacroix and founded the journal *L'Artiste* before concentrating on teaching drama.

111 "Mademoiselle, you": Charles Monselet. *Le musée secret de Paris* (Paris: Michel Lévy Frères, 1870).

112 "The theatre, you understand": *Le Mousquetaire,* 1 April 1855.

112 "It's there above all": Saint-Victor, *Le théâtre contemporain.*

113 It was sent to the *distributeur des faveurs:* Marie addresses the recipi-

ent as "My little monsieur Amant," which may be her misspelling of the Christian name "Amand" (she even misspells her own name at the end), or it may be a deliberate play on the word *amant,* French for "lover."

113   "Once again I'm asking": Quoted in Lucien-Graux, *Les factures de la dame aux camélias.*

114   "Vendu a Madame Dupleci": Gros, *Une courtisane romantique.*

114   It is her way of alluding: In Frederick Ashton's ballet *Marguerite and Armand,* Margot Fonteyn, "for reasons of modesty connected with the novel," insisted on wearing only white flowers. The designer Cecil Beaton, however, appears not to have known about the tradition linked to the display of red blooms, as he intended, says his biographer Hugo Vickers, "to put red camellias on most of Margot Fonteyn's gowns."

115   And with several friends and acquaintances in common: George Sand makes no mention of Marie in her journals and letters—not even during the course of her long correspondence with Alexandre Dumas fils. Dumas, though, must have read *Isidora,* as he answered the scholars who had criticized him for spelling camellia with a single 'l' with the comment "It's because Madame Sand used this word as I did, and I would rather write badly with her example than write well with that of others." Marie, however, may also have been guilty of plagiarism. One of the habitués of the Café de Paris was one M. Lautour-Mezeray, known as "l'homme au camélia" because of his habit of never appearing in public without a single white bloom in his buttonhole (as in Lami's *Le foyer de la danse,* where he is pictured leaning against a pillar, languidly eyeing a ballerina). She would undoubtedly have known Lautour-Mezeray, who belonged to her set, and they might even have discovered that they came from the same Orne district of Normandy. Albert Vandam implies, however, that he would not have approved of Marie's "usurpation" of his signature camellia, on which he must have spent no less than fifty thousand francs. "It was more than an ornament to him . . . he looked upon it as a talisman." When Dumas fils's novel appeared, l'homme au camélia voiced his resentment of its title: "It injures my own."

115   "one immense Belshazzar's hall": Lord Beaconsfield, *Correspondence with His Sister, 1832–1852* (London: John Murray, 1886). Letter of 16 January 1843.

116   "Your conversation tonight interested me": Quoted in Gros, *Une*

courtisane romantique. First printed in *L'amateur d'autographes,* no. 18 (April 1865) as the only letter of MD to have been sold at auction, first in the collection of Trémont (1852) and then in that of Laverdet (1861).

117 "When we were installed": Mané, *Le Paris viveur* (Paris: E. Dentu, 1862).

117 The beautiful grace which he brought: This all sounds entirely plausible, except for the fact that Henri de Pené would have been only fourteen years old at the time. It could be argued, though, that he was an exceptionally precocious student, as he had established himself as a political columnist by the age of nineteen. Also, if Marie had been approached by teenagers, it would explain her initial hesitation about accepting their invitation. "You know, don't you, that an Opera ball is every schoolboy's dream," remarks the narrator of Alexandre Dumas fils's *La vie à vingt ans* (Paris: Michel Lévy Frères, 1854). "I sold my dictionaries in order to go," replies his friend.

—And did you have fun?

—Well, every time a woman approached, I trembled for fear that she might speak to me.

—Why did you go then?

—So that the next day I could tell my friends I'd been, and because I wanted to give myself the air of a debauched rake.

Vienne's far less persuasive version has Perregaux falling in love at first sight with Marie seated in her box at the Opéra.

117 Count Edouard de Perregaux: Vienne disguises him as "Robert de Saint-Yves," a name he may have taken from the original French translation of Verdi's *La Traviata,* in which the surname of the heroine, Violetta, Marie's operatic counterpart, is de Saint-Ys.

117 "Mlle A.O.": Edition of 8 May 1843.

121 The tone of a formal, impatient note: No trace of evidence exists for this voyage, but her most reliable biographer, the scholarly Johannes Gros, was convinced that a large medallion called *Tête d'étude avec fleurs,* which appeared at the Salon of 1849, was a portrait of Marie painted in Rome. Its subsequent disappearance makes his claim impossible to verify.

121 "After her death a copy of the novel": Claudin, *Mes souvenirs.* Charles Matharel de Fiennes claimed to have seen a portrait, "painted by a master," which was a version of Greuze's famous work *Jeune fille à*

la cruche cassée; instead of the broken vase, a symbol of lost virginity, "Marie holds in her hand the immortal book of Abbé Prévost" (*L'Entr'acte,* 10 and 11 February 1852).

122 their passion was a source of misery: In Dumas's novel, it is Armand who sends Marguerite a copy of the book, wanting to draw her attention to their resemblance to Prévost's lovers. (It is inscribed "Manon to Marguerite. Humility" and signed "Armand Duval.") Realizing that he cannot change his mistress's life, Armand resolves to change his own; he starts gambling in order to meet their expenditure and discovers this to be an effective distraction. "Jealousy would have kept me awake . . . while gambling gave a new turn to the fever which would otherwise have preyed upon my heart." Ned, however, could not bring himself to be complicit.

123 Ned Perregaux had acquired: There is no entry of a sale in the name of Perregaux—or anyone else associated with Marie—in the listings of the region's notary at the time, Léon Armand Gaucheron, whose records are held in Montigny Archives. According to Vienne, though, the Perregaux family had their own notary in Paris, but with no knowledge of a name, it is impossible to trace a confirmation of the property sale. An article in *La Gazette de Bougival* (undated clipping in the collection of Jean-Marie Choulet) is illustrated with a photograph of the house—now a suburban villa—believed to have been Marie's. No source of evidence is given for this, nor for the following claim: "Marie Duplessis lived on the Ile de la Chaussée, the eastern tip of which is known as Ile Gautier (Marguerite's surname)."

125 is said to have been frequented by Marie: Called La Camélia in response to local lore, the restaurant still exists today and has one Michelin star.

125 As a laureate of Chantilly: With thoroughbreds costing fabulous prices there were only nine of the Jockey Club's three hundred members wealthy enough to *faire courir*—to own and raise racehorses. Edouard de Perregaux was one of them.

125 "enormous debts and terrifying losses": *Le Siècle,* 8 May 1843.

126 "It's a very agreeable surprise": Quoted in Choulet, *Promenades à Paris et en Normandie avec la dame aux camélias.*

127 "But he kept Alphonsine out of sight": Quoted in Nicholas John, *Violetta and Her Sisters.*

127 "I adore you": This is the passage read aloud by Armand in the play, after which he remarks, "She's right, but she does not love, because love knows no reason."

128 "lady companion": *Faculté de droit de Toulouse* (Toulouse: Caillol et Baylac, 1869).

131 "a free, blissful society": Quoted in Prasteau, *The Lady of the Camellias: A Story of Marie Duplessis.*

132 But even a century earlier: In John Neumeier's 1978 ballet version, the heroine is shadowed by a second ballerina in the role of Manon, who becomes the amoral, materialistic doppelgänger of loving, tender Marguerite.

132 "At the beginning of the third act": Quoted in Vandam, *An Englishman in Paris,* vol. 1.

133 "Mme la Comtesse Deperegaud": Lucien-Graux, *Les factures de la dame aux camélias.*

PART FOUR: MARGUERITE

139 "a great similarity with her own": Hays, *L'Ancien Merlerault.*

139 "as a work of charity": Quoted in Georges Soreau *La Vie de la dame aux camélias* (Paris: Editions de la *Revue de France,* 1898).

139 "She was discovered twelve years later": Parent-Duchâtelet, *La prostitution à Paris au XIXe siècle.*

143 Count von Stackelberg had come back: Baden-Baden's Liste des Etrangers records that "Stackelberg, baron de, Russe" was staying in the town (without his wife, who went earlier that summer) between 21 August and 22 September—a period coinciding exactly with the dates that Ned Perregaux had been alone in Spa. But if Marie was reunited with Stackelberg in Baden-Baden she left no evidence to confirm it.

143 "Have you given it": "Méjannes," column in *Gil Blas,* 18 October 1887.

144 it was back in rue d'Antin: Joséphine Bloch, aka Marix, posed for two Ary Scheffer paintings in 1837 when she was fifteen. A Scheffer oil painting given the title *Marie Duplessis, la dame aux camélias,* was sold at an auction in Fontainebleau in November 1996, but the pensive girl sitting in an armchair bears little resemblance to Marie. Catalogue from the collection of Jean Hournon.

145 "an arsenal of the most elegant coquetterie": Henry Lumière, "La

dame aux camélias: Une lettre inédite de Marie Duplessis," La Revue Normande, 1900.

146 "She particularly owed her fortune": *Le Corsaire,* 8 March 1852.

146 "a thousand plots": Vandam, *An Englishman in Paris,* vol. 1.

147 "interested her far less": Gros, *Une courtisane romantique.*

147 The cause of tuberculosis would not be discovered: Evading the medical profession for centuries, the means of transmission was not known until the German bacteriologist Robert Koch identified the bacillus, subsequently given his name. R.T.H. Laënnec, one of the most revered figures in the history of French medicine, regarded the question of contagion as "highly dubious . . . In France, at least, it does not seem to be," he wrote in 1818, his opinion still virtually unquestioned by physicians forty years later.

147 "elixir of long life": Catalogue for Hôtel Drouot sale, 28 June 2004, from the collection of Jean Darnel.

147 "with perfect mediocrity": *Le Corsaire,* 4 April 1852.

147 "the coming of old age": Dumas fils, *La dame aux camélias.*

149 "You're wasting your time, Marquis": There is a very similar exchange in the novel between Marguerite and the Count de N.

—How are you this evening?

—Bad, Marguerite replies dryly.

—Is it because I'm inconveniencing you?

—Perhaps.

—What a way to receive me! What have I done, dear Marguerite?

—My dear friend, you haven't done anything. I am ill, and I need to rest, so you will oblige me by leaving. What bores me is not being able to return in the evening without you appearing five minutes later. What exactly do you want? That I become your mistress? Well, I've already told you a hundred times no. That you annoy me horribly, and that you should fix your attention on someone else. . . . Look, Nanine [her maid] is back; she will show you to the door. Goodnight.

150 Some chroniclers of Marie's: According to Johannes Gros, Ned "certainly provided Dumas with several character traits for the suitor," while the historian R. du Mesnil du Buisson cites evidence for this in the scene where the Count de N. pulls out a splendid pocket watch and announces that it is time for him to go to his club. The Swiss Perregauxs were famous watchmakers, and Ned himself

owned a magnificent example encased in gold and engraved with his entwined initials and the family coat of arms.

151 The veteran actor Marie Bouffé: *Le dîner de Madelon* was a one-act vaudeville by Désaugiers. Davesne's *Le père Turlututu* had Bouffé as the lead, and the program included Racine's *Phèdre* with Jacques-Charles Odry, *La Basquaise* by Fusch and Mlle Bertin, and *Premières armes de Richelieu,* starring Virginie Déjazet. The performance concluded with the two-act *Le gamin de Paris,* by Bayard and Van den Bruck; a polka, *Le pas de la sylphide;* followed by a quadrille in which various artists appeared. "Then M. Cavallo, the pianist, played several pieces of his own composition," wrote Paul d'Ariste. "A rather overloaded programme, as one can see." *La vie et le monde du boulevard (1830–1870)* (Paris: Jules Tallandier, 1930).

151 "Her name on the posters": Eugène Pierron, *Virginie Déjazet* (Paris: Bolle-Lasalle, 1856).

151 "Every member of the press" and "She spoke in all the jargons": Eugène de Mirecourt, *Déjazet* (Paris: Gustave Havard, 1855).

152 "She was alone there": If this was the same gala night, then it must have been Stackelberg, not Ned Perregaux, who provided the box for Marie—not surprisingly, as the price for a stage box at a special benefit performance such as this was "enough to keep a family for six months." Jules Janin, *L'Artiste,* 1 December 1851; Dumas fils, *Théâtre complet,* vol. 3: Notes.

153 Alexandre was eyeing but Marie: Marie could have been collecting the bronze frame itemized on her Susse account as paid for by Ned and engraved with the Perregaux arms. Susse was also the dealer of sculptures by James Pradier, whose wife, Louise, had seduced Dumas fils in 1843 and was the model for the nymphomaniac heroine of his novel *L'affaire Clemenceau.*

153 "She wore a muslin dress": Dumas fils (preface by André Maurois), *La dame aux camélias.* Years later, Dumas fils bought Marie's chain from an antiquarian—"links of two centimetres separated by a tarnished little pearl"—which he gave to his daughter Jeanine d'Hauterive-Dumas, who wore it as a necklace.

154 Forced to pay his creditors: Alexandre Dumas fils is listed among the contributors to *Sylphide* from June–November 1843, and has a poem, *"À une jeune fille,"* in its July issue. In *Paris Elégant* (1 Octobre 1844) is a piece published under his own name, a tribute to the writer Joseph Méry.

155 "I know of no two characters": Quoted in F.W.J Hemmings, *The King of Romance: A Portrait of Alexandre Dumas* (London: Hamish Hamilton, 1979).

156 "We went together": Quoted in Gros, *Une courtisane romantique.*

156 "What are you complaining about?": Quoted in Viel-Castel, *Mémoires.*

156 "If you have spent a little too much time": *Paris Elégant,* 1 October 1844.

157 "She gave me to understand": Quoted in Edith Saunders, *The Prodigal Father: Dumas Père et Fils and* The Lady of the Camellias (London: Longmans, Green and Co., 1951).

157 On one such day: In the notes he gave to prepare the actors for a new production of his play, Dumas fils declared this to have been "a fine day in September '44"—the date every biographer and Dumas scholar, from André Maurois to Claude Schopp, has used to mark the beginning of his liaison with Marie. But not only was Alexandre involved with his actress in September 1844—their breakup, which caused him to "shed hot tears," was at the beginning of October—Marie had not yet moved in to boulevard de la Madeleine, where the events Dumas fils describes took place. Their first meeting must have been after January 1845, when she left rue d'Antin, and as both Marie and Eugène were present at the Variétés gala of February 25, it seems likely that Alexandre was there too. His reason for predating his first encounter with Marie by six or seven months—and presumably also for using her previous address in the novel—can only have been to make their affair appear more significant: she was, after all, the most profound influence on his career. Albert Vandam was right in saying that Dumas fils "had not seen half as much of Alphonsine Duplessis during her life as is commonly supposed."

157 "[He] went over": Dumas fils, *Théâtre complet,* vol. 3: *Notes.*

158 "I remember exactly": Ibid.

159 with Dumas's assurance: "At this point the narrative of the novel, Chapter X," he told his actors, "is even more faithful to the truth than the play. The whole novel conforms, more than the play, to actual events in this little drama of love."

159 "the same supper": Ibid.

160 "is likely to coat these" and "We know": Quoted in David S. Barnes, *The Making of a Social Disease: Tuberculosis in Nineteenth-Century France* (Berkeley: University of California Press, 1995).

160 "You don't have a father": Dumas fils, introduction to *L'affaire Clemenceau: Mémoire de l'accusé* (Paris: Michael Lévy Frères, 1869).

161 "fired with proselytizing," Edmund Gosse, introduction to *The Lady of the Camellias* (London: William Heinemann, 1902).

162 "One morning I left at eight": Gros, *Une courtisane romantique.*

162 Marie Duplessis's new *amant de cœur:* The cause of an acrimonious end to Rachel's relationship with Count Alexandre in March 1845.

162 "He was famous among our generation": Letter to Calmann Lévy, printed in the 1886 edition of *La dame aux camélias* (Paris: Maison Quantin).

163 "As soon as a woman takes my arm": Quoted in Saunders, *The Prodigal Father.*

163 "Everyone turned to look": Villemessant, *Mémoires d'un journaliste: deuxième série: Les hommes de mon temps* (Paris: E. Dentu, 1872).

163 "He benefited from the myth": F. W. J. Hemmings, *The King of Romance.*

164 "causing problems": Dumas fils, letter to Joseph Méry, 18 October 1844, quoted in Saunders, *The Prodigal Father.*

165 "or else an effect of her state of health": Dumas fils (preface by André Maurois), *La dame aux camélias.*

165 "He was not bound to let the public know": Vandam, *An Englishman in Paris,* vol. I.

166 "So it's you, is it?": *Le Mousquetaire,* 1 April 1855.

168 "I hope you weren't in love": Ibid.

168 "more closely bound to the other": Hemmings, *The King of Romance.*

168 She had an Englishman: This may well have been Beau Brummel's friend Lord Alvanley (1798–1849), a keen rider to hounds, who was equally at home in French and English society. A witty bachelor and host, he was known to be recklessly extravagant, with a wide acquaintance of the world and proficiency in several languages.

168 "Dear Adet": Quoted in Choulet, *Promenades à Paris et en Normandie avec la dame aux camélias.*

169 "He always had" and "One often hears": Quoted in Marietta Martin, *Le Docteur Koreff (1783–1851): Un aventurier intellectuel sous la Restauration et la Monarchie de Juillet* (Paris: Edouard Champion, 1925).

170 "He is no longer received": Ibid.

170 "It always improves the appetite": Admiralty surgeon J. H. Whelan,

MD, RN, cites half a dozen case histories, one being a twenty-five-year-old sailor who suffered night sweats, coughing, and anorexia until tuberculin and strychnine injections cured him "in three weeks." "Strychnine-Tuberculin Treatment in Tuberculosis," *The British Medical Journal,* 16 May 1914.

170 Seeing how ill she was: "He was a curious character, this lord A.," Méjannes continues. "He came to Paris and bought half a dozen horses from Tony, telling him to keep them for a month or two as he was going to Brighton and would return for them. He left, made two or three world trips, and when he came back to Paris after several years in Japan, he had completely forgotten about the thoroughbreds that were awaiting collection.

170 a magnificent pair of thoroughbreds: Roqueplan, *Parisine.*

171 "In the woods": Michael Gustave du Puynode, "Marie Duplessis," *L'Artiste,* 1 novembre 1849.

171 "My very dear Marie": Quoted in Choulet, *Promenades à Paris et en Normandie avec la dame aux camélias.* The opening chimes almost exactly with the first lines of Armand's letter: 'Adieu, my dear Marguerite; I am neither rich enough to love you as I would like to, nor poor enough for you to love as you would like. Let's then forget, you a name to which you must be virtually indifferent, me, a happiness which appears to me impossible.' "

172 "What makes this one unique": Gros, *Une courtisane romantique.*

173 "It was 7 October 1845": Quoted in Henri Blaze de Bury, *Mes études et mes souvenirs: Alexandre Dumas, sa vie, son temps, ses œuvres* (Paris: Calmann Lévy, 1885).

173 "She walked on the muddy floor" . . . "very much astonished": Jules Janin, Preface to Dumas, *La dame aux camélias* (Paris: A. Sadot, 1851).

173 "for a week at the most": Liszt to his mother, Anna, 18 October 1845. Liszt, *Selected Letters,* trans. and ed. Adrian Williams (Oxford: Clarendon Press, 1998).

PART FIVE: THE COUNTESS

177 "a delirium unparalleled" and subsequent quotes on d'Agoult and Liszt: Eleanor Perényi, *Liszt.*

178 "If she tries to take Cosima": Ibid.

178 "People were hoping his work would fail": Adrian Williams, *Portrait of Liszt by Himself and His Contemporaries* (Oxford: Clarendon Press, 1990).

179 "Very happy to see me": Letter of 25 October 1845. Janin, 735 *lettres à sa femme.*

179 "Pompous nonsense": Letter of 10 August 1845. Ibid.

179 "There were more caps" . . . "It seemed": Janin, preface to *La dame aux camélias.*

180 "a very conspicuous" . . . "She has taken a fancy to you": *François Liszt: Recollections of a Compatriot* (London: Ward & Downey, 1887).

180 "as if the air were peopled with spirits": Amy Fay, quoted in Perényi, *Liszt.*

181 "set [her] dreaming" . . . "We were very much surprised": Janin, preface to *La dame aux camélias.*

181 "I am convinced that the lady": Ibid.

182 "We embarked at once upon elevated subjects": Quoted in Alan Walker, *Franz Liszt,* vol. 1: *The Virtuoso Years 1811–1847* (New York: Alfred A. Knopf, 1990).

182 "listening with uninterrupted attention": Janin, preface to *La dame aux camélias.*

182 "If a salonnière": Martin, *Le Docteur Koreff.*

183 "Koreff said the other day": 17 January 1840. Liszt and d'Agoult, *Correspondance.*

184 "abominable inventions" . . . "such that old vignerons": Banville, *Mes souvenirs.*

184 "The Lady of the Camellias had her own salon": Houssaye, *Man about Paris.*

184 "I shall not live" and following quotes: 2 May or 2 June 1847. Liszt and d'Agoult, *Correspondance.*

185 "the illustrious pianist L.": Roqueplan, *Parisine.*

185 "I have never told you": 1 May 1847. Liszt and d'Agoult, *Correspondance.*

185 "excitements . . . leading to disgust": 8 December 1842. Ibid.

185 "I shan't be able": 1 May 1847. Ibid.

186 "it's risky to tie me down": Quoted in Perényi, *Liszt.*

186 "I want to breathe": Ibid.

186 "the only reasonably possible journey": 1 May 1847. Liszt and d'Agoult, *Correspondance.*

186 at Jules Janin's house: Marie d'Agoult had mocked his "ridiculous

patronage of Janin," but Liszt defended his decision as "an affectionate courtesy on my part, in recognition of his past and present kindnesses."

186 "You would have looked in vain": Janin, preface to *La dame aux camélias.*

187 "as generous with Marie": Roqueplan, *Parisine.*

187 "Her beautiful hair" . . . "Only a few amateurs": Janin, preface to *La dame aux camélias.*

188 "Indiscriminately, she looked here and there": Ibid.

190 "Edward de Perregaux, 29 years: Choulet, *Promenades à Paris et en Normandie avec la dame aux camélias.*

191 "not the status . . . it was the title": In fact, Edouard de Perregaux was not entitled to call himself count until the death of his elder brother in 1857.

191 "Mme la Comtesse Deperegaud": Lucien-Graux, *Les factures de la dame aux camélias.*

191 "Mme la Comtesse du Plessis": Henry Lyonnet, La dame aux camélias *d'Alexandre Dumas fils* (Paris: Société Française d'Editions Littéraires et Techniques, 1930).

192 inspired by the stuffed green lizard: "Marie loved this lizard with tenderness, and kept it with her always," writes Charles du Hays in his article "The Ring and the Lizard," in *Récits du coin du feu: Autour du Merlerault* (Alençon, 1886). Wondering what became of it, he says, "It has slipped without doubt, like all the rest into the pits of misery which swallowed up everything." Far from it: Marie's wizened little lizard is now on display in its original case in Gacé's Musée de la Dame aux Camélias.

193 "I can see her now": Hays, *L'ancien Merlerault.*

196 mistress for ten years of . . . the author of *Carmen:* Mérimée's novella (more famous in Bizet's opera adaptation) had been published the previous year.

196 "A delicious young man": Ambroise Colin in Gros, *Une courtisane romantique.*

197 "Over there is the Ocean": Jules Janin, *Journal des Débats,* undated, in the collection of Jean-Marie Choulet.

197 "She had gained admission": Janin, preface to *La dame aux camélias.*

198 Vienne describes him as being very close to Liszt: "It may be impossible to identify with certainty Liszt's 'Teutonic' friend, though several individuals could fit the bill," says his biographer Alan Walker.

The archives of the Hôtel Meurice in Paris, where Vienne says "Prince Paul" kept a suite, might have provided a name, but documents from that period no longer exist. One possible contender is the Austro-Hungarian Count Ladislaus Koszielsky, an acquaintance of Liszt and (according to Janka Wohl) a lover of Marie. In his castle of Bertholdstein near Vienna, he showed Wohl a number of paintings, which he said were portraits of Marie, but none has been made public. Koszielsky, though, does not match Vienne's description of the young man as a member of a royal family. The details he gives are tantalizingly exact. Beneath the off-putting exterior, he was endearing and extremely generous—"a dream protector," Vienne says. "The sweetest, and least jealous suitor of any she knew." He claims that it was Prince Paul, an excellent musician himself, who had bought Marie her valuable piano. "He got Liszt to agree to try it out, after first having given her a lesson." This, however, is refuted by the date recorded in the Pleyel inventory: in July 1846, when the piano was purchased, Liszt had been gone from Paris for six months.

199   "Dear friend,": Lucien-Graux, *Les factures de la dame aux camélias.*

199   "In Spa no other fever" . . . "Our fair friend": Janin, preface to *La dame aux camélias.*

201   "When the night was pitch black": Matharel de Fiennes, *L'Entr'acte,* 10 and 11 February 1852.

202   "Mon cher Monsieur": In a boxed set of 3 volumes of *Dame aux Camélia* Miscellany, Bibliothèque de la Comédie-Française.

203   "The undersigned doctors are of the opinion": Davaine/Chomel prescriptions printed in Gros, *Une courtisane romantique.*

207   "Although everything there is luxurious" . . . "in a fine, anglicised hand" . . . "Monsieur": Henry Lumière, "La Dame aux Camélias: Une lettre inédite de Marie Duplessis," *La Revue Normande,* 1900.

207   "nest of pink silk" . . . "so deliciously pretty": Ibid.

208   "such a noble person": Claude Vento, *Les peintres de la femme* (Paris: E. Dentu, 1888).

208   "Ask for 200 francs": Vento, *Les peintres de la femme.* Marie had already made a gift to Tony of the Olivier aquarelle of herself. (In the 1872 edition of *La dames aux camélias,* the portrait is described as "Given by Mlle MD herself to M. T." However, he may not have commissioned the Chaplin painting. An article published in *Le Livre* by the Count G. de Contades (December 10, no. 72, 1885) claims that this was paid for by Count Pierre de Castellane. "A lost wager, accord-

ing to one source, a votive offering of love, according to another." In Contades's version, Chaplin is taken to visit Marie, who is in bed but delighted to see him, and Marie immediately suggests several poses. A simple sketch that allowed him to work on the portrait in his studio was lent to Contades by Chaplin to reproduce in his article.

209   the discovery that year of the explosive: Three different chemists, working independently, had all made the discovery in 1846. The German-Swiss Christian Schönbein had spilled a bottle of nitric acid on his kitchen table and mopped it up with a cotton apron, which he then hung on a stove to dry. Soon afterward it exploded.

209   "Two lackeys . . . set her down": Alfred Delvau, *Les lions du jour* (Paris: E. Dentu, 1867).

210   "the halo of a saint": Quoted in Barnes, *The Making of a Social Disease.*

210   "Her faded" . . . "She was already mortally ill": Saint-Victor, *Le théâtre contemporain.*

212   "His mother listened to him": *L'Epoque,* 9 February 1847.

212   "All the poor of Paris and Spain": Villemessant, *Mémoires d'un journaliste: Scènes intimes.*

213   "Celebrated for more than a title": *L'Epoque,* 9 February 1847.

213   "Why, Madame?": Matharel de Fiennes, *L'Entr'acte,* 10 and 11 February 1852.

214   "Go quickly to her": *Revue Encyclopédique,* 15 February 1896.

214   "If I had happened to be in Paris": 2 May or 2 June. Liszt and d'Agoult, *Correspondance.*

214   "banned from the bedroom": Matharel de Fiennes, *L'Entr'acte,* 10 and 11 February 1852.

214   "Forty-eight hours before": Amédée Achard (Grimm) in *L'Epoque,* 9 February 1847.

215   "Oh, I'm dying!" and following descriptions of Marie's final moments: Matharel de Fiennes, *L'Entr'acte,* 10 and 11 February 1852.

215   That evening Clotilde answered the door to Romain: Vienne says that he returned to Paris on Tuesday, 20 February, but, writing forty years later, he has forgotten the exact date. He must have meant Tuesday, 2 February (the 20th, a Saturday, is the date of Marguerite's death in the novel).

216   "The tenderness and touching taste": Roqueplan, *Parisine.*

218   The church was still hung with black draperies: In the announce-

ment of Marie's death in *Les Petites Affiches, Le Constitutionnel et Le Moniteur des Ventes,* she is plain "Mlle Plessis."

218 "Olympe A.": "Méjannes," column in *Gil Blas,* 18 October 1887.

219 thoroughbred "of superb genealogy": Gros, *Une courtisane romantique.*

219 Clotilde was "hunted down": Matharel de Fiennes, *L'Entr'acte,* 10 and 11 February 1852.

220 In the novel: Could Dumas fils himself have been there observing Ned? He had learned of Marie's death when he was in Marseille, but had returned to Paris by February 12 or 13. The exhumation took place on the 16th. In the first two editions of the novel the cemetery is described as Père Lachaise, not Montmartre, but this may just be another of Dumas fils's amendments of the facts. There is no written evidence of his presence at the exhumation (undisclosed to all but Ned Perregaux, the grave diggers, and the prefect of police). But how else was he able to describe the procedure in such grim detail?

222 "delivered up to sepulchral worms": 1 May 1847. Liszt and d'Agoult, *Correspondance.*

222 "I've always felt that I'll come back to life": Matharel de Fiennes, *L'Entr'acte,* 10 and 11 February 1852.

POSTSCRIPT

223 "a rich and elegant property" . . . "After the death": Gros, *Une courtisane romantique.*

224 "The greatest medical practitioner": Letter (in French) from Dickens to Comte d'Orsay, Paris, March 1847, in Pontavice de Heussey, *L'inimitable Boz.*

224 "For my part": Ibid.

224 "the gaudy and ghastly": Dickens, letter to the Rev. Edward Tagart, 28 January 1847. Pilgrim edition of *The Letters of Charles Dickens,* vol. 5: 1847–1849, ed. Graham Storey and K. J. Fielding (Oxford: Clarendon Press, 1981).

224 "with a dreadful insatiability": John Forster, *The Life of Charles Dickens* (London: Cecil Palmer, 1928).

224 "Everyone whom": Letter to d'Orsay, in Pontarice du Heussey, *L'inimitable Boz.*

225 "each object speak": Dumas fils, "M.D.," in *Péchés de jeunesse.*

225 "This one was dead": Dumas fils, *La dame aux camélias.*

225 "For it is there, in the past": Dumas fils, "M.D.," in *Péchés de jeunesse.*

226 Delphine had held back: In an unpublished letter dated 28 October 1869, Gustave Le Vavasseur describes an encounter with Delphine that took place at a notary's office in Vimontier (Frederick R. Koch Collection, Beinecke Rare Book and Manuscript Library, Yale University). "The unhappy Plessis girl" admitted being in miserable circumstances, he says, having sold every item she had inherited and lost twenty thousand francs through speculation. She was trying to negotiate a loan and was considering selling the last remaining thing of value, which was Vidal's portrait *Marie Duplessis aux bains des Pyrénées*. The fact that it was found in an attic a century later by her descendents suggests that Delphine either changed her mind or did not find a buyer.

226 "Did he intend to give the courtesan's": Boudet, *La fleur du mal*.

228 But the explanation: Letter to Calmann Lévy, printed in the 1886 edition of *La dame aux camélias* (Paris: Quantin).

229 Count de G. who "launched" . . . "no more than": Dumas fils, *La dame aux camélias*.

229 "It's a history": Saint-Victor, *Le théâtre contemporain*.

229 "The habitués": Vandam, *An Englishman in Paris*, vol. 1.

230 "Acting on impulse": Gustave Le Vavasseur, in *L'almanach de l'Orne*, 1895.

230 "The Faubourg St Germain" . . . "Haughty with men": Elisabeth de Gramont, *Pomp and Circumstance*, trans. Brian W. Downs (New York: Jonathan Cape's Harrison Smith, 1979).

231 "My dear count": Alice Ozy to Théophile Gautier, Letter 960, 14? March 1847. Claudine Lacoste-Veysseyre, ed., *Théophile Gautier, correspondance générale 1846–1848*, vol. 3 (Geneva and Paris: Librairie Droz, 1988).

231 "an amiable and witty": Alice Ozy to Théophile Gautier, Letter 162, Gautier correspondence, Lovenjoul Collection, Bibliothèque de l'Institut de France.

231 "And he has kept": Mané, *Le Paris viveur.*

232 "very extraordinary and distinguished": Quoted in Perényi, *Liszt*.

232 "It was the last": Iassy, May or June 1847.

232 "He loved to lay stress": Wohl, *François Liszt*.

233 "with his inventive intelligence": Le Vavasseur, in *l'Almanach de l'Orne*, 1895.

233 "the phantom who had haunted": Ibid.

Bibliography

Frequently Cited Sources

Choulet, Jean-Marie. *Promenades à Paris et en Normandie avec la dame aux camélias.* Paris: Editions Charles Corlet, 1998.

Dumas fils, Alexandre. *La dame aux camélias.* Preface by André Maurois. Paris: Collection Folio Classique, Gallimard, 1975.

———. *Théâtre complet.* Vol. 3, *Notes.* Paris: Calmann Lévy, 1898.

Gros, Johannes. *Une courtisane romantique, Marie Duplessis.* Paris: Au Cabinet du Livre, 1929.

Hays, Charles du. *L'ancien Merlerault: Récits chevalins d'un vieil éleveur.* Paris: Morris Père et Fils, 1885.

Janin, Jules. Preface to *La dame aux camélias.* Paris: A. Cadot, 1851.

Judith, Julie Bernat. *La vie d'une grande comédienne: Mémoires de Madame Judith de la Comédie-Française et souvenirs sur ses contemporains.* Edited by Paul Gsell. Paris: J. Tallandier, 1911.

Matharel de Fiennes, Charles. *L'Entr'acte,* 10 and 11 February 1852.

"Méjannes." Column in *Gil Blas,* 18 October 1887.

Mesnil, E. du. *L'Intermédiaire des Chercheurs et Curieux.* 10 September 1890.

Roqueplan, Nestor. *Parisine.* Paris: J. Hetzel et Cie, 1868.

Vandam, Albert. *An Englishman in Paris,* vol. 1. New York: D. Appleton & Co., 1892.

Further Reading

Alméras, Henri d'. *La vie parisienne sous le règne de Louis-Philippe.* Paris: Albin Michel, no date.

Anon. *La grisette à Paris et en province. Sa vie, ses moeurs, son caractère, ses joies, ses espérances, ses tribulations.* Paris: Renault, 1843.

Anon. *Paris dansant; ou, Les filles d'Hérodiade.* Paris: J. Bréauté, 1845.

Ariste, Paul d'. *La vie et le monde du boulevard (1830–1870) (Un Dandy: Nestor Roqueplan).* Paris: Jules Tallandier, 1930.

Banville, Théodore de. *Mes souvenirs.* Paris: G. Charpentier, 1882.

————. *Les Parisiennes de Paris.* Paris: M. Lévy Frères, 1866.

————. *Petites études, Paris vécu.* Paris: G. Charpentier, 1883.

Barnes, David S. *The Making of a Social Disease: Tuberculosis in Nineteenth-Century France.* Berkeley: University of California Press, 1995.

Beach, Vincent W. *Charles X of France: His Life and Times.* Boulder, Colo.: Pruett, 1971.

Beaconsfield, Lord. *Correspondence with His Sister, 1832–1852.* London: John Murray, 1886.

Beauvoir, Roger de. *Voluptueux Souvenirs; ou, Le Souper des Douze* (avec la réproduction de 12 figures libre de Devéria). Paris: Romainville, pour la bibliothèque de "Disciples d'Eros," date unknown.

Bertaut, Jules. *Le Boulevard.* Paris: Jules Tallandier, 1957.

Blessington, Countess of. *The Idler in France,* vols. 1 and 2. London: Henry Colburn, 1841.

Bordeaux, Michèle, et al. *Madame ou Mademoiselle?: Itineraires de la solitude feminine, 19–20me siècle.* Paris: Montalba, 1984.

Castelnau, Jacques. *En remontant les grands boulevards.* Paris: Le Livre Contemporain, 1960.

Claudin, Gustave. *Mes souvenirs: Les boulevards de 1840–1870.* Paris: Calmann Lévy, 1884.

Claretie, Jules La. *Vie à Paris.* Paris: Bibliothèque-Charpentier, 1911.

Contades, Comte G. de. *Portraits et fantaisies.* Paris: Maison Quantin, 1887.

Corbin, Alain. *Women for Hire: Prostitution and Sexuality in France after 1850.* Cambridge, Mass. London: Harvard University Press, 1990.

Czapska, Maria. *Une famille d'Europe Centrale 1772–1914.* Paris: Plon, 1972.

Delvau, Alfred. *Les lions du jour.* Paris: E. Dentu, 1867.

Disraeli, Benjamin. *Letters,* vols. I, II, V. Toronto, Buffalo, London: University of Toronto Press, 1982.

Dumas, Alexandre. *Lettres à mon fils.* Edition présentée et annotée par Claude Schopp. Paris: Mercure de France, 2008.

Dumas fils, Alexandre. *L'affaire Clemenceau: Mémoire de l'accusé.* Paris: Michael Lévy Frères, 1869.

————. *The Lady of the Camellias.* With a critical introduction by Edmund Gosse. London: William Heinemann, 1902.

————. *Péchés de jeunesse.* Paris: Fellens et Dufour, 1847.

Félice, Raoul de. *La Basse-Normandie.* Paris: Hachette, 1907.

Foulkes, Nick. *Last of the Dandies.* New York: St. Martin's Press, 2003.

Gramont, E[lisabeth] de, ex-Duchesse de Clermont-Tonnerre. *Pomp and Circumstance.* Trans. Brian W. Downs. New York: Jonathan Cape & Harrison Smith, 1929.

Gribble, Francis. *Dumas, Father and Son.* London: Eveleigh Nash & Grayson, 1930.

Grunwald, Constantin de. *Le Duc de Gramont, gentilhomme et diplomate.* Paris: Hachette, 1950.

Guitry, Sacha. *Cinquante ans d'occupations.* Paris: Le Grand Livre du Mois, 1993.

Hemmings, F.W.J. *The King of Romance: A Portrait of Alexandre Dumas.* London: Hamish Hamilton, 1979.

Henriot, Emile. *Portraits de femmes d'Héloïse à Katherine Mansfield.* Paris: Albin Michel, 1951.

Houssaye, Arsène. *Man about Paris.* Trans. and ed. Henry Knepler, London: Victor Gollancz, 1972.

————. *La péchéresse,* Paris: M. Lévy Frères, 1863.

————. *Souvenirs de jeunesse.* Paris: Flammarion, 1896.

Hugo, Victor. *Choses vues.* Paris: Mondiale, 1957.

James, Henry. *The Scenic Art: Notes on Acting and the Drama, 1872–1901.* London: Rupert Hart-Davis, 1949.

Janin, Jules. *735 lettres à sa femme.* Textes décryptés, classés et annotés par Mergier-Bourdeix. 3 vols. Paris: C. Klincksieck, 1973–79.

John, Nicholas, ed. *Violetta and Her Sisters: "The Lady of the Camellias"; Responses to the Myth.* London: Faber & Faber, 1994.

Landor, Walter Savage. *Letters and Other Unpublished Writings.* Ed. Stephen Wheeler. London: Richard Bentley and Son, 1897.

Liszt, Franz. *Selected Letters.* Trans. and ed. by Adrian Williams. Oxford: Clarendon Press, 1998.

Liszt, Franz, and Marie d'Agoult. *Correspondance.* Présentée et annotée par Serge Gut et Jacqueline Bellas. Paris: Fayard, 2001.

Loliée, Frédéric. *The Gilded Beauties of the Second Empire.* London: John Long, 1909.

Madden, R. R. *The Literary Life and Correspondence of the Countess of Blessington,* vols. 1–3. London: T. C. Newby, 1855.

Mané [pseudonym of Henri de Pené]. *Le Paris viveur.* Paris: E. Dentu, 1862.

Mansel, Philip. *Paris Between Empires, 1814–1852.* London: John Murray, 2001.

Martin, Marietta. *Le Docteur Koreff (1783–1851): Un aventurier intellectuel sous la restauration et la Monarchie de Juillet.* Paris: Edouard Champion, 1925.

Maupassant, Guy de. *Le colporteur.* Edition présentée, établie et annotée par Marie-Clare Bancquart. Paris: Gallimard, 2006.

Maurois, André. *Three Musketeers: A Study of the Dumas Family.* Trans. Gerard Hopkins. London: Jonathan Cape, 1957.

Morrison, Alfred. *The Collection of Autograph Letters and Historical Documents: The Blessington Papers.* Printed for private circulation, 1895.

Murger, Henri. *Scènes de la vie de bohème.* Paris: Calmann Lévy, 1886.

Musset, Alfred de. *Etudes d'histoire romantique.* Vol. 1 (1848–1914). Paris: Societé du *Mercure de France,* 1907.

Nesselrode, Comte de. *Lettres et papiers, 1760–1850.* Paris: A. Lahure, 1904.

Noël, Benoit, and Jean Hournon. *La Seine au temps des canotiers.* Paris: ROM Productions, 1997.

Parent-Duchâtelet, Alexandre. *La prostitution à Paris au XIXe siècle.* Paris: Editions du Seuil, 1981.

Perényi, Eleanor. *Liszt.* London: Weidenfeld & Nicolson, 1974.

Plancy, Baron de. *Souvenirs et indiscrétions d'un disparu.* Paris: Paul Ollendorff, 1892.

Pontavice de Heussey, Robert du. *L'inimitable Boz: Etude historique et anecdotique sur la vie et l'oeuvre de Charles Dickens.* Paris: Maison Quantin, 1889.

Prévost, d'Exiles, Antoine-François. *Histoire du chevalier Des Grieux et de Manon Lescaut.* Paris: Gallimard, 2008.

Price, David. *Cancan!* London: Cygnus Arts, 1998.

Richardson, Joanna. *The Courtesans: The Demi-Monde in Nineteenth-Century France.* London: Weidenfeld & Nicolson, 1967.

———. *Théophile Gautier: His Life and Times.* London: Max Reinhardt, 1958.

Roqueplan, Nestor. *Regain: La vie parisienne.* Paris: Librairie Nouvelle, 1853.

Rousseau, Jean-Jacques. *La nouvelle Héloïse.* Paris: Garnier, 1963.

Sadleir, Michael. *Blessington-D'Orsay: A Masquerade.* London: Constable, 1947.

Saint-Pierre, Bernardin de. *Paul and Virginia.* Trans. Helen Maria Williams. London: F. C. and J. Rivington, 1822.

Saint-Victor, Paul de. *Le théâtre contemporain.* Paris: C. Lévy, 1889.

Sand, George. *Isidora*. Paris: Editions Sercap, 1982.

Saunders, Edith. *The Prodigal Father: Dumas Père et Fils and* The Lady of the Camellias. London: Longmans, Green and Co., 1951.

Seymour, Bruce. *Lola Montez: A Life*. New Haven, Conn.: Yale University Press, 1996.

Texier, Edmond. *Tableau de Paris*. Paris: Paulin et Le Chevalier, 1852–53.

Vento, Claude. *Les peintres de la femme*. Paris: E. Dentu, 1888.

Vérel, Charles. *Nonant-le-Pin, ses foires et son marché, etc.* Alençon: Vve A. Laverdure, 1914.

Viel-Castel, Horace de. *Mémoires sur la règne de Napoléon III, 1851–1864.* Paris: Chez Tous les Libraires, 1883.

Villemessant, H. de. *Mémoires d'un journaliste: deuxième serie: Les hommes de mon temps.* Paris: E. Dentu, 1872.

———. *Mémoires d'un journaliste: Scènes intimes.* Paris: E. Dentu, 1876.

Walker, Alan. *Franz Liszt*. Vol. 1, *The Virtuoso Years, 1811–1847.* New York: Alfred A. Knopf, 1990.

Wharton, Edith. *Beatrice Palmato*. Appendix to R. W. B. Lewis, *Edith Wharton: A Biography*. London: Constable, 1975.

Williams, Adrian. *Portraits of Liszt by Himself and His Contemporaries.* Oxford: Clarendon Press, 1990.

Wissant, Georges de. *Cafés and Cabarets*. Paris: Jules Tallandier, 1928.

Wohl, Janka. *François Liszt: Recollections of a Compatriot.* Trans. B. Peyton Ward. London: Ward & Downey, 1887.

Yriarte, Charles. *Les cercles de Paris 1828–1864.* Paris: Dupray de la Mahérie, 1864.

Zola, Emile. *L'assommoir.* Paris: Livre de Poche, 1996.

———. *The Belly of Paris.* Trans. with an introduction and notes by Brian Nelson. Oxford: Oxford University Press, 2007.

———. *Nana.* Trans. with an introduction and notes by Douglas Parmee. Oxford: Oxford University Press, 1998.

Index

ILLUSTRATION CREDITS ·

Watercolor by Camille-Joseph-Etienne Roqueplan © Bridgeman Art Library/ Musée de la Ville de Paris, Musée Carnavalet, Paris, France/Giraudon.

Photograph of Nestor Roqueplan. From Jean-Louis Tamvaco, *Les Cancans de l'Opéra: Chroniques de l'Académie Royale de Musique et du théâtre à Paris sous les deux restaurations*, fig 159. Paris: CNRS Editions, 2000. Collection of Jean-Louis Tamvaco.

Drawing by Viset (Luc Lafnet). From Johannès Gros, *Une courtisane romantique: Marie Duplessis*. Paris: Au Cabinet Du Livre, 1929; photograph by Ross MacGibbon.

La Chaumière (1834). Lithograph by Nicolas-Eustache Maurin © Musée Carnavalet/ Roger-Viollet.

Le foyer de la danse (1841). Lithograph by Eugène Lami. Collection of M. Lopez.

L'Enchantresse Espagnole (1847). Lithograph by J. G. Middleton; engraved by George Zobel. Collection of The Australian Ballet Collection, donated 1998. Performing Arts Collection, Arts Centre Melbourne.

Interior of an Opera Box (1843). Original steel engraving drawn by Eugène Lami; engraved by H. Robinson.

Frontispiece to *La vérité sur la dame aux camélias* by Romaine Vienne. (1888). Photograph by Ross MacGibbon.

Congress of Vienna (1819). Engraving by Jean Godefroy. Collection of the State Hermitage Museum.

Die Allee im Bereich der Klesterwiese (1840). From Heike Kronendett, *Die Lichtentaler Allee im Wandel der Zeit*. Baden-Baden: Stadtmuseum Baden-Baden und Autoren, 2005.

Painting of Duke Agenor de Guiche by Count d'Orsay. Collection of The Beinecke Rare Book and Manuscript Library, Yale University.

Drawing of Count Edouard Perregaux. From Raymond Morel et al., *Au Pays d'Argentelles: La Revue Culturelle de l'Orne*, fig. 28. Rouen: No. 3. January–March 1983.

Engraving of Alexandre Dumas fils by Charles Geoffroy. Collection of Bibliothèque Nationale de France.

Illustration Credits

Self-portrait (circa 1855), photograph by Olympe Aguado © RMN-Grand Palais / Art Resource, NY. Collection of Musée d'Orsay.

Portrait of Franz Liszt by Henri Lehmann (1839) © Musée Carnavalet/Rober-Viollet.

Portrait of Marie Duplessis by Charles Chaplin (1846). Photograph by Ross MacGibbon. Collection of Musée de la Dame aux Camélias.

Portrait of Alphonsine's mother Marie Plessis. Photograph by Ross MacGibbon. Collection of Musée de la Dame aux Camélias.

Skeleton of a lizard. Photograph by Ross MacGibbon. Collection of Musée de la Dame aux Camélias.

Photograph of the tomb of Marie Duplessis © Albert Harlingue/Roger-Viollet.

Lithograph of Marietta Piccolomini by Émile Desmaisons (1855). Collection of Bibliothèque Nationale de France.

Lithograph of Eugénie Doche as Marguerite in *La Dame aux Camélias* by Richard Buckner. Collection of Musée Carnavalet, Paris.

Photograph of Sarah Bernhardt as Marguerite in *La Dame aux Camélias* (1882). Collection of Bibliothèque Nationale de France.

Eleonora Duse by d'E. Kaulbach (1885). Collection of Musée de la Scala, Milan.

Still from *Camille* (1936), directed by George Cukor © Photofest.

Photograph of Maria Callas as Violetta by Houston Rogers (1958) in Nicola Rescigno's production of *La Traviata*, Covent Garden.

Photograph of Margot Fonteyn and Rudolf Nureyev (1963) by Michael Peto © University of Dundee The Peto Collection.

Photograph of Isabelle Huppert in *Lady of the Camellias* (1981) © Cevallos/Sygma/Corbis.

Photograph of Anna Netrebko in *La Traviata* (2005) © Klaus Lefebvre.

Photograph of Tamara Rojo and Sergei Polunin © 2011 Royal Opera House/Tristram Kenton.

A NOTE ABOUT THE AUTHOR

Julie Kavanagh is the author of *Secret Muses: The Life of Frederick Ashton* and *Nureyev*. She lives in London, Wales, and Salento with her husband and two sons.

A NOTE ON THE TYPE

The text of this book was set in Garamond No. 3, named
for Claude Garamond (ca. 1480–1561). This particular
version is based on an adaptation by Morris Fuller Benton.

Composed by North Market Street Graphics,
Lancaster, Pennsylvania
Printed and bound by RR Donnelley,
Harrisonburg, Virginia
Designed by Maria Carella